The Handbook of French Fantastic Radio & Television

OTHER RELEVANT TITLES FROM BLACK COAT PRESS

by *Jean-Marc & Randy Lofficier*
The French Fantasy Treasury 1: The World's Edge (ISBN 978-1-61227-544-4)
The French Fantasy Treasury 2: Myths & Legends (ISBN 978-1-61227-545-1)
The French Fantasy Treasury 3: Far Realms (ISBN 978-1-61227-546-8)
Shadowmen: Heroes and Villains of French Pulp Fiction (ISBN 978-0-9740711-3-8)
Shadowmen 2: Heroes and Villains of French Comics (ISBN 978-0-9740711-8-3)
The Handbook of French Science Fiction (ISBN 978-1-64932-161-9)
The Handbook of French Fantasy & Supernatural Literature (ISBN 978-1-64932-165-7)
The Handbook of French Fantastic Cinema (ISBN 978-1-64932-166-4)

by *Brian Stableford*
The Plurality of Imaginary Worlds: The Evolution of French Roman Scientifique (ISBN 978-1-61227-503-1)
Tales of Enchantment and Disenchantment: A History of Faerie, with an Exemplary Anthology of Tales (ISBN 978-1-61227-838-4)

The Handbook of French Fantastic Radio & Television

by

Jean-Marc & Randy Lofficier

A Black Coat Press Book

Acknowledgements: Portions of this book have appeared in *French Science Fiction, Fantasy, Horror & Pulp Fiction* published in 2000 by McFarland.

Copyright © 2023 by Jean-Marc & Randy Lofficier.
Cover illustration *L'Homme Sans Visage* Copyright © 2023.

Visit our website at www.blackcoatpress.com

ISBN 978-1-64932-196-1. First Printing. May 2023. Published by Black Coat Press, an imprint of Hollywood Comics.com, LLC, P.O. 18321 Ventura Blvd., Suite 915, Tarzana, CA 91356. All rights reserved. Except for review purposes, no part of this book may be reproduced or transmitted in any form or by any means, electronic or mechanical, including photocopying, recording, or by any information storage and retrieval system, without permission in writing from the publisher. The stories and characters depicted in this novel are entirely fictional. Printed in the United States of America.

TABLE OF CONTENTS

Foreword 7
TELEVISION 11
  Overview 11
  Series 15
  Telefilms 141
RADIO 191
  Overview 191
  Serials 193
  Radio Plays 235
Index 243

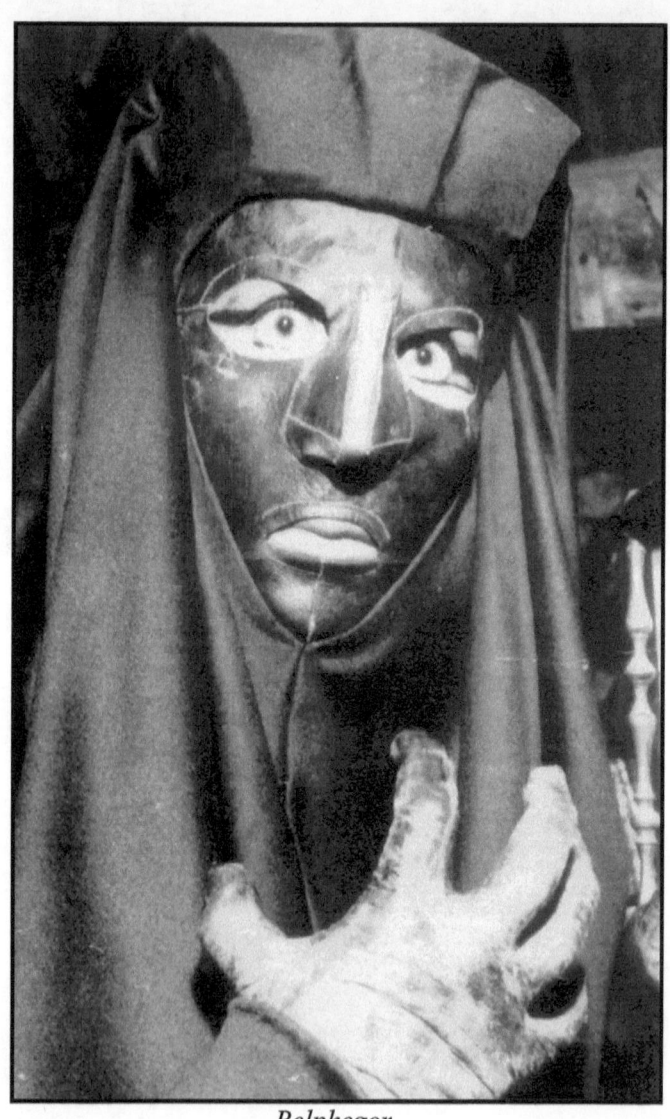

Belphegor

Foreword

When embarking on any study about science fiction or fantasy, it is often customary to start with an attempt to define these genres.

In French, the word "*fantastique*" carries with it a much larger definition, or "semantic field", than its approximate English equivalent—fantasy. Because it is easy to lose oneself in complex arguments about definitions, about what belongs to the genre and what does not, we subscribe to Pierre Gripari's simple definition: "The *fantastique* is everything that is not rational".

Within this definition, science fiction can be viewed, as Belgian writer Jacques Sternberg once did, as nothing more than a *succursale* [a branch] of the *fantastique*.

For the purpose of these handbooks, science fiction is defined as works appealing to the head, the intellect and the mind, and not the heart. Its true roots lie with humanism, the Renaissance, and the 18th century *Esprit des Lumières*, or Age of Enlightenment. It is, ultimately, based on logic, on science and on testing hypotheses. Science fiction, even when used as a social allegory, which it often is, always relies on a shared pretense of verisimilitude between the writer and his reader.

Fantastique, on the other hand, encompasses all of that which appeals to the heart, to the emotions, to the soul. It relies on irrational beliefs, a sense of the *merveilleux*. It stems from faith; faith in established religions as well as in folkloric legends; faith in ancient or modern myths, such as what is commonly known as the occult or, more accurately, what the French dub *ésotérisme* [*esoterica*], meaning that which is hidden, occult, obscure or secret. Faith traditionally opposes science and material progress, which science fiction, naturally, embraces and advocates.

These, then, are our terms of reference, the canvas against which we propose to paint the history of French fantastic cinema and television.

It will not escape the knowledgeable reader's attention that large sections of this book (and its two companion volumes, *The Handbook of French Fantasy & Supernatural Fiction* and *The Handbook of French Science Fiction*) first appeared in our 800-page bibliographical work, *French Science Fiction, Fantasy, Horror and Pulp Fiction: A Guide to Cinema, Television, Radio, Animation, Comic Books and Literature from the Middle Ages to the Present*, published 2000 by McFarland. According to *The Encyclopedia of Science Fiction*, "the Lofficier text covers the French fantastic with a comprehensiveness and intensity equaled only by the central texts of English-language bibliography and reference".

It should also be understood that, throughout this book, we have used the word "French" in the sense of French-language, that is to say, including Belgian, Swiss and French-Canadian works whenever appropriate We have, however, strived to identify such non-French-national works and/or authors. Also, animated theatrical features and television programs will be the subject of a fourth book in this series; only live action films and television are included in this volume.

Finally, no project of this type is ever perfect, or complete. We have tried to be as comprehensive as possible and correct all mistakes that appeared in the

McFarland tome. Nevertheless, in a book of this scope, no matter how careful one is, omissions are still bound to creep in, as well as the occasional mistake. We will be grateful to anyone pointing out such errors or omissions to us, for future reference and inclusion in subsequent reprints.

While we have listed new films and television up to 2022, we have wisely left the analysis of French Fantastic cinema in this new century to future genre historians.

Jean-Marc & Randy Lofficier

Tout Spliques Etaient les Borogoves

TELEVISION

Overview

First, a brief historical note about French Television: it was first called RTF, for *Radio Télévision Française*, and changed its name to ORTF in 1964, when it was split into two, then later, three channels. In 1975, these channels were eventually dubbed TF1, A2 and FR3, the latter functioning as a regional channel. French television was partially privatized in 1987, with TF1 becoming private, and A2 (later renamed FR2) and FR3 remaining public. Other private channels, such as Channel 5, M6, Arte, etc., and pay cable channel, Canal-Plus, were also added to the broadcasting spectrum in the 1980s.

French television has traditionally created less original fiction programming than American or British television, because it has relied on a greater diversity of types of programs, including movies, foreign imports, variety, music, sports, round-table discussions, documentaries, ballet, opera, etc. Whatever series it has produced have generally been either historical or police series, two genres at which French television has fairly excelled.

Science fiction and *fantastique* have, therefore, been mostly relegated to literary adaptations of Jules Verne, Marcel Aymé, and, more rarely, Maurice Renard, as well as the stable of ever-popular pulp authors such as

Gaston Leroux, Maurice Leblanc, Arthur Bernède, Marcel Allain & Pierre Souvestre, and Gustave Le Rouge.

The most memorable of these literary adaptations were made in the 1960s and 1970s and deserve to be singled out here. They included:

* Claude Barma's *Belphegor* (1965), an overnight ratings sensation and cult series.

* Claude Santelli's series of 1960s Jules Verne adaptations.

* Jean Kerchbron's remarkable version of Gustav Meyrinck's *Golem* (1967).

* Jacques Champreux teaming up with Pierre Prévert for *Les Compagnons de Baal* [*The Companions of Baal*] (1968) and with Georges Franju for *L'Homme sans Visage* [*The Faceless Man*, translated as *Shadowman*] (1975).

* Maurice Cravenne's versions of Gaston Leroux's *La Poupée Sanglante* [*The Bloody Puppet*] (1976) and Maurice Leblanc's *L'Île aux Trente Cercueils* [*The Island of the Thirty Coffins*] (1979).

* And, finally, Maurice Frydland's wonderfully over-the-top adaptation of Gustave Le Rouge's *Le Mystérieux Docteur Cornelius* [*The Mysterious Dr. Cornelius*] (1984).

Notable, made-for-television genre fare included:

* Claude Guillemot's fondly remembered and short-lived *La Brigade des Maléfices* [*The Brigade of Spells*] (1970).

* Jean Dréville and Noël-Noël's time travel saga *Le Voyageur des Siècles* [*The Traveler of the Centuries*] (1971).

* The interesting, but often tame, *Aux Frontières du Possible* [*At the Frontiers of the Possible*] (1971, 1974).

* And, finally, writer Alain Page's thrilling mini-series *Les Compagons d'Eleusis* [*The Brotherhood of Eleusis*] (1975) and *Le Mutant* (1978).

Also notable was producer Michel Subiela's *Le Tribunal de l'Impossible* [*The Tribunal of the Impossible*] which, from 1967 to 1974, presented a series of made-for-television features dealing with all the various facets of the fantastique, the paranormal and the unexplained.

Sadly, as French television became increasingly privatized and commercial in the early 1980s, it almost entirely stopped producing new genre programs, instead relying increasingly on inexpensive foreign imports. A few low-budget genre productions were made on regional channels, but these were not especially well made, nor did they have any significant impact on the ratings.

However, this changed again in the 1990s samnd 2000s, during which a large number of homegrown cop shows were made: *Maigret, Navarro, Nestor Burma, Commissaire Leclerc, Julie Lescault*, to name but a few of the more famous. Despite of this abundance of new French productions, and the local success of American genre series such as *The X-Files*, French television producers generally remained shy about making new genre series.

A few notable exceptions include *Contact, David Nolande, Eternelle* and the very popular *Kamelott*.

Arsène Lupin

Series

Our definition of "series" includes the following types of programs:
Regular Series: hero-driven, open-ended, on-going, self-contained stories, with recurring characters.
Mini-Series: a single story, with beginning, middle and end, split into various episodes for programming purposes.
Anthologies: series of unrelated, self-contained stories with no recurring characters.

Ad Vitam (Arte, col., six 50 min. episodes, 8-22 November 2018)
Dir: Thomas Cailley, Manuel Schapira; *Wri*: Thomas Cailley, Sébastien Mounier.
Cast: Yvan Attal (Darius), Garance Marillier (Christa), Anne Azoulay, Niels Schneider, Victor Assié.
Story: When we think we have conquered death, the bodies of seven suicides are discovered, all minors. Darius, a 120-year-old cop, leads the investigation with Christa, a rebellious and rebellious young girl.

Aéroport 2000 [*Airport 2000*] (A2, col., three 60 min. episodes, 1980)
Only episode 2 of this airport-themed anthology series belonged to the science fiction genre.
2. *Charter 2020* (19 April 1980)
Dir: Pierre Lary; *Wri*: Fernand Pluot, Pierre Lary.

Cast: Georges Marchal, Tsilla Chelton, Alexandre Rignault, Daniel Mesguich.
Story: A Concorde lands in 2020 in a future where women reproduce by parthenogenesis.

L'Agence Nostradamus [*The Nostradamus Agency*] (RTF, B&W., nine 15 min. episodes, 9-27 October 1950)
Dir: Claude Barma; *Wri*: Jean-Luc Dumayet, Pierre Dumayet.
Cast: Denise Provence (Dominique), Jacques-Henry Duval (Robert), Tsilla Chelton, Jean-Claude Deret, Pierre Goutas, Jean-Paul Moulinot, Michèle Brabo, Cora Camoin, Pierre Moncorbier, Henri Demay, Gisèle Chilton, Geneviève Morel, Jean-Jacques Daubin, Roger Saltel, Pierre Goutas, Bernard Hubrenne.
Story: A duo of private detectives investigates a series of murders involving a marriage agency, the Nostradamus Agency, which organizes encounters based on the astrological sign of the suitors.
Episodes 1. *Un Vaudor est toujours debout !* [*A Vaudor Always Stands*] (9/19/50) ; 2. *Double enquête chez l'Astrologue* [*Twin Inquiry at the Astrologer's*] (11/10/50) ; 3. *Rendez vous avec l'Amour* [*Rendez-vous with Love*] (13/10/50) ; 4. *La Nuit des Horoscopes* [*Night of the Star Charts*] (16/10/50) ; 5. *La Dernière Menace* [*The Last Menace*] (18/10/50) ; 6. *Trop d'eau dans le Whisky* [*Too Much Water in the Whiskey*] (20/10/50) ; 7. *Le Secret d'Angélique* [*Angelique's Secret*] (23/10/50) ; 8. *La Vengeance des Astres* [*The Stars' Revenge*] (25/10/50) ; 9. *Sous le Signe de Saturne* [*Under the Sign of Saturn*] (27/10/50).
Note: This was the first French TV series ever created.

Alice, Où es-tu? [*Alice, Where Are You?*] (ORTF 1, col., twenty 13 min. episodes, August-October 1969)
Dir: Paul Siegrist; *Wri*: Jean Canolle, Gérard Lucas, Pierre Zimmer.
Cast: Alain Chevallier (Antoine), Hariette Ariel (Alice).
Story: A young employee leaves his job to pursue a mysterious young woman across the world.
Note: French-Swiss co-production.

L'Alphomega (ORTF 1, col., six 60 min. episodes, 26 February-2 April 1973)
Dir/Wri: Lazare Iglésis.
Cast: Henri Virlojeux (Tonton), André Weber (Biceps), Sylvie Kuhn (Petite Pomme), Jean Gras, Darlan Leroy.
Story: Two former resistance fighters, Tonton and Biceps, are contacted by their superior to find the Alphomega said to contain a secret that would enable its holder to become master of the world.

Arsène Lupin (Radio-Canada, B&W., thirteen 25 min. episodes, July-September 1960)
Dir: René Verne; *Wri*: André Giroux, Roger Lemelin, based on the novels by Maurice Leblanc.
Cast: Jean Gascon (Lupin), Guy Sanche (Beautrelet).
Story: Adaptation of *The Hollow Needle*.

Arsène Lupin (ORTF 2, col., twenty-six 60 min. episodes, 1971, 1973-74)
Regular Cast: George Descrières (Lupin), Yvon Bouchard (Grognard), Marthe Keller (Natacha), Roger Carel (Guerchard).
Based on the novels by Maurice Leblanc.
Season 1:

1. *Le Bouchon de Cristal* [*The Cristal Topper*] (18/03/71)
Dir: Jean-Pierre Decourt; *Wri*: Jacques Nahum, René Wheeler.
Guest Cast: Daniel Gélin, Nadine Alari.
Story: A politician blackmails the government with secret information.

2. *Victor de la Brigade Mondaine* [*Victor From the Vice Squad*] (25/03/71)
Dir: Jean-Pierre Decourt; *Wri*: Claude Brulé.
Guest Cast: Bernard Lavalette, Pierre Massimi.
Story: Lupin impersonates a police detective.

3. *Arsène Lupin contre Herlock Sholmes* [*Arsène Lupin vs Herlock Sholmes*] (1/04/71)
Dir: Jean-Pierre Decourt; *Wri*: Claude Brulé.
Guest Cast: Henri Virlojeux (Herlock Sholmes), Charles Millot.
Story: Lupin and Sholmes match wits.

4. *L'Arrestation d'Arsène Lupin* [*The Capture of Arsène Lupin*] (8/04/71)
Dir: Jean-Pierre Decourt; *Wri*: Claude Brulé.
Guest Cast: William Sabatier, Robert André.
Story: Lupin is arrested on a liner.

5. *L'Agence Barnett* [*The Barnett Agency*] (15/04/71)
Dir: Jean-Pierre Decourt; *Wri*: Jacques Nahum, René Wheeler.
Guest Cast: Jacques Balutin, Teddy Bilis.
Story: Lupin impersonates a private eye.

6. *La Demoiselle aux Yeux Verts* [*The Lady with Green Eyes*] (22/04/71)
Dir: Dieter Lemmel; Wri: Albert Simonin, Rolf & Alexandra Becker.
Guest Cast: Kathrin Ackermann (Lady Bakefield), Josef Fröhlich.
Story: Lupin seeks a hidden treasure and teams up with a daring female thief.

7. *La Chaîne Brisée* [*The Broken Chain*] (29/04/71)
Dir: Paul Cammermans; *Wri*: Jean Marcillac, Jacques Armand.
Guest Cast: Sjoukje Hooymaayer, Fons Rademakers.
Story: Lupin in Holland.

8. *La Femme aux Deux Sourires* [*The Woman with Two Smiles*] (6/05/71)
Dir: Marcello Baldi; *Wri*: Albert Simonin, Duccio Tessari, Adriano Barraco.
Guest Cast: Raffaela Cara, Mario Bernardi.
Story: Lupin pursues a mysterious woman in Italy.

9. *La Chimère du Calife* [*The Caliph's Chimera*] (13 May 1971)
Dir: Dieter Lemmel; *Wri*: Albert Simonin, Rolf & Alexandra Becker.
Guest Cast: Gunnar Moller, Bernd Schäfer.
Story: Lupin in Germany.

10. *Une Femme contre Arsène Lupin* [*A Woman vs. Arsène Lupin*] (20/05/71)
Dir: Tony Flaadt; *Wri*: Jacques Armand.
Guest Cast: Louis Arbessier, Juliette Mills, François Simon.

Story: Lupin outwits a gang of jewel thieves.

11. *Les Anneaux de Cagliostrio* [*The Rings of Cagliostro*] (27/05/71)
Dir: Wolf Dietrich; *Wri*: Georges Grammont, Rolf & Alexandra Becker.
Guest Cast: Christine Buchegger (Countess Cagliostro), Hans Holt, Kitty Speiser.
Story: In Wien, Lupin meets the beautiful Countess Cagliostro.

12. *Les Tableaux de Tornbüll* [*The Tornbüll Paintings*] (3/06/71)
Dir: Dieter Lemmel; *Wri*: Georges Grammont, Rolf & Alexandra Becker.
Guest Cast: Kathrin Ackermann (Lady Bakefield), Hubert Mittendorf, Conny Collins.
Story: Lupin teams up with Lady Bakefield again.

13. *Le Sept de Coeur* [*The Seven of Hearts*] (19/06/71)
Dir: Jean-Louis Colant; *Wri*: Nathan Grigorieff.
Guest Cast: Janine Patrick, Roger Dutoit, Raoul de Manez (Maurice Leblanc).
Story: Lupin tells Maurice Leblanc how he recovered the plans of a secret weapon.

Season 2:
14. *Herlock Sholmes Lance un Défi* [*Herlock Sholmes Throws a Challenge*] (18/12/73)
Dir: Jean-Pierre Desagnat; *Wri*: Claude Brulé.
Guest Cast: Henri Virlojeux (Sholmes), Sophie Agacinski, Bernard Dhéran.
Story: Lupin and Sholmes match wits again.

15. *Arsène Lupin Prend des Vacances* [*Arsène Lupin Takes a Holiday*] (20/12/73)
Dir: Jean-Pierre Desagnat; *Wri*: Nathan Grigorieff, Albert Simonin.
Guest Cast: Claude Degliame, Daniel Sarry.
Story: Lupin seeks the secret of "813."

16. *Le Mystère de Gesvres* [*The Gesvres Mystery*] (22/12/73)
Dir: Jean-Pierre Desagnat; *Wri*: Albert Simonin.
Guest Cast: Bernard Giraudeau (Beautrelet), Thérèse Liotard.
Story: Lupin hides behind the secret of the Hollow Needle.

17. *Le Secret de l'Aiguille* [*The Secret of the Needle*] (25/12/73)
Dir: Jean-Pierre Desagnat; *Wri*: Albert Simonin.
Guest Cast: Bernard Giraudeau (Beautrelet), Henri Virlojeux (Sholmes), Catherine Rouvel.
Story: Sholmes and Beautrelet compete to solve the mystery of the Hollow Needle.

18. *L'Homme au Chapeau Noir* [*The Man with the Black Hat*] (27/12/73)
Dir: Jean-Pierre Desagnat; *Wri*: Claude Brulé.
Story: Lupin protects a woman's inheritance (a river carrying gold nuggets). Last appearance of Herlock Sholmes.

19. *L'Écharpe Rouge* [*The Red Scarf*] (29/1273)
Dir: Jean-Pierre Desagnat; *Wri*: Claude Brulé.
Guest Cast: Sacha Pitoëff, Prudence Harrington.

Story: Lupin seeks a precious sapphire.

20. *La Demeure Mystérieuse* [*The Mysterious House*] (5/01/74)
Dir: Jean-Pierre Desagnat; *Wri*: Georges Berlot.
Guest Cast: Evelyne Dress, Marika Green.
Story: Lupin solves the mystery of an ancient house.

21. Les Huit Coups de l'Horloge [*The Eight Strikes of the Clock*] (12/01/74)
Dir: Jean-Pierre Desagnat; *Wri*: Robert Scipion, Claude Brulé.
Guest Cast: Corinne Le Poulain, François Maistre.
Story: Lupin unmasks a serial killer.

22. *La Dame au Chapeau à Plumes* [*The Lady with the Feathered Hat*] (19/01/74)
Dir: Wolf Dietrich; *Wri*: Rolf & Alexandra Becker.
Guest Cast: Fritz Muliar, Christine Böhm.
Story: Lupin meets Sigmund Freud in Wien.

23. *La Danseuse de Rottenburg* [*The Dancer from Rottenburg*] (26/01/74)
Dir: Fritz Umgelter; *Wri*: Rolf & Alexandra Becker.
Guest Cast: Dagmar Heller, Charlotte Kerr.
Story: Lupin saves a girl from committing suicide.

24. *Le Film Révélateur* [*The Revealing Film*] (2/02/74)
Dir: Fritz Umgelter; *Wri*: Rolf & Alexandra Becker.
Guest Cast: Maria Korber, Marie Versini.
Story: Lupin replaces a famous actor to steal a diamond.

25. *Double Jeu* [*Double Game*] (9/02/1974)
Dir: Fritz Umgelter; *Wri*: Rolf & Alexandra Becker.
Guest Cast: Andrea Dahmen, Gunther Sporrle.
Story: Lupin proves a Baroness is innocent of murder.

26. *Le Coffre-Fort de Madame Imbert* [*Mrs. Imbert's Safe*] (16/02/74)
Dir: Jean-Pierre Desagnat; *Wri*: Albert Simonin.
Guest Cast: Pascale Roberts, Jean-Pierre Rambal.
Story: Lupin commits a daring burglary.

Arsène Lupin Joue et Perd [*Arsène Lupin Plays and Loses*] (A2, col., six 52 min. episodes, 12-27 December 1980)
Dir: Alexandre Astruc; *Wri*: Alexandre Astruc, Roland Laudenbach, based on the novels by Maurice Leblanc.
Cast: Jean-Claude Brialy (Lupin), Christiane Kruger (Dolores), Maurice Biraud (Weber), François Maistre (Valenglay), Marco Perrin (Gourel), François Perrot (Altenheim), Jacques Dacqmine, Philippe Mareuil, Elyette Damian, Sacha Briquet, Jeanne Goupil, Hubert Deschamps, Serge Berry, Gérard Buhr, René Bovloc, Valérie Pascal.
Story: Lupin seeks to solve mystery of "813" which might change the map of Europe.

Le Retour d'Arsène Lupin (FR3, col., twelve 55 min., episodes, 10 November 1989-26 January 1990)
Regular Cast: François Dunoyer (Lupin), Paul Le Person (Ganimard), Eric Franklin (Grognard).
Prod: Jacques Nahum based on the novels by Maurice Leblanc

1. *Le Médaillon du Pape* [*The Pope's Medallion*] (10/11/89)
Dir: Vittorio Barino; *Wri*: Francis Lacassin, Michel Subiela.
Guest Cast: Catherine Alric, Nando Gazzolo.
Story: A priceless medallion is stolen in Locarno.

2. *Lenormand, Chef de la Sûreté* [*Lenormand, Head of the Sûreté*] (17/11/89)
Dir: Michel Wyn; *Wri*: Philippe Delannoy, Jacques Nahum.
Guest Cast: Yolande Folliot.
Story: Lupin impersonates the Head of the Sûreté.

3. *La Camarade Tatiana* [*Comrade Tatiana*] (24/11/89)
Dir: Jacques Besnard; *Wri*: Albert Kantof, Jacques Nahum.
Guest Cast: Susanna Hoffmann.
Story: Lupin is hired to steal a previous Russian icon.

4. *Le Triangle d'Or* [*The Golden Triangle*] (1/12/89)
Dir: Philippe Condroyer; *Wri*: Patrick Besson, Philippe Delannoy, Jacques Nahum.
Guest Cast: Sophie Barjac, Jacques Boudet, Didier Flamand, Roland Lesaffre.
Story: Lupin seeks to reciver a stolen treasure in gold.

5. *Un Savant bien tranquille* [*A Quiet Scientist*] (8/12/89)
Dir: Michel Boisrond; Wri: Daniel Goldenberg, David Lachterman, Jacques Nahum.
Guest Cast: Daniel Goldenberg, Anna Condo.
Story: Lupin impersonates Albert Einstein.

6. *Les Flûtes enchantées* [*The Enchanted Flutes*] (15/12/89)
Dir: Theo Mezger; *Wri*: François Chevalier, Philippe Delannoy.
Guest Cast: Fritz Bachschmidt.
Story: A Baroness steals from Lupin.

7. *Le Canon de Junot* [*Junot's Cannon*] (22/12/89)
Dir: Michel Wyn; *Wri*: Jacques Nahum.
Guest Cast: Maria Blanco, Alexandre Sousa.
Story: Lupin steals a historical cannon from the Invalides Museum.

8. *Les Dents du Tigre* [*The Teeth of the Tiger*] (29/12/89)
Dir: Theo Mezger; *Wri*: Mohamed Boudjera.
Guest Cast: Sabine Kaack, Michael Schwarzmaier.
Story: Lupin unmasks a murderer who left a bite mark behind.

9. *Un Air Oublié* [*A Forgotten Sonata*] (5/01/90)
Dir: Michel Boisrond; *Wri*: Robert Scipion, Krzysztof Teodor Toeplitz.
Guest Cast: Gabriela Kownacka, Katarzyna Kozak.
Story: Lupin travels tio Poland to investigate the murder of a pianist.

10. *La Sorcière aux Deux Visages* [*The Two-Faced Witch*] (12/01/90)
Dir: Michel Wyn; *Wri*: Mohamed Boudjera, Michel Wyn.
Guest Cast: Laetitia Gabrielli.
Story: A girl steals a painting fton Lupin's home.

11. *La Comtesse de Cagliostro* [*Countess Cagliostro*] (19/01/90)
Dir: Jordi Cadena; *Wri*: Philippe Delannoy , Jacques Nahum, Bernard Stora.
Guest Cast: Alicia Moro (Countess Cagliostro), Hermann Bonnín, Artur Costa.
Story: Lupin matches wits with Countess Cagliostro in Barcelona.

12. *Le Bijou Fatidique* [*The Fateful Jewel*] (26/01/90)
Dir: Serge Friedman; *Wri*: Serge Friedman, Jacques Nahum.
Guest Cast: Ena Begovic, Branko Cvejic, Rade Serbedzija (Sholmes).
Story: During the attack perpetrated on the person of King Alexander of Yugoslavia, in Marseilles, a watch of great value disappeared. Herlock Sholmes is tasked with finding her.

Les Nouveaux Exploits d'Arsène Lupin (FR3, col., eight 90 min. episodes, 1996-97)
Regular Cast: François Dunoyer (Lupin), Paul Le Person (Ganimard), Franck Capillery (Grognard).
Prod: Jacques Nahum, based on the novels by Maurice Leblanc

1. *La Tabatière de l'Empereur* [*The Emperor's Snuff Box*] (20/05/95)
Dir: Alain Nahum; *Wri*: Jacques Avanac, Albert Kantof.
Guest Cast: Edward Zentara, Henryk Bista, Katarzyna Walter, Agnieszka Wagner, Gabriela Kownacka.

Story: Lupin travels to Poland to investigate the death of a friend.

2. *La Robe de Diamants* [*The Diamond-Studded Dress*] (3/06/95)
Dir: Nicolas Ribowski; *Wri*: Jacques Nahum, Philippe Delannoy.
Guest Cast: Michèle Laroque, Patrice Kerbrat, Thiam, Roland Lesaffre, Antoine Duléry.
Story: A masked man steal a precious dress Lupin was planning to steal.

3. *Requins à la Havane* [*Sharks in Havana*] (167/06/95)
Dir: Alain Nahum; *Wri*: Jacques Avanac, Albert Kantof.
Guest Cast: Jacqueline Arenal, Carlos Cruz, Broselandia Hernandez Boudet.
Story: Lupin meets Ernest Hemingway and Lucky Luciano in Cuba.

4. *Rencontre avec le Dr. Freud* [*Arsène Lupin Meets Dr.Freud*] (*9/09/95*)
Dir: Vittorio Barino; *Wri*: Albert Kantof, Jacques Nahum.
Guest Cast: Eva Grimaldi, Ugo Pagliai, Rugger de Daninos, Silvano Tranquilli, Tamara Dona, Rosetta Salata, Pier Senarica
Story: Lupin is after a map of Libyan oil wells when he meets Sigmund Freud.

5. *Le Masque de Jade* [*The Jade Mask*] (4/11/95)
Dir: Philippe Condroyer; *Wri*: Philippe & Mariette Condroyer.

Guest Cast: Charlotte Kady, Corinne Touzet, Bruno Raffaelli, Yann Babilée, Aurélien Wiik, Christine Lemler.
Story: The Nazis are after a jade necklace that contains a new formula.

6. *Herlock Sholmes s'en mêle* [*Herlock Sholmes Steps In*] (9/12/95)
Dir: Alain Nahum; *Wri*: Jacques Avanac, Albert Kantof, Philippe Delannoy.
Guest Cast: Vania Tzvetkova, Joseph Sartchadjiev.
Story: Someone impersonating Lupin steals a collection of paintings.

7. *Les Souterrains Étrusques* [*The Etruscean Tunnels*] (10/02/96)
Dir: Vittorio de Sisti; *Wri*: Jacques Nahum, Christian Watton, based on an idea by Richard Caron.
Guest Cast: Vittoria Belvedere, Pier Paolo Capponi, Augusto Zucchi, Stafania Orsola Garrello, Paolo Maria Scalondro, Marina Giulia Cavalli, Vincenzo Crocitti.
Story: In Italy, Lupin impersonates a murdered priest.

8. *L'Étrange Demoiselle* [*The Strange Damsel*] (7/07/96)
Dir: Marc F. Voizard; *Wri*: Pierre Billon, Victor Harrouch.
Cast: Claude Préfontaine, Gabriel Gascon, Macha Limonchik.
Story: In Montreal, Lupin solves a 10 years-old mystery.

Lupin (Netflix, col., ten 50 min. episodes, 2021)

Dir: Louis Leterrier, Marcela Said, Ludovic Bernard, Hugo Gélin; *Wri*: George Kay, François Uzan, based on the character created by Maurice Leblanc.
Cast: Omar Sy (Assane Diop/Lupin), Ludivine Sagnier, Clotilde Hesme, Hervé Pierre (Pellegrini), Soufiane Guerrab.
Story: The father of professional thief Assane Diop was framed for the theft of a diamond necklace by his employer, Hubert Pellegrini, and hangs himself in his prison cell. Twenty-five years later, inspired by the *Arsène Lupin* books, Assane sets out to get revenge on the Pellegrini family.

Astrolab 22 (TF1, col., thirteen 26-min. episodes, 15 June-7 July 1985)
Dir: Pierre Sisser; *Wri*: Pierre Sisser, Roland Portiche, based on a story by Essam El Maghraby.
Cast: Pierre Londiche, Jean-Yves Gautier, Vincent Siegrist, Véronique Prune, Bruno Guillain.
Story: A group of space cadets live aboard a space station and explore the planets of the solar system.
Note: French-Saudi co-production.

Les Atomistes [*The Atom-Smashers*] (ORTF 1, B&W., twenty-six 13 min. episodes, 12 February-18 March 1968)
Dir: Léonard Keigel; *Wri*: Bernard Thomas, Agnès Van Parys, Michel Levine.
Cast: Marc Michel, Jacques Debary, Simone Bach, Alain Nobis, Philippe Rouleau.
Story: Nuclear scientists create a crystal that boosts human powers. But foreign spies loom.
Episodes: 1-5. *Le Recrutement* [*The Recruiting*]; 6-10. *La Découverte* [*The Discovery*]; 11-15. *L'Espionnage*

[*Spies*]; 16-20. *L'Accident* [*The Accident*]; 21-26. *La Crise* [*Crisis*].

Au-delà des Murs [*Beyond the Walls*] (ARTE, three 45 min., episodes, 22 September 2016)
Dir: Hervé Hadmar; *Wri*: Sylvie Chanteux, Hervé Hadmar, Marc Herpoux.
Cast: Veerle Baetens, Geraldine Chaplin, François Deblock, Lilas-Rose Gilberti.
Story: Lisa, a young speech therapist, moves into a strange house which she mysteriously inherited, and discovers hidden rooms and corridors far larger than what the old mansion could contain.
Note: Belgian coproduction.

Aux Frontières du Possible [*To the Frontiers of the Possible*] (ORTF 2, col., thirteen 60 min. episodes, 1971, 1974)
Dir: Victor Vicas, Claude Boissol. *Wri*: Henri Viard, Jacques Bergier, based on his book *L'Espionnage scientifique* (1971)
Regular Cast: Pierre Vaneck (Yan Thomas), Elga Andersen (Barbara Andersen) (10 eps), Jean-François Rémi (Courtenay-Gabor), Yvette Montier (secretary), Eva Christian (Christa Neumann, eps. 9-11 only), Roger Rudel (Commissioner Chalier, eps. 1-6 only).
Story: Two young scientists, Thomas and Andersen, work for the BIPS (International Bureau of Scientific Protection) and investigate unexplained phenomena. The answers are always based on new, cutting edge scientific discoveries.
1st Season:
  1. *Le Dossier des Mutations V* [*The V-Mutation File*] (4/10/71)

Dir: Victor Vicas; *Wri*: Jacques Bergier, Jean Sacha.
Guest Cast: François Chaumette, François Jaubert, Robert Lombard.
Story: Can a plum tree be genetically modified to grow diamonds?

2. *Attention Névroses Mentales* [*Beware Mental Neuroses*] (11/10/71)
Dir: Victor Vicas; *Wri*: Jacques Bergier, Jean Sacha.
Guest Cast: Philippe Mareuil, Alan Scott, Jerry Brouer, Michel Garland.
Story: Returned astronauts exhibit mysterious signs of depression.

3. *Terreur au Ralenti* [*Terror in Slow Motion*] (18/10/71)
Dir: Claude Boissol; *Wri*: Jacques Bergier, Jean Sacha.
Guest Cast: Michel Garnier, Jean-Pierre Lorrain, Géo Beuf.
Story: A man has the power to make people move in slow motion.

4. *Menaces sur le 6ème Continent* [*Threats on the 6th Continent*] (25/10/71)
Dir: Claude Boissol; Wri: Jacques Bergier, Jean Sacha.
Guest Cast: André Oumansky, Jean Lemaître, Max Amyl.
Story: Is there intelligent life under water?

5. *L'Homme Radar* [*The Radar Man*] (4/11/71)
Dir: Victor Vicas; *Wri*: Jacques Bergier, Jean Sacha.

Guest Cast: Robert Dalban, Françoise Giret, Hubert Deschamps.
Story: Scientists are killed in mysterious plane crashes.

6. *Protection Spéciale Ultra-Sons U* [*Special Protection Ultrasound U*] (11/11/71)
Dir: Claude Boissol; *Wri*: Jacques Bergier, Jean Sacha.
Guest Cast: Jacques Harden, Max Desrau, Marc de Georgi.
Story: A criminal ring designed the ultimate spying device.

2nd Season:
7. *Le Dernier Rempart* [*The Last Rampart*] (23/02/74)
Dir: Claude Boissol; *Wri*: Henri Viard.
Guest Cast: Georges Atlas, Olivier Mathot, Med Hondo, Eva Saint-Paul, Jess Hahn.
Story: A Parisian suburb lives under a mysterious spell.

8. *Le Cabinet Noir* [*The Black Cabinet*] (2/03/74)
Dir: Victor Vicas; *Wri*: Henri Viard.
Guest Cast: Herta Kravina, Joachim Rake.
Story: Seemingly random murders are committed in the cinemas.

9. *Les Hommes Volants* [*The Flying Men*] (9/03/74)
Dir: Claude Boissol; *Wri*: Henri Viard.
Guest Cast: Martti Katajisto, Soila Komi, Eero Kosteikko, Pertti Melasniemi.

Story: The BIPS investigate UFO sightings in Finland.

10. *Meurtres à Distance* [*Remote Murders*] (16/03/74)
Dir: Claude Boissol; *Wri*: Henri Viard.
Guest Cast: Michel Auger, Nicole Dessailly, Georges Géret.
Story: Something is interfering with a telepathic communication experiment aboard a nuclear submarine.

11. *Alerte au Minotaure* [*Minotaur Alert*] (23/03/74)
Dir: Victor Vicas; *Wri*: Henri Viard.
Guest Cast: Jenny Arasse, Jacques Berthier, Michel Creton, Serge Sauvion, Philippe Brigaud.
Story: A new method of doping.

12. *Les Créateurs de Visible* [*The Creators of Visible*] (30/03/74)
Dir: Victor Vicas; *Wri*: Henri Viard.
Guest Cast: Louis De Santis, Guy Lecuyer, Aubert Pallascio, Gilles Pelletier.
Story: Someone creates lifelike optical illusions of dead political leaders.

13. *L'Effaceur de Mémoire* [*The Memory Eraser*] (6/04/74)
Dir: Victor Vicas; *Wri*: Henri Viard.
Guest Cast: Don Arrès, Paul Guèvremont, Roland Chenail, Gratien Gelinas, Monique Miller.
Story: A series of mysterious attacks of amnesia.

Marcel Aymé (A2, col., five 60 min. episodes, 1977-91)

Five delightful adaptations of Marcel Aymé's classic tales starring Michel Serrault produced by Pierre Tchernia.

1. *Le Passe-Muraille* [*The Walker Through the Walls*] (24/12/77)
Dir/Wri: Pierre Tchernia.
Cast: Michel Serrault, Andréa Ferréol, Marco Perrin, Jean Obé, Pierre Tornade, Raoul Curet, Michel Muller, Georges Atlas, Roger Carel, Michel Tugot, Robert Rollis.
Story: A meek civil servant discovers that he has the ability to walk through walls and becomes a master thief.

2. *La Grâce* [The Grace] (21/04/79)
Dir/Wri: Pierre Tchernia.
Cast: Michel Serrault, Rosy Varte, Roger Carel, Ginette Garcin, Serge Bento, Annie Le Youdec.
Story: A saintly man is given a halo and must learn to sin to be rid of it.

3. *Lucienne et le Boucher* [*Lucienne and the Butcher*] (1983)
Not a genre story.

4. *L'Huissier* [*The Bailiff*] (3/01/91)
Dir: Pierre Tchernia; *Wri*: Jean-Claude Grinberg.
Cast: Michel Serrault, Judith Magre, Maurice Chevit, Daniel Prévost, Jean-Paul Roussillon, Pierre Tornade, Georges Wilson.
Story: A mean-spirited bailiff dies and is sent back to Earth for a second chance.

5. *Héloïse* (23/0191)

Dir/Wri: Pierre Tchernia.
Cast: Michel Serrault, Françoise Arnoul, Roger Carel, Pierre Doris, Jean Rougerie, Jacqueline Danno, Bernard Woringer.
Story: A meek photographer turns into a woman at night.

La Belle et son Fantôme [*The Beauty and her Ghost*] (RTF, B&W., thirteen 30 min. episodes, 1962)
Dir/Wri: Bernard Hecht.
Cast: Philippe Ogouz (Charles-Auguste Bauvallet), Anne Tonietti (Barbara), Jacques Monod (Deodat), Josette Vardier (Minna), Jean-Paul Moulinot (Walter), Jean-Marc Tennberg (Poinsot), Bernard Woringer (Oreste), Harry Max, Charles Lavialle, Raymond Jourdan, Madeleine Damiens, Henri Lambert, Annick Allières.
Story: Amateur detective Charles-Auguste Bauvallet and the beautiful Barbara investigate the gothic mysteries surrounding a haunted castle.
Note: The character of Charles-Auguste Bauvallet was first created by Bernard Hecht in 1959 for another (non genre) television series entitled *Bastoche & Charles-Auguste*.
Episodes: 1. *Le Prince de Comagène* [*The Prince of Comagène*] (7/04/62); 2. *Le Château de Lestrange* [*Castle Lestrange*] (14/04/62) ; 3. *La Nuit Fantôme* [*The Ghostly Night*] (21/04/62); 4. *La Fiancée du Premier Clerc* [*The First Clerk's Fiancée*] (28/04/62) ; 5. *Barbara, Morte ou Vivante* [*Barbara, Dead of Alive*] (5/05/62); 6. *La Nuit de Gustave* [*Gustave's Night*] (12/05/62); 7. *Rencontre avec l'Homme Aquarium* [*Meeting the Aquarium Man*] (19/05/62); 8. *Troisième Nuit au Château* [*Third Night at the Castle*] (26/05/62);

9. *Charles-Auguste perd la Partie* [*Charles-Auguste loses a Hand*] (2/06/62); 10. *Minna de Lestrange* (9/06/62); 11. *La Villa Rose* [*The Pink Villa*] (16/06/62); 12. *Week-End pour Charles-Auguste* [*Charles-Auguste's Week-End*] (23/06/62); 13. *Le Puit de la Cave* [*The Cellar's Pit*] (30 /06/62)

Belphegor, ou Le Fantôme du Louvre [*Belphegor, or The Phantom of the Louvre*] (ORTF 1, B&W., four 70 min. episodes, 1965)
Dir: Claude Barma; *Wri*: Claude Barma, Jacques Armand, based on the novel by Arthur Bernède.
Cast: Juliette Gréco (Laurence Borel/Belphegor), René Dary (Commissioner Ménardier), Yves Rénier (André Bellegarde), Christine Delaroche (Colette Ménardier), François Chaumette (Boris Williams), Sylvie (Lady Hodwin), Héléna Bossis (Irène Nando), Paul Cambo, François Chodat, Paul Crauchet, René Alone, Sylvain Levignac, Marguerite Muni, Christian Lude, Jacky Calatayud, Raymond Devime, Jacques Dynam, Maurice Gautier, Germaine Ledoyen, Robert Lombard, Jean Mauvais, Jean Michaud, Pascal Mazzotti, Alain Mottet, Nathalie Nerval, Hubert Noel, Pierre Palau, Marcelle Ranson, Nicolas Vogel, Jean-Pierre Zola.
Story: A ghostly presence is haunting the Louvre. In reality, it is a medium (Laurence) who is manipulated by a secret society led by Boris Williams. They are looking for an ancient alchemical treasure hidden inside the statue of the god Belphegor. The villains are unmasked by André Bellegarde, an enterprising student, and his girlfriend Colett
Episodes: 1. *Le Louvre* (6/03/65); 2. *Le Secret du Louvre* [*The Secret of the Louvre*] (13/03/65); 3. *Les Rose-Croix*

[*The Rosicrucians*] (20/03/65); 4. *Le Rendez-Vous du Fantôme* [*Rendezvous with the Phantom*] (27/03/65).
Note: When in costume, Belphegor is played by Isaac Alvarez, a mime.

Bing (FR3, col., three 60 min. episodes, 1991)
Dir: Nino Monti; *Wri*: Nino Monti, Henri Slotine, based on the novel *All Right, Everybody Off The Planet* by Bob Ottum.
Cast: Jean-François Garreaud (Bing/Dieudonné), Jean-Paul Farré (Fiddle), Claire Nadeau (Gabrielle), Marcel Philippot (Narbonne), Valentin Traversi (Destournelles), Sophie Carle (Marie-Lou), Marina Pastor (Ginny), Christian Jolibois (Prof. Brisebois), Marie-Claude Vermorel (Paola).
Story: Alien visitors send one of their own, Bing, disguised as a journalist, to help Earth decrypt their message, which reads "We come in Peace." In spite of his ignorance of human relationships, Bing stages a successful first contact.
Episodes: 1. *Bing* (3/05/91); 2. *Touche Pas à mon Antenne* [*Don't Touch My Antenna*] (10/05/91); 3. *Où sont les Confitures?* [*Where's The Jam?*] (17/05/91).

Bing II (FR3, col., two 90 min. episodes, 29 /30 December 1992)
Dir: Nino Monti; *Wri*: Henri Slotine, based on the characters created by Bob Ottum in his novel *All Right, Everybody Off The Planet*.
Cast: Jean-François Garreaud (Bing/Dieudonné), Jean-Paul Farré (Fiddle), Claire Nadeau (Gabrielle), Marcel Philippot (Narbonne), Valentin Traversi (Destournelles), Sophie Carle (Marie-Lou), Marina Pastor (Ginny), Christian Jolibois (Prof. Brisebois), Marie-Claude Ver-

morel (Paola), Paul Guers (Gen. Bassompierre), Katherine Erhardy (Felicity).
Story: The Aliens leave Earth and erase all memories of their visit, but have mistakenly left behind an "egg" containing their knowledge. Bing returns to Earth to retrieve it. Eventually, he and his human friends use it to build a new Noah's Ark-like spaceship and leave Earth for a more peaceful planet.

Bob Morane (ORTF 2, B&W., twenty-six 30 min. episodes, 1965)
Regular Cast: Claude Titre (Bob Morane), Billy Kearns (Bill Ballantine).
Story: Based on a long-running series of popular, YA novels by Henri Vernes featuring the intrepid French major Robert Morane and his sidekick, a hulking Scotsman named Bill Ballantine.
Note: Whereas most of the novels contain science fiction or fantasy elements (such as a deadly Fu Manchu-like enemy called Monsieur Ming and the recurring appearances of a friendly Time Patrol from the future), only a few of the television episodes do.
Season 1:

1. *Le Cheik Masqué* [*The Masked Sheik*] (28/03/65)
Dir: Robert Vernay; *Wri*: Gilles Coroner.
Guest Cast: Katrin Schaake, Robert Favard.
Story: Bob Morane and Bill Ballantine are sent to the Middle East to thwart a conspiracy in a Forbidden City.
Note: Original story.

2. *Rafales en Méditerranée* [*Storm Over the Mediterranean*] (4/04/65)

Dir: Robert Vernay; *Wri*: Claude Denys, based on *Trafic aux Caraïbes* by Henri Vernes.
Guest Cast: Claire Maurier, Herbert Knippenberg.
Story: Morane fights a ring of smugglers.

3. *Le Témoin* [*The Witness*] (11/04/65)
Dir: Robert Vernay; *Wri*: Claude Denys.
Guest Cast: Helga Kruck.
Story: Morane protects a schoolteacher who witenessed a crime.
Note: Original story.

4. *Le Prince* [*The Prince*] (18/04/65)
Dir: Raymond Bailly; *Wri*: Claude Denys.
Guest Cast: Douglas Read, Reinhard Kolldehoff.
Story: Morane impersonates an escape artist.
Note: Original story.

5. *Le Tigre des Lagunes* [*The Lagoon Tiger*] (25/04/65)
Dir: Robert Vernay; *Wri*: Robert Vernay, Solange Térac, based on the novel by Henri Vernes.
Guest Cast: Ursule Felsner, Med Hondo, Jean Franval.
Story: Morane defeats a famous pirate.

6. *Le Club des Longs Couteaux* [*The Club of the Long Knives*] (2/05/65)
Dir: Robert Vernay; *Wri*: Gilles Coroner, based on the novel by Henri Vernes.
Guest Cast: Erika Remberg, Jean-Pierre Zola.
Story: Morane tackles a Chinese Tong.

7. *La Galère Engloutie* [*The Sunken Galley*] (9/05/65)
Dir: Pierre Malfille; *Wri*: Gilles Coroner, based on the novel by Henri Vernes.
Guest Cast: Marianne Lutz, Pierre Risch.
Story: Morane goes looking for an underwater treasure.

8. *Le Démon Solitaire* [*The Lone Demon*] (16/05/65)
Dir: Robert Vernay; *Wri*: Robert Vernay, Solange Térac, based on the novel by Henri Vernes.
Guest Cast: Noële Noblecourt, Alexandre Rignault.
Story: Morane goes after a wild horse.

9. *Complot à Trianon* [*Plot at the Trianon*] (23/05/65)
Dir: Raymond Bailly; *Wri*: J. M. Arlaud, Henri Vernes.
Guest Cast: Arthur Allan, Biggi Freyer.
Story: Morane prevents a political assassination.
Note: Original story.

10. *La Voix du Mainate* [*The Mynah's Voice*] (30/05/65)
Dir: Robert Vernay; *Wri*: Régine Artarit, based on the novel by Henri Vernes.
Guest Cast: Alain Nobis, Sarah Sanders.
Story: A Mynah bird has been taught secret information.

Échec à la Main Noire [*The Black Hand in Check*] (6/06/65)
Dir: Robert Vernay; *Wri*: Robert Vernay, Solange Térac, based on the novel by Henri Vernes.

Guest Cast: Reinhard Kolldehoff, Anne Crelli.
Story: Morane vs. the Mafia.

12. *Les Semeurs de Foudre* [*The Sowers of Lightning*] (13/06/65)
Dir: Pierre Malfille; *Wri*: Régine Artarit, based on the novel by Henri Vernes.
Guest Cast: Gunter Meisner, Harline Respati, Jean Michaud.
Story: A gang of villains use controlled lightning as their weapon.

13. *La Vallée des Brontosaures* [*The Valley of the Brontosauri*] (20/06/65)
Dir: Robert Vernay; *Wri*: J. M. Arlaud, based on the novel by Henri Vernes.
Guest Cast: Claude Cerval, Ellen Farner.
Story: Morane locates a hidden graveyard of dinosaurs.

Season 2:

14. *Le Temple des Crocodiles* [*The Temple of the Crocodiles*] (27/06/65)
Dir: Robert Vernay; *Wri*: Robert Vernay, Solange Térac, based on the novel by Henri Vernes.
Guest Cast: Robert Barré, Clément Harari, Helga Münster.
Story: Morane discovers a lost Egyptian temple.

15. *Mission pour Montellano* [*Mission to Montellano*] (19/09/65)
Dir: Robert Vernay; *Wri*: Gilles Coroner, based on *Mission pour Thule* by Henri Vernes.
Guest Cast: Kerstin De Ahna, José Noguéro.

Story: Morane transports an invaluable rocket part.

16. *La Cité des Sables* [*The City of the Sands*] (26/9/65)
Dir: Robert Vernay; *Wri*: Robert Vernay, Solange Térac, based on the novel by Henri Vernes.
Guest Cast: Jacky Calatayud, Walter Gnilka.
Story: A Middle-Eastern adventure.

17. *La Rivière de Perles* [*The River of Pearls*] (3/10/65)
Dir: Robert Vernay; *Wri*: Claude Denys, Henri Vernes.
Guest Cast: André Fouché, Gabriel Gobin, Lucien Hubert.
Story: In Hong Kong, Morane searches for a valuable necklace.
Note: Later novelized by Henri Vernes.

18. *Le Lagon aux Requins* [*The Shark Lagoon*] (10/10/65)
Dir: Pierre Malfille; *Wri*: Claude Denys, based on the novel by Henri Vernes.
Guest Cast: Bernard Charlan, Margit Saad.
Story: Morane fights a gang of pirates.

19. *Mission à Orly* [*Mission at Orly*] (17/10/65)
Dir: Robert Vernay; *Wri*: Régine Artarit, Henri Vernes.
Guest Cast: Claude Evrard, Jean Saudray, Mitsouko.
Story: Morane prevents a kidnapping.
Note: Later novelized by Henri Vernes.

20. *Le Gardian Noir* [*The Black Guardian*] (24/10/65)
Dir: Pierre Malfille; *Wri*: Claude Denys.
Guest Cast: Jack Berard, Marie-Claude Breton.
Story: Morane thwarts a plot among the Gypsies.
Note: Original story.

21. *L'Héritage du Flibustier* [*The Freebooter's Inheritance*] (31/10/65)
Dir: Robert Vernay; *Wri*: Robert Vernay, Solange Térac, based on the novel by Henri Vernes.
Guest Cast: Yves Barsacq, Jean Houbé.
Story: A treasure hunt.

22. *Les Joyaux du Maradjah* [*The Jewels of the Maharadjah*] (7/11/65)
Dir: Robert Vernay; *Wri*: Claude Denys, based on the novel by Henri Vernes.
Guest Cast: Anne Carrère, Emilio Carrer.
Story: Morane stops a revolution.

23. *La Fleur du Sommeil* [*The Flower of Sleep*] (14/11/65)
Dir: Robert Vernay; *Wri*: Régine Artarit, based on the novel by Henri Vernes.
Guest Cast: Frances Martin, Jean Rupert.
Story: Morane fights an opium trafficking ring.

24. *Le Camion Infernal* [*The Truck from Hell*] (21/11/65)
Dir: Robert Vernay; *Wri*: Claude Denys, Henri Vernes.
Guest Cast: Roland Armontel, Hellmut Grube, Antoine Marin.

Story: Morane accepts a suicide mission.
Note: Later novelized by Henri Vernes.

25. *Les Forbans de l'Or Noir* [*The Black Gold Villains*] (28/11/65)
Dir: Robert Vernay; *Wri*: J. M. Arlaud, Henri Vernes.
Guest Cast: Georges Demas, Pierre Gualdi, Olivier Mathot.
Story: Morane thwarts a sabotage ring.
Note: Original story.

26. *Le Dragon des Fenstone* [*The Fenstone Dragon*] (5/12/65)
Dir: Robert Vernay; *Wri*: J. M. Arlaud, based on the novel by Henri Vernes.
Guest Cast: Michel Dacquin, Hubert de Lapparent, Raoul Delfosse.
Story: A fake dragon is used to divert attention from a crime.

La Brigade des Maléfices [*The Brigade of Spells*] (ORTF 2, col., six 60 min.
episodes, 1971)
Dir: Claude Guillemot; *Wri*: Claude Jean-Philippe, Monique Lefebvre, Claude Guillemot.
Regular Cast: Léo Campion (Inspector Gaston Martin Paumier), Marc Lamole (Albert), Jacques François (Police Commissioner), Jean-Claude Balard (Inspector Muselier).
Story: Inspector Paumier and his faithful assistant Albert investigate supernatural mysteries. Their rival, skeptic inspector Muselier, always tries and fails to find a rational explanation for each mystery.

1. *Les Disparus de Rambouillet* [*Disappearances in Rambouillet*] (2/08/71)
Guest Cast: Jean-Pierre Andreani (Lancelot), Roger Riffard, Sylvie Fennec (Fairy), Virginie Vignon (Musidora).
Story: Fairies are responsible for men disappearing in a forest near Paris.

2. *La Septième Chaîne* [*The Seventh Channel*] (9/08/71)
Guest Cast: Pierre Brasseur (The Devil), Olivier Lebeaut, Sybille Maas, Jacques Serres.
Story: The Devil uses television to drive people to commit murder.

3. *Voir Vénus et Mourir* [*To See Venus And Die*] (16/08/971)
Guest Cast: Philippe Clay (Adonis), Anny Duperey (Venusine), Gérard Lartigau.
Story: A beautiful Venusian goes after a con artist selling interplanetary vacations.

4. *La Créature* [*The Creature*] (23/08/71)
Guest Cast: Pierre Brasseur (The Devil), Claude Brasseur, Catherine Jacobsen (The Creature), Albert Simono,
Story: The Devil uses a beautiful, soulless woman to drive people to suicide.

5. *Les Dents d'Alexis* [*Alexis' Teeth*] (30/08/71)
*Guest C*ast: Pierre Vernier (Alexis de Sambleux), Karyn Balme, Jean-Marie Rivière.
Story: An unhappy vampire falls in love with his dentist, thus lifting his curse.

6. *Le Fantôme des HLM* [*The Ghost of the Housing Project*] (6/09/71)
Guest Cast: Gérard Séty (Anatole the Ghost), Paul Villé (Marquis de Palaiseau).
Story: The ghost of a 17th century nobleman haunts a housing project.

Calls (Canal-Plus, twenty-seven 10 to 15 min. eps., 2017-20)
Created by: Timothée Hochet; *Wri*: Timothée Hochet, Clémence Setti, Norman Tonnelier, Lucas Pastor.
Cast: Mathieu Kassovitz, François Civil, Marina Foïs, Charlotte Le Bon, Gaspard Ulliel.
Concept: Told through a series of interconnected phone conversations, these conversations chronicle the mysterious story of a group of strangers whose lives are thrown into disarray in the lead-up to an apocalyptic event.

Season 1 (10 eps, 15 December 2017-12 January 2018): 1. *Appels téléphoniques Paris-New York (2028)*; 2. *Masques faciaux de plongées (Océan Atlantique) (2026)*; 3. *Appel enregistré 17 (Nancy) (2004)*; 4. *Sources multiples (Servon, France) (2027)*; 5. *Répondeurs téléphoniques (Paris) (2028)*; 6. *Prises son d'un long-métrage (Forêt Domaniale d'Orléans) (2028)*; 7. *Archives NASA (ISS) (2028)*; 8. *Talkies Walkies (Magicland) (2027)*; 9. *Boîte Noire (Boeing 747) (2025)*; 10. *Sources multiples (Lieu inconnu, France) (1999)*.

Saison 2 (27 May 2019): 1. *Sleep Recordin App / Appels Téléphoniques (Huesca, Espagne) - Dans le noir (2024)*; 2. *Appels Téléphoniques (New York) - Le rendez-vous (2001)*; 3. *Enregistrement radiophonique (Paris) – L'auditeur (2021)*; 4. *Cassette dictaphone EL3581 (France) - Souvenirs audio : 05/1958, 07/1958, 11/1958, 03/1959, 11/1959, 01/1960, 05/1960, 11/1962, 01/1963, 11/1963, 12/1963, 04/1965, 06/1965, 02/1966, 05/2006*; 5. *Appels téléphoniques Service d'Aide à l'Enfance (Val-de-Marne, France) (2001)*; 6. *Documentaire Audio / Prise Son Binaural (2CXF+P6 Belvédère, France) - Sous la terre (???)*; 7. *Répondeur / Appels / Dictaphone (Ile-de-France) - Le dernier message (2026)*; 8. *Dictaphone (Savoie) - Better Call Satan (2023)*; 9. *Fichier son micro voiture (Les Brugassières, France) - La route (2028)*; 10. *Micro-trottoir / Rushs Son / Appel (France) - Chasseur de fantômes (2002)*.

Season 3 (10 December 2020): 1. *Appel téléphonique – L'Égarée (???)*; 2. *Conversation téléphonique (Le Mans, France) - Le Lâche (2023)*; 3. *Enregistrement de caméras (Beaujan, France) – L'Innocente (???)*; 4. *Dictaphone d'Anne Larcher (Meaux, France) - La Cène (2023)*; 5. *L'Oubliée (???)*; 6. *Conférence de presse NASA (Houston) - Les Écoutants (2028)*; 7. *Les Autres (???)*.

Note: An American remake of the series has been available on the Apple TV+ platform since March 19, 2021.

Les 100 Tours de Centour [*The Hundred Tricks of Centour*] (French-Canadian TV, col, 105 15 min. episodes, 27 September 1971-24 March 72)
Dir/Wri: Guy Sanche.
Cast: Roland Chenail, Julien Genay (Verbo), Yves Massicotte (Centour), Ghyslain Tremblay (Pico), Camille Ducharme, Madeleine Sicotte.

Story: Verbo, a genie, is trying to recapture Centour, another genie. Verbo's constant companion is Pico, a young human male whose family is often the target of Centour's tricks.
Note: The show's main purpose was language acquisition.

Chéri-Bibi (ORTF 1, col. forty-six 15 min episodes, 16 December 1974-18 February 1975)
Dir: Jean Pignol; *Wri*: A.D.G., Jean Pignol, based on the novels by Gaston Leroux.
Cast: Hervé Sand (Chéri-Bibi), Danièle Lebrun (Cécily), Jean Lefèbvre (La Ficelle), Malka Ribowska (Comtesse), Daniel Emilfork (Kanak), Roger Vattier (Commandant), Marguerite Cassan (Soeur Ste. Marie), Jean Herbert, Pierre Jatet, Alexandre Rignault, Antoine Marin, Georges Montillier, Bernard Charnacé, Katia Tchenko, Virginie Vignon, Nadine Benoît, Muse Dalbray, Mireille Audibert, Laurent Douieb, Jean Saudray, Marcel Champel, Jean Mauvais, Henri Jouf, Pierre Bolo.
Story: After being unjustly incarcerated, the amazingly strong Cheri-Bibi and La Ficelle are sent to Devil's Island. They take over the prison ship and later rescue some shipwrecked people, including the beautiful Cecily who is fianced to the evil Maxime du Touchais. Dr. Kanak kills Maxime and grafts his face on Cheri-Bibi who hopes to start a new life.

Les Classiques de l'Étrange [*Classics of the Strange*]
Prod: Michel Subiela.
Concept: This anthology series was intended to take over from *Le Tribunal de l'Impossible* (see below), with a program of four films per year, all adapted from the best

literary material. Unfortunately, it was cancelled soon after the first episode and subsequent productions were aired independently at random dates.

1. *La Main Enchantée* [*The Enchanted Hand*] (ORTF 1, col., 90 min., 5/10/74)
Dir: Michel Subiela; *Wri*: Michel Subiela, Francis Lacassin, based on a story by Gérard de Nerval.
<u>Cast</u>: Pierre Maxence, Nathalie Juvet, Alain Mottet, Thierry Dufour, Roland Monod, Serge Lhorca.
Story: A magician gives a man a spell which makes his right hand invincible, but it no longer obeys his will.

2. *Le Péril Bleu* [*The Blue Peril*] (A2, col., 90 min., 31/03/75)
Dir: Jean-Christophe Averty; *Wri*: Claude Veillot, based on the novel by Maurice Renard.
Cast: Jean-Roger Caussimon, Bernard Valdeneige, Michel Modo, Erik Colin, France Dougnac, Yvonne Clech, Nicole Norden.
Story: In 1914, mysterious aliens abduct people to study humankind.

3. *Le Collectionneur de Cerveaux* [*The Brain Collector*] (A2, col., 90 min., 23/10/76)
Dir/Wri: Michel Subiela, based on the story "Robots Pensants" [*Thinking Robots*] by George Langelaan.
Cast: Claude Jade, François Dunoyer, André Reybaz, Roger Crouzet, Thierry Murzeau.
Story: Count Saint-Germain grafts human organs inside robot bodies to build perfect androids.

Les Compagnons de Baal [*The Brotherhood of Baal*] (ORTF 1, B&W., seven 60 min. episodes, 1968)

Dir: Pierre Prévert; *Wri*: Jacques Champreux.
Cast: Jean Martin (Hubert de Mauvouloir), Jacques Champreux (Claude), Martine Redon (Liliane), René Dary (Commissioner), Raymond Bussières (Diogenes), Jacques Monod, Catherine Alcover, Pierre André Krol, René Lefèvre, Jean Herbert, Roger Desmare, Patrick Lancelot, François Dyrek, André Rousselet, Gérard Larcebeau, Claire Nadeau.
Story: Claude, a journalist, unmasks a centuries-old criminal conspiracy, the Brotherhood of Baal, led by the mysterious Hubert de Mauvouloir, a man who may be the Count of Saint-Germain.
Episodes: 1. *Le Secret de Diogène* [*Diogenes' Secret*] (12/07/68); 2. *Les Mystères de l'Île Saint-Louis* [*The Mysteries of île Saint-Louis*] (29/07/68); 3. *Le Spectre Rouge* [*The Red Spectre*] (5/08/68); 4. *L'Inquiétant Professeur* [*The Disturbing Professor*] (19/08/68); 5. *La Nuit du Huit de Trèfle* [*The Night of the Eight of Clubs*] (26/08/68); 6. *L'Héritage de Nostradamus* [*The Legacy of Nostradamus*] (2/09/68); 7. *L'Éveil de Liliane* [*Liliane Awakens*] (9/09/68).

Les Compagnons d'Eleusis [*The Brotherhood of Eleusis*] (TF1, col., thirty 15 min. episodes, 26 September-16 November 1975)
Dir: Claude Grinberg; *Wri*: Alain Page.
Cast: Marcel Dalio (Mafel), Bernard Alane (Vincent), Thérèse Liotard (Sophie), Catherine Sellers (Emmanuelle), Hubert Gignoux (Verdier), Pierre Tabard (Beaumont), Yves Bureau, Gabriel Cinque, Jacques Goasguen, Maurice Travail, Pierre Hentz, Jean-Jacques Lagarde, Jean Turlier, Jean Berger, Raoul Delfosse.

Story: A secret society of modern alchemists decides to use vast quantities of gold to destroy the modern world's emphasis on material values.

Contact (TF1, eight 49-min. episodes, 17 décembre 2015-26 octobre 2017)
Created by: Jean-Yves Arnaud, Delinda Jacobs.
Dirs: Frédéric Berthe, David Morley, Elsa Bennett, Hippolye Dard.
Wri: Delinda Jacobs, Christophe Carmona, Hervé Korian, Marine Ruini, Eliane Vigneron, Pennda Ba.
Cast: Thomas Jouannet (Thomas Adam), Alexis Loret (Éric Adam), Amélie Remacle (Nathalie Adam), Louvia Bachelier (Maya Adam), Charlie Joirkin (Isabelle Adam), Ingrid Donnadieu (Mélanie), Hélène Seuzaret (Captain Ortiz), Alexandra Campanacci, Sara Mortensen, Julien Boisselier, Jérémie Covillault, Daniel Njo Lobé, Jean-Marc Michelangeli.
Story: Thomas has the gift of seeing the memories left on an object by the person who touched it last. For 10 years, he has collaborated with the FBI. Back in France, he finds himself at the heart of the investigations led by his brother, Eric, a police lieutenant, in Aix-en-Provence.
Episodes: 1. *Untitled* (12/17/2015); 2. *Untitled* (12/17/2015); 3. *L'homme sans visage* [*The Faceless Man*] (10/12/2017); 4. *Une vie pour une autre* [*One Life for Another*] (10/12/2017); 5. *Instinct maternel* [*Maternal Instinct*] (10/19/2017); 6. *Romain* (10/19/2017); 7. *Tatouages* [*Tattoos*] (10/26/2017); 8. *Derrière les murs* [*Behind the Walls*] (10/26/2017).

Les Contes du Chat Perché [*The Tales of the Crouching Cat*, A.K.A. *The Wonderful Farm*] (ORTF 2, col., thirteen 20-min., episodes, December 1968)

Dir: Arlen Papazian; *Wri*: Albert Husson, based on the tales by Marcel Aymé.

Regular Cast: Christine Chicoine (Delphine), Marie-Claude Breton (Mariette), André Julien (Father), Odette Picquet (Mother).

Guest Cast: Armand Maistre, Pierre Gualdi, Françoise Bertin, Bernard Tirli, Yveline Moatti, and the voices of Yves Mathieu, Alexandre Rignault, Jean Valton, Roger Carel, Marguerite Cassan, Françoise Arnaud.

Story: On a farm, two little girls communicate with the animals, and have a series of adventures.

Episodes: 1. *Les Boîtes de Peinture* [*The Paint Boxes*] (21/12/68); 2. *L'Âne et le Cheval* [*The Ass and the Horse*] (22/12/68); 3. *Les Vaches* [*The Cows*] (23/12/68); 4. *La Patte du Chat* [*The Cat's Paw*] (24/12/68); 5. *Le Problème* [*The Problem*] (25/12/68); 6. *Le Petit Coq Noir* [*The Little Black Rooster*] (26/12/68); 7. *Le Chien Aveugle* [*The Blind Dog*] (27/12/68); 8. *Le Cerf et le Chien* [*The Deer and the Dog*] (28/12/68); 9. *Le Paon* [*The Peacock*] (29/12/68); 10. *Les Boeufs* [*The Ox*] (30 /12/68); 11. *Le Canard et la Panthère* [*The Duck and the Panther*] (31/12/68); 12. *Le Mouton* [*The Sheep*] (1/01/69); 13. *Le Loup* [*The Wolf*] (2/01/69).

Coplan FX-18 (A2, six 90 min. episodes, 1989-91)

Story: The adventures of Francis Coplan, Agent FX-18, are the French equivalent of *James Bond*. The novels were published by Editions Fleuve Noir, and written by Paul Kenny, a pseudonym of writers Jean Libert & Gaston Vandenpanhuyse. Each episode begins with a problem directly or indirectly targeting the security of France. Agent FX-18 is then summoned by the head of his department, nicknamed the "Old Man." Exotic ad-

ventures ensue with plenty of dastardly villains and beautiful femme fatales.
Regular Cast: Philippe Caroit (Coplan), Pierre Dux (Mr. Pascal, aka Le Vieux).

1. *Coups Durs* [*Hard Blows*] (16/04/89)
Dir: Gilles Behat; *Wri*: Gilles Behat, Philippe Madral.
Guest Cast: Daniel Olbrychski, Manfred Andrae, Isabelle Renauld, Kristina Van Eyck.

2. *L'Ange et le Serpent* [*The Angel and the Snake*] (17/09/89)
Dir: Peter Kassovitz; *Wri*: Pierre Geller, Dominique Robelet, based on the novel by Paul Kenny.
Guest Cast: Claire Nebout, Jacques Denis, Jean-Pol Dubois, Gérard Caillaud.

3. *Le Vampire des Caraïbes* [*The Caribbean Vampire*] (22/10/89)
Dir: Yvan Butler; *Wri*: Tito Topin, based on the novel *Diplomatie de la Terreur* by Paul Kenny.
Guest Cast: Patricia Millardet, Pierre Julien, France Zobda.

4. *Vengeance à Caracas* [*Revenge in Caracas*] (3/12/89)
Dir: Philippe Toledano; *Wri*: Philippe Madral.
Guest Cast: Patachou, Ruddy Rodriguez, Eva Mondolfi.

5. *La Filière Argentine* [*The Argentinian Network*] (3/03/91)

Dir: Roger Andrieux; *Wri*: Roger Andrieux, Claude Veillot, Nancy Heikin-Pepin, based on the novel by Paul Kenny.
Guest Cast: Sylvie Orcier, Jean-Pierre Kalfon.

6. *Retour aux Sources* [*Back to the Basics*] (1991)
No information available.

Les Corbeaux [*The Crows*] (TF1, col., two 90-min. episodes, 26 January-2 February 2009)
Dir: Régis Musset; *Wri*: Sergio Gobbi, Laurent Scalese.
Cast: Astrid Veillon (Sonia), Jean-Pierre Michaël, Anne Charrier, Frédéric Pellegeay, Zoé Duthion, Zacharie Chasseriaud, Fabio Zenoni, Delphine Grandsart, Catherine Sola, Jean-Pierre Malignon.
Story: Climate change has disrupted the migration of crows, who find themselves disoriented on an island in Brittany. Sonia, a doctor, her autistic granddaughter, Estelle, and Thomas, an ornithologist investigating the strange behavior of birds, are confronted with the violence of the crows.

David Nolande (FR2, col., six 52 min. episodes, 12 September-20 December 2006)
Dir: Nicolas Cuche; *Wri*: Joël Houssin.
Cast: Frédéric Diefenthal (David Nolande), Elsa Kikoïne, Édouard Montoute, Jean-Louis Foulquier, Emmanuel Patron.
Story: David Nolande, drunk, swerves off the highway to avoid a black dog and kills an old Gypsy fortuneteller. After being found not guilty of negligent homicide, another Gypsy curses him, telling him that he will have to save many lives in order to make up for the death of the

old woman and for each life he fails to save, one of his own loved ones will die.

Episodes: 1. *Peine perdue* [*Wasted Effort*]; 2. *La Proie des Flammes* [*Victim of the Flames*]; 3. *L'Horloge du Destin* [*The Clock of Fate*]; 4. *Crescendo*; 5. *Chiens Méchants* [*Beware the Dogs*]; 6. *La Carte du Diable* [*The Devil's Card*].

Dead Landes (FR4, col., ten 25 min. episodes, 3 December-17 December 2016)
Dir: François Descraques; *Wri*: François Uzan, François Descraques (eps. 1, 2, 10), Éric Vérat (eps. 3, 8), Éric Delafosse (eps. 4, 9), Claire Le Luhen (eps. 5, 6, 7).
Cast: Thomas VDB, Julie Farenc-Deramond, Yacine Belhousse, Sören Prévost, Adrianna Gradziel, David Salles.
Story: While two documentary filmmakers follow the end of holidays in a campsite of the French Landes, a supernatural disaster strikes the small community. From then on, the two cameramen will try to record what seems to be the end of the world.

Episodes. 1. *Et sa Colère s'abattit* [*And His Wrath Fell*]; 2. *Et l'Horizon s'enflamma* [*And the Horizon Took Fire*]; 3. *Et les Ténèbres s'épaissirent* [*And Darkness Grew*]; 4. *Et un Étranger apparut* [*And a Stranger came*]; 5. *Et les Premiers nés moururent* [*And the First Born died*]; 6. *Et la Fièvre les consuma* [*And the Fevers Took them*]; 7. *Et les Voix se turent* [*And the Voices Grew Silent*]; 8. *Et l'Espoir s'éteignit* [And Hope Died]; 9. *Et les Morts se relevèrent* [*And the Dead Rose Up*]; 10. *Et la Spirale se referma* [*And the Spiral Closed*].

Note: *Dead Floor* was a web-series in five episodes, describing events taking place in parallel to those portrayed in the TV series. It follows the misadventures of five medical students, who have come to celebrate the end of their exams at a nightclub in the region. When the fog appears, they too find themselves stuck in the area.

De Bien Étranges Affaires [*Some Very Strange Affairs*] (FR3, col., six 60 min. episodes, 1982)

1. *La Soucoupe de Solitude* [*A Saucer of Loneliness*] (8/09/82)
Dir: Philippe Monnier; *Wri*: Philippe Monnier, Michel Picard, based on a story by Theodore Sturgeon initially published in *Galaxy* in 1953.
Cast: Catherine Leprince, André Valardy, Valerio Popesco.
Story: One evening, a dysphoric visual artist receives a visit from a tiny flying saucer which seems to communicate with her, but the young woman loses consciousness. The secret services seize the mini-starship and harass the message recipient.
Note: The story was adapted again by David Gerrold as part of the new *Twilight Zone* on CBS on 27 September 1986, starring Shelley Duvall.

2. *L'Ami Étranger* [*The Alien Friend*] (15/09/82)
Dir: Patrick Jamain; *Wri*: Philippe Setbon.
Cast: Ottavia Piccolo, Marcel Bozzuffi, Roland Bertin.
Story: A man meets a girl who is the exact double of a girl he loved twenty years ago. In reality, she is an alien who has been sent to study mankind.

3. *Lourde Gueuse* [*Heavy Iron*] (22/09/82)
Dir/Wri: Jean-Luc Miesch, based on a story by Jean-Pierre Andrevon.

Cast: Franco Interlenghi, Eddie Constantine, Michel Robin, Isabelle Lacamp, Elisabeth Bourgine, Christian Bouillette.
Story: The crew of a spaceship revolts against their captain.

4. *L'Amour qui Tue* [*The Killing Love*] (29/09/82)
Dir/Wri: Laurent Heynemann, based on the story *The Price of Synergy* by Theodore Sturgeon.
Cast: Patrick Chesnais, Stefania Casini, Philippe Lemaire, Jean-Paul Muel, Daniel Laloux.
Story: A drug kills its victims during lovemaking.

5. *Un Homme Ordinaire* [*An Ordinary Man*] (6/10/82)
Dir: Juan Luis Buñuel; *Wri*: Hélène Peycharand, based on the short story *Programmation* by Raoul Gamond.
Cast: David Pontremoli, Michel Auclair, Hélène Peycharand, Danielle Godet.
Story: In a chaotic post-nuclear future, androids learn to become human.

6. *Le Triangle à Quatre Côtés* [*The Four-Sided Triangle*] (13/10/82)
Dir: Jean-Claude Lubtchansky; *Wri*: Jean-Claude Lubtchansky, Paul Gégauff, based on the novel by William Temple originally published as a short story in *Amazing* in 1939 and expanded in 1949.
Cast: Maria Rosaria Ommaggio, Alain Maratrat, François Marthouret, Gabriel Jabbour.
Story: A girl who is loved by two men is duplicated by the one she has refused.

Note: This novel was also adapted as a 1952 Hammer Film directed by Terence Fisher, starring Barbara Payton.

Déjà Vu (France 2, fifty-two 216-min. episodes, October 2007-December 2009)
Dir: Youcef Hamidi, Alain Rudaz, Thean-Jeen Lee; *Wri*: Eric Vérat, David Paillot, Hadrien Soulez Larivière, Marie Duroy, Pierre Monjanel, Claire Paoletti, Olivier Dehors, Thomas Martinetti, Christophe Martinolli.
Cast: Leslie Coutterand (Alexandra Casala), Eléa Clair, Arnaud Cordier, Pierre-Antoine Damecour, André Marcotte, Anton Khan, Daphné Hacquard.
Story: Young Alexandra is endowed with supernatural powers after an accident. She can relive scenes from her life at will.

La Dernière Vague [*The Last Wave*] (France 2, six 52-min. episodes, 21 October-4 November 2019)
Dir: Rodolphe Tissot; *Wri*: Raphaëlle Roudaut, Alexis Le Sec, Sophie Hiet.
Cast: David Kammenos, Marie Dompnier, Arnaud Binard, Lola Dewaere, Capucine Valmary, Guillaume Cramoisan, Gaël Raës, Roberto Calvet, Théo Christine, Olivier Barthélémy, Isabel Otero, Alexia Barlier, Odile Vuillemin.
Story: In a peaceful seaside resort in the Landes, everything changes with the arrival of a mysterious cloud which causes the disappearance of ten people. Later, they reappear without memories of their disappearance. Some find themselves changed and endowed with strange powers...
Episodes: *1. Cinq heures [Five Hours]; 2. Le Retour [The Return]; 3. Révolte [Rebellion]; 4. Déflagration*

[Conflagration]; 5. Boomerang; 6. Les Messagers [The Messengers].

Deux Ans de Vacances [*A Two Years' Vacation*, transl. as *Adrift in the Pacific*] (ORTF 1, col., six 60 min. episodes, 1 June-15 July 1974)
Dir: Gilles Grangier; *Wri*: Claude Desailly, based on the novel by Jules Verne.
Cast: Franz Seidenschwan, Didier Gaudron, Marc di Napoli, Dominique Planchot, Frédéric Duru, Rainer Basedow, Werner Pocchard.
Story: Two shipwrecked teenagers strugglie to escape pirates in the South Pacific.

Disparitions [*Disappearances*] (France 3, twelve 52-min. episodes, 1 November-6 December 2008)
Dir: Robin Davis, Olivier Jamain, Bruno Gantillon; *Wri*: Nicolas Durand-Zouky, Yves Ramonet, Jacques Mazeau, Fabienne Facco, Sylvie Chanteux.
Cast: Agathe de La Boulaye (Claire), Thomas Sanchez (Andreu), Jérôme Bertin (Antoine), Georges Corraface (Sormand), Gilles Guérin, Katia Cuq, Samira Lachhab, Cédric Chevalme, Laurent Collombert, Jeanne Goupil, Valeria Cavalli, Virginie Desarnauts.
Story: Antoine, a police officer specializing in investigating sects, is dispatched to Toulouse to investigate a crime involving a macabre ritual. He meets his former college professor, Raphaël Sormand, who is the father of the victim. The circumstances of the crime have strange similarities with a fifteen years-old tragedy involving Antoine and Raphaël, which caused to lose Claire, the woman he loved. Today, Claire is stuck in a wheelchair. As she prepares to take up a position as a hospital psy-

chiatrist, the mediumnic powers that she thought she had lost with the use of her legs manifest themselves again...

Dorothée, Danseuse de Corde [*Dorothy, the Rope Dancer*] (A2, col., three 60 min. episodes, 1983)
Dir: Jacques Fansten; *Wri*: Michel Favart, Jacques Fansten, based on the novel by Maurice Leblanc.
Cast: Fanny Bastien (Dorothée), Macha Méril, Féodor Atkine, Patrick Fierry, Jean-Denis Filliozat, Bruno Bouillon, Arnaud Giordano.
Story: A young circus acrobat solves the mystery of the treasure of the Kings of France.
Episodes: 1. *L'Assassin du Prince d'Argonne* [*The Murderer of the Prince d'Argonne*] (21/12/83); 2. *In Robore Fortuna* (22/12/83); 3. *Le Testament du Marquis de Beaugreval* [*The Testament of the Marquis de Beaugreval*] (28/12/82).

La Double Vie de Théophraste Longuet [*The Double Life of Théophraste Longuet*] (TF1, col., three 90 min. episodes, 1981)
Dir: Yannick Andrei; *Wri*: Jean-Claude Carrière, based on the novel by Gaston Leroux.
Cast: Jean Carmet (Théophraste), Geneviève Fontanel (Marcelline), Gabriel Cattand, Nicolas Silberg (Cartouche), Michel Duchaussoy, Gabriel Jabbour, Jean-Claude Carrière (Eliphas), Marie Bunel, Nicole Carrière.
Story: Théophraste, a retired merchant, finds himself possessed by the spirit of notorious 18th century highwayman Cartouche.
Episodes: 1. *Le Mystère* [*The Mystery*] (27/10/81); 2. *Le Combat* [*The Fight*] (29/10/81); 3. *Le Trésor* [*The Treasure*] (30 /10/81).

La Duchesse d'Avila [*The Duchess of Avila*] (ORTF 2, col., four episodes of 70, 130, 55 and 100 min., 4-25 July 1973)
Dir: Philippe Ducrest; *Wri*: Philippe Ducrest, Véronique Castelnau, Roger Caillois, based on Jan Potocki's *Ms. found in Zaragoza*.
Cast: Jean Blaise (Alphonse), José-Luis de Villalonga, Evelyne Eyfel (aka Véronique Castelnau), Sylvie Bréal, Jacqueline Laurent, Michel de Ré, Pierre Piéral, François Maistre, Serge Marquand, Jacques Morel, Jean Martin, Jean Franval.
Story: Alphonse, a young Spanish nobleman, embarks on a fantastic journey.

L'Effondrement [*The Collapse*] (Canal+, eigh 15-to-25 mins. episodes, 11 November-2 December 2019)
Dir/Wri: « Les Parasites » i.e.: Guillaume Desjardins, Jérémy Bernard, Bastien Ughetto.
Cast: Bellamine Abdelmalek, Roxane Bret, Philippe Rebbot, Christelle Cornil, Thibault de Montalembert, Audrey Fleurot.
Story: This series follows diverse individuals and families, at different times and places, as they seek to survive in a society that is collapsing around them, starting on D-Day+2.
Episodes: 1. *D+2/Le Supermarché [The Supermarket]; 2. D+5/La Station-service [The Service Station]; 3. D+6/L'Aérodrome [The Airport]; 4. D+25/Le Hameau [The Hamlet]; 5. D+45/La Centrale [The Station]; 6. D+50/La Maison de retraite [The Retirement Home]; 7. D+170/L'Île [The Island]; 8. D-5/L'Émission [The Broadcast].*

Emma (TF1, col., two 52 min. episodes, October 2016)

Dir: Alfred Lot; *Wri*: Manon Dillys, Sébastien Le Délézir.
Cast: Solène Hébert (Emma), Patrick Ridremont, Slimane Yefsah, Sabrina Seyvecou, Vanessa Larré.
Story: A young policewoman, Emma, 25, turns out to be an android.
Episodes: 1. *Question de confiance* [*A Matter of Trust*]; 2. *Mort aux Vainqueurs* [*Death to the Winners*].

Éternelle [*Eternal*] (M6, six 52 min. episodes ,30 July-13 August 2009)
Dir: Didier Delaître; *Wri*: Joël Houssin
Cast: Claire Keim (She), Guillaume Cramoisan (Dr. Voline), Boris Terral, Antoine Duléry, Arthur Jugnot, Elsa Mollien, Asil Rais, Audrey Fleurot, Serge Riaboukine.
Story: Dr. Voline knocks down a naked young woman with his 4x4. Transported to the hospital, she doesn't remember anything and is declared carrier of an unknown virus. Refusing to be separated from Voline, "She" discovers her ability to read thoughts and exchange memories with those she meets.
Episodes: 1. *Rencontre par accident* [*Accidental Encounter*]; 2. *La Télépathe* [*The Telepath*]; 3. *Bactérie inconnue* [*Unknown Bacteria*]; 4. *Plante disparue* [*Extinct Plant*]; 5. *Sang contaminé* [*Contaminated Blood*]; 6. *Disparition inquiétante* [*Troubling Disappearance*].
Note: This series gives no explanation to the multiple mysteries it created: who is "She"? Where does she come from? Who is the mysterious biker who follows her? etc.

Fantômas (A2, col., four 90-min. episodes, 1980)

A series of films based on the popular novels by Marcel Allain & Pierre Souvestre published between 1911 and 1913.
Regular Cast: Helmut Berger (Fantômas), Jacques Dufilho (Juve), Pierre Malet (Fandor), Gayle Hunnicut (Lady Beltham).
Story: Arch-criminal Fantômas outwits Police Commisionner Juve and journalist Jerôme Fandor.

1. *L'Échafaud Magique* [*The Magic Scaffold*] (4/10/80)
Dir: Claude Chabrol; *Wri*: Bernard Revon, based on Book 1 of the series by Allain & Souvestre.
Guest Cast: Kristina Van Eyck (Princess Danidoff), Pierre Douglas (Judge Fuselier), Mario David (Nibet), Hélène Duc.
Story: Fantômas sends an innocent man to the guillotine.

2. *L'Étreinte du Diable* [*The Devil's Hug*] (11/10/80)
Dir: Juan Luis Buñuel; *Wri*: Bernard Revon, based on Book 2 of the series by Allain & Souvestre.
Guest Cast: Pierre Douglas (Judge Fuselier), Jean-Paul Zehnacker, Hélène Peycharand.
Story: Fantômas infiltrates the Paris underground.

3. *Le Mort qui Tue* [*The Dead Man Who Kills*] (18/10/80)
Dir: Juan Luis Buñuel; *Wri*: Bernard Revon, based on Book 3 of the series by Allain & Souvestre
Guest Cast: Kristina Van Eyck (Princess Danidoff), Pierre Douglas (Judge Fuselier), Mario David (Nibet), Maxence Mailfort, Véronique Delbourg, Philippe Laudenbach, Victor Garrivier, Danielle Godet.

Story: Fantômas impersonates a banker and uses a glove made with human skin to leave false fingerprints behind.

4. *Le Tramway Fantôme* [*The Phantom Trolley*] (25/10/80)
Dir: Claude Chabrol; *Wri*: Bernard Revon, based on Book 5 of the series by Allain & Souvestre
Guest Cast: Peter Wolfsberger, Claudia Messner, Marieli Frohlich.
Story: Fantômas kidnaps a king.

Fantômette (FR3, col., twenty-one 30 min. episodes, April-May 1993)
Based on the popular YA novels by Georges Chaulet.
Regular Cast: Katia Sourzac (Fantômette/Françoise), Justine Fraioli (Boulotte), Sabine Franquet (Ficelle), Bertrand Lacy (Oeil-de-Lynx), Arsène Jiroyan (Navarin).
Story: A teenage girl, Françoise, takes on the identity of costumed crime fighter Fantômette to thwart evil.

1. *Fantômette et le Clone* [*The Clone*] (20/04/93)
Dir: Christiane Spiero; *Wri*: Pascal Bancou.
Guest Cast: Bruno Raffaelli (Silver Mask).

2. *Fantômette est givrée* [*Fantômette is crazy*] (21/04/93)
Dir: Christiane Spiero; *Wri*: Pascal Bancou.
Guest Cast: Bruno Raffaelli, Dominique Sarrazin.

3. *Fantômette et l'Eau Rouge* [*The Red Water*] (22/04/93)
Dir: Marco Pauly; *Wri*: Brigitte Aymard.

Guest Cast: Michel Crémadès (Le Furet), Éric Leblanc (Bulldozer).

4. *Fantômette et le Secret de la Couronne* [*The Crown's Secret*] (23/04/93)
Dir: Unknown; *Wri*: Unknown.
Guest Cast: Unknown.

5. *Fantômette contre le Colonel X* [*Colonel X*] (26/04/93)
Dir: Christiane Lehérissey; *Wri*: Christian Bouveron.
Guest Cast: Christine Reverho (Cynica), Myriam Moszko (Colonel X), Julia Fink.

6. *Prise de tête pour Fantômette* [*Fantômette Struggles*] (27/04/93)
Dir: Christiane Lehérissey; *Wri*: Stéphane Barbier, Jean-Guy Gingembre.
Guest Cast: Christine Reverho.

7. *Fantômette et la Carnimousse* [*The Carnimoss*] (28/04/93)
Dir: Christiane Spiero; *Wri*: Gérard Bitton, Michel Munz.
Guest Cast: Grégory Cantien (Molécule), Bruno Raffaelli, Céline Carrié.

8. *Fantômette et la Malédiction de la Bague-Serpent* [*The Curse of the Snake-Ring*] (29/04/93)
Dir: Unknown; *Wri*: Unknown.
Guest Cast: Unknown.

9. *Fantômette et le Passé Recomposé* [*The Rebuilt Past*] (30/04/93)

Dir: Christiane Lehérissey; *Wri*: Christian Bouveron.
Guest Cast: Christine Reverho, Grégory Cantien, Florence Rougé.

10. *Fantômette Chasse Gardée* [*Private Turf*] (3/05/93)
Dir: Unknown; *Wri*: Unknown.
Guest Cast: Unknown.

11. *Fantômette et la Photo Interdite* [*The Forbidden Photo*] (4/05/93)
Dir: Marco Pauly; *Wri*: Isabelle Dubernet, Éric Führer.
Guest Cast: Michel Crémadès, Éric Leblanc.

12. *Fantômette et les Habits du Ciel* [*The Sky Clothes*] (5/05/93)
Dir: Christiane Lehérissey; *Wri*: Brigitte Aymard, Stéphane Barbier.
Guest Cast: Christine Reverho, Jacques de Candé (Poison), Bénédicte Mathieu, Christophe Guybet.

13. *Fantômette au Bal des Empereurs* [*The Emperors' Ball*] (6/05/93)
Dir: Unknown; *Wri*: Unknown.
Guest Cast: Unknown.

14. *Fantômette et le Temps du Magicien* [*Time of the Wizard*] (7/05/93)
Dir: Christiane Lehérissey; *Wri*: Christian Bouveron.
Guest Cast: Christine Reverho, Félix Marek (Magirex), Kamel Sherif.

15. *Fantômette et le Collier de Rahpsaskou* [*The Necklace of Rahpsasku*] (10/05/93)
Dir: Marco Pauly; *Wri*: Patrick Hutin.
Guest Cast: Michel Crémadès, Éric Leblanc.

16. *Fantômette et le Vol Parfait* [*The Perfect Robbery*] (11/05/93)
Dir: Christiane Spiero; *Wri*: Patrick Hutin.
Guest Cast: Michel Crémadès, Éric Leblanc.

17. *Fantômette et la Framboisy Connection* (12/05/93)
Dir: Christiane Spiero; *Wri*: Patrick Hutin.
Guest Cast: Michel Crémadès, Éric Leblanc, Serge Riaboukine.

18. *Fantômette contre Mettofan* (13/05/93)
Dir: Christiane Spiero; *Wri*: Patrick Hutin.
Guest Cast: Michel Crémadès, Éric Leblanc.

19. *Fantômette et l'Os Préhistorique* [*The Prehistoric Bone*] (14/05/93)
Dir: Christiane Spiero; *Wri*: Céline Caussimon, Frédéric Reverend.
Guest Cast: Bruno Raffaelli, Jean-Pierre Rambal (Fossilius).

20. *Fantômette et le Brouilleur d'âmes* [*The Soul Scrambler*] (17/05/93)
Dir: Christiane Spiero; *Wri*: Gérard Bitton, Michel Munz.
Guest Cast: Bruno Raffaelli, Katherine Erhardy.

21. *Fantômette contre le Masque d'Argile* [*Clay Mask*] (18/05/93)
Dir: Christiane Spiero; *Wri*: Gérard Bitton, Michel Munz.
Guest Cast: Bruno Raffaelli.

Le Grand Secret [*The Great Secret*] (A2, col., six 60 min. episodes, 6 January-10 February 1989)
Dir: Jacques Trébouta; *Wri*: André Cayatte, Claude Veillot, Mark Princi, based on the novel by René Barjavel.
Cast: Claude Rich, Louise Marleau, Peter Sattmann, Fernando Rey, Richard Munch, Paul Guers, Martine Sarcey.
Story: An Indian scientist discovers a virus which confers immortality, but because it is contagious, it threatens the security of the world. The immortals are secretly exiled to a forbidden island in the Pacific.

Greco (FR2, col., six 52 min. episodes, 2007)
Regular Cast: Philippe Bas (Greco), Audrey Lunati, Maxime Leroux, Mata Gabin, Anne Canovas, Farida Rahouadj.
Story: Greco, a police officer, can see ghosts after being wounded in the head. He helps them by solving their murders.

1. *Contact* (11/05/2007)
Dir/Wri: Philippe Setbon.
Guest Cast: Katherine Erhardy, Hubert Koundé, Sophie de La Rochefoucauld.

2. *La Deuxième Silhouette* [*The Second Silhouette*] (11/05/2007)
Dir/Wri: Philippe Setbon.

Guest Cast: Sarah Stern, Valérie Stroh, Luis Marquez.

3. *Corps et âme* [*Body and Soul*] (18/05/2007)
Dir/Wri: Philippe Setbon.
Guest Cast: Veronica Novak, Lionnel Astier, Hervé Laudière, Anne Canovas.

4. *Fille de quelqu'un* [*Someone's Daughter*] (18/05/2007)
Dir/Wri: Philippe Setbon.
Guest Cast: Cris Campion, Joël Demarty, Venantino Venantini, Pierre Deny.

5. *Mon Assassin* [*My Murderer*] (25/05/2007)
Dir/Wri: Philippe Setbon.
Guest Cast: Thérèse Roussel, Audrey Fleurot, Catherine Marchal, Thomas Cerisola, Catherine Salviat.

6. *Petite Julie* [*Little Julie*] (25/05/2007)
Dir/Wri: Philippe Setbon.
Guest Cast: Philippe Polet, Stéphan Guérin-Tillié, Pascal Elso, Soizic Deffin, Véronique Prune.

La Guerre des Insectes [*The War of the Insects*] (A2, col., four 60 min. episodes, 20-28 March 1981)
Dir: Peter Kassovitz; *Wri*: Giulio Questi, based on the novel by Jean Courtois-Brieux.
Cast: Mathieu Carrière, Patrick Chesnais, Victoria Tennant, Miguel Fernandez, André Oumansky, Anémone, Bernard-Pierre Donnadieu, Marie-Pierre Casey.
Story: A mutated breed of insects threatens to create worldwide starvation by destroying all food supplies on Earth.

Les Habits Noirs [*The Black Coats*] (ORTF 1, B&W., thirty-one 15 min. episodes, 16 October - 24 November 1967)
Dir: René Lucot; *Wri*: Jacques Siclier, based on the novels by Paul Féval.
Cast: Jean-François Calvé (Lecoq), Jean-Pierre Bernard (André Maynotte), Julia Dancourt (Julie Maynotte), Jean Lanier (Colonel Bozzo-Corona), François Dalou (J.-B. Schwartz), Bernard Jousset, Renée Barell, Gilette Barbier, Raymond Jourdan, Raoul Curet, Roger Jaquet, Maïa Simon, Annie Siniglia, Jean-Pierre Brunot, Jean-Pierre Leroux, Gilles Guillot.
Story: André Maynotte is framed for a burglary he did not commit. He discovers that the real villains are a Mafia-like secret society, the Black Coats, whose mysterious leader, Colonel Bozzo-Corona, may be hundreds of years old. His adversary is the ruthless Lecoq, inspired by the real-life Vidocq.

Hero Corp (col., 921 episodes in total, broken down as follows:
Created by: Simon Astier, Alban Lenoir.
Main Cast: Simon Astier (John), Alban Lenoir (Klaus), Sébastien Lalanne (Doug), Gérard Darier (Steve), Agnès Boury (Mary), François Podetti (Burt), Arnaud Joyet (Stan), Philippe Noël (Cécil), Etienne Fague (Mique), Aurore Pourteyron (Jennifer), Stéphanette Martelet (Miss Moore), Christian Bujeau (Ethan Grant, The Lord), Lionnel Astier (Neil Mac Kormack), Arnaud Tsamere (Karin), Jennie-Anne Walker (Claudine), Émilie Arthapignet (Héléna), Josée Drevon (Mégane), Hubert Saint-Macary (Matthew Hoodwink), Didier Bénureau (Laurence Hawkins), Jacques Fontanel (Théo-

dore), François Frapier (Kyle), Jacques Ville (John Sr.), Erik Gerken (Valur), Patrick Vo (Micheng), Charles Clément (Eraste), Michel Courtemanche (Benedict), Jean-Luc Couchard (Dan), Disiz (Guy), Nathalie Roussel (Jane), Jonathan Cohen (Julien), Oldelaf (Jean-Marc).
Story: Following a war in the 1980s, the Hero Corp agency brings together all superheroes in order to maintain peace. In a secret site in France, former heroes can find a calm and peaceful life. Twenty years later, this is shattered when the supervillain known as The Lord returns.

Season 1: Comédie+, fifteen 26 minutes episodes (October 25-December 6, 2008)
Dirs: Simon Astier, Xavier Matthieu, Sébastien Lalanne, Arnaud Joyet, Aurélien Portehaut, Alban Lenoir; *Wri*: Simon Astier, Xavier Matthieu.
Guest Cast: Maurice Lamny, Jonathan Lambert.
Episodes: 1. *Le Village* [*The Village*]; 2. *Le Test* [*The Test*]; 3. *Le Grand Départ* [*The Great Departure*]; 4. *Révélations* [*Reveals*]; 5. *Recherches* [*Searches*]; 6. *Retour aux Sources* [*Back to the Basics*]; 7. *À l'intérieur* [*Inside*]; 8. *Nouvelle Donne* [*New Deal*]; 9. *Emplettes* [*Purchases*]; 10. *L'Alerte* [*The Alert*]; 11. *Chez l'Habitant* [*At Home*]; 12. *Nouvelle Peau* [*New Skin*]; 13. *Die Hard*; 14. *Duel*; 15. *Après le Calme* [*After the Quiet*].

Season 2: Comédie+, fifteen 26 minutes episodes (January 8-29, 2010)
Dir: Simon Astier; *Wri*: Simon Astier, Claire Alexandrakis, Aude Blanchard, Arnaud Joyet.
Guest Cast: Christophe Arnulf, Alexandre Astier, Lilly Eïdo, Constance Pittard, Malik Issolah, Pascal

Légitimus, Pierre Palmade, Patrick Puydebat, Bérengère Krief, Dorian Bisson, Christophe Vandevelde.
Episodes: 1. *La Tempête* [*The Tempest*]; 2. *La Leçon* [*The Lesson*]; 3. *Ex-æquo*; 4. *La Mine* [*The Mine*]; 5. *Au Pied des Murs* [*At the Feet of the Walls*]; 6. *Nouveau Toit* [*New Roof*]; 7. *Intrus* [*Intruder*]; 8. *Du Bon Côté* [*On the Right Side*]; 9. *Servir l'Homme* [*To Serve Man*]; 10. *Dix-sept Survivants* [*17 Survivors*]; 11. *Retrouvailles* [*To Meet Again*]; 12. *Stratèges* [*Strategists*]; 13. *Instructions*; 14 & 15. *Une Nouvelle Ère* [*A New Era*].

Season 3: France 4, thirty-six 7 minutes episodes (October 21-December 6, 2013)
Dir: Simon Astier; *Wri*: Simon Astier, Claire Alexandrakis.
Guest Cast: Justine Le Pottier, Valentine Revel, Manu Payet, Baptiste Lecaplain, Jean-Luc Lemoine, Grégoire Ludig, David Marsais, Cyril Guei, Nicolas Gerout.
Episodes: Épisode 0; 1-5. *Un Nouveau Monde* [*A New World*]; 6-10. *Hero Corp*; 11-15. *Amour et Jeux* [*Love and Games*]; 16-20. *Nouvelles Vies* [*New Lives*]; 21-26. *Plans*; 27-30. *À sa Place* [*In His Place*]; 31-35. *H*.

Season 4: France 4, nineteen 13 minutes episodes (December 19, 2014-January 23, 15)
Dir: Simon Astier; *Wri*: Simon Astier, Claire Alexandrakis.
Guest Cast: Antoine Cholet, Pascal Demolon, Juliette Plumecocq-Mech, Muranyi Kovacs, Stéphane Gourdon, Stéphan Wojtowicz, Fred Scotlande, Davy Mou-

rier, Quentin Baillot, Jean Lescot, Tété, Antoine Gouy.
Episodes: 1. *H*; 2. *Enfermés* [*Locked in*]; 3. *Des Innocents* [*The Innocents*]; 4. *Échappées* [*The Escapees*]; 5. *De Bon Matin* [*Early Morning*]; 6. *Jusqu'en Enfer* [*All the way to Hell*]; 7. *Aie Confiance* [*Trust Me*]; 8. *En Avance* [*Early*]; 9. *Trafics* [*Traffic*]; 10. *Jour de Fête* [*Holiday*]; 11. *Sa Place* [*His Place*]; 12. *Feu aux Poudres* [*Light the Powder*]; 13. *Neil*; 14. *Tenèbres* [*Darkness*]; 15. *La Clef* [*The Key*]; 16. *Le Plan* [*The Plan*]; 17. *Le Réveil* [*The Awakening*]; 18 & 19. *La Fin* [*The End*].

Season 5: France 4, eight 26 minutes episodes (except ep.8 which is 50 min) (May 24-June 7, 2017) plus 2 webisodes streamed on facebook.
Dir: Simon Astier; *Wri*: Simon Astier.
Guest Cast: Guillaume Bats, François Briault, Julien Josselin, Jonathan Cohen, Julien Schmidt, Laura Balasuriya, Nicolas Berno, Franck Beckmann.
Episodes: Numbered 1 to 8 (no titles).
Note: Additionally, three web series were produced by Studio 4: 1. *Les Survivants* [*The Survivors*], eleven 7 minutes episodes (2012); 2. *Les Prémonitions de Kyle* [*Kyle's Premonitions*], eight episodes (2013); 3. *La Voie de Klaus* [*Klaus' Way*] (2014).

Histoires Étranges [*Strange Tales*] (FR 3, col., four 90 min. episodes, 1980)
Prod: Pierre Badel, Chantal Rémy.
Story: Pierre Badel plays himself as a filmmaker investigating the supernatural.
   1. *Un Rêve* [*A Dream*] (9/02/80)

Dir/Wri: Pierre Badel, based on a story by Ivan Turgenev.
Cast: Philippe Duclos, Geneviève Mnich, William Coryn, Dominique Paturel.
Story: A child dreams of his father who vanished during World War I.

2. *La Loupe du Diable* [*The Devil's Magnifying Glass*] (23/02/80)
Dir/Wri: Pierre Badel, based on the story *The Portrait* by Nikolai Gogol.
Cast: Rosy Varte, Pierre Michael, Gabriel Jabbour, Pierre Destailles.
Story: An actress's life is plagued by a cursed painting.

3. *La Morte Amoureuse* [*The Loving Dead*] (9/03/80)
Dir/Wri: Peter Kassovitz, based on a story by Théophile Gautier.
Cast: François Marthouret, Jean Martin, Gérard Desarthe, Laura Condamines.
Story: A man's retina preserves the image of the dead woman he once loved.

4. *Le Marchand de Sable* [*The Sandman*] (22/03/80)
Dir/Wri: Pierre Badel, based on a story by E.T.A. Hoffmann.
Cast: Paul Le Person, Nathalie Nell, André Landais, Alain Berteau, Elisabeth Bourguine, Victor Garrivier, Thérèse Liotard, Daniel Russo.
Story: A student recognizes his father's murderer in a painting.

Histoires Extraordinaires [*Extraordinary Tales*] (FR 3, col., six 60 min. episodes, 1981)
Based on stories by Edgar Allan Poe.

1. *Le Joueur d'Echecs de Maelzel* [*Maelzel's Chess Player*] (7/02/81)
Dir: Juan Luis Buñuel; *Wri*: Hélène Peycharand, Juan Luis Buñuel.
Cast: Jean-Claude Drouot, Diana Bracho, Martin Lasalle.
Story: Maetzel creates a chess-playing android.

2. *Le Scarabée d'Or* [*The Gold Beetle*] (21/02/81)
Dir: Maurice Ronet; *Wri*: Napoléon Murat, Maurice Ronet.
Cast: Vittorio Caprioli, Dominique Zardi.
Story: A macabre treasure hunt.

3. *Ligeia* (7/03/81)
Dir: Maurice Ronet; *Wri*: Napoléon Murat, Maurice Ronet.
Cast: Georges Claisse, Josephine Chaplin, Arielle Dombasle.
Story: A man's dead wife returns to haunt him.

4. *Le Système du Docteur Goudron et du Professeur Plume* [*The System of Dr. Tarr & Professor Feather*] (21/03/81)
Dir: Claude Chabrol; *Wri*: Paul Gégauff.
Cast: Jean-François Garreaud, Coco Ducados, Pierre Le Rumeur, Vincent Gauthier, Ginette Leclerc, Noële Noblecourt, Jacques Galland.
Story: The inmates take over the asylum.

5. *La Lettre Volée* [*The Purloined Letter*] (4/04/81)

Dir/Wri: Ruy Guerra.
Cast: Vittorio Caprioli, Pierre Vaneck.
Story: Detective Dupin must find a stolen document.

6. *La Chute de la Maison Usher* [*The Fall of the House of Usher*] (12/04/81)
Dir: Alexandre Astruc; *Wri*: Pierre Pelegri.
Cast: Fanny Ardant, Pierre Clémenti, Mathieu Carrière, Jacques Dacqmine.
Story: A family curse and a premature burial haunt an ancient house.

Histoires Insolites [*Weird Tales*] (ORTF 1, col., six 55 min. episodes, 1974)

1. *Monsieur Bébé* [*Mister Baby*] (19/10/74)
Dir: Claude Chabrol; *Wri*: Roger Grenier, based on the story *Good and Loyal Services* by Julio Cortazar.
Cast: Daniel Ollier, Denise Gence, François Perrot, Philippine Pascal, Max Doelnitz, Jean-Marie Bernicat.
Story: An old cleaning woman is hired to take care of the mysterious "Mister Baby."

2. *Les Gens de l'Été* [*The Summer People*] (26/10/74)
Dir: Claude Chabrol; *Wri*: Roger Grenier, based on a story by Shirley Jackson.
Cast: Madeleine Ozeray, François Vibert, Jean-Paul Frankeur, Charles Charras.
Story: A retired couple falls in love with a holiday town.

3. *Une Invitation à la Chasse* [*An Invitation to a Hunt*] (2/11/74)

Dir: Claude Chabrol; *Wri*: Paul Gégauff, based on a story by George Hitchcock.
Cast: Jean-Louis Maury, Margarethe Trotta, Jean Martin, Dominique Zardi, Henri Attal, Michèle Alexandre.
Story: An accountant is invited to a hunting party organised by the local nobleman.

4. *Nul n'est Parfait* [*Nobody's Perfect*] (9/11/74)
Dir: Claude Chabrol; *Wri*: Roger Grenier, based on a story by Georges Mandel.
Cast: Michel Duchaussoy, Caroline Cellier.
Story: Every morning, a man tries, unsuccessfully, to murder his wife.

5. *Un Jour comme les Autres avec des Cacahuètes* [*A Day Like Any Other, With Peanuts*] (23/11/74)
Dir: Édouard Molinaro; *Wri*: Roger Grenier, based on a story by Shirley Jackson.
Cast: Jean-Pierre Darras, Marie-Hélène Breillat, Christine Kaufmann, Bernard Lecoq.
Story: A strange man who does good deeds always gives peanuts away afterwards.

6. *Parcelle Brillante* [*Shining Particle*] (30/11/74)
Dir: Christian de Chalonge; *Wri*: Roger Grenier, based on a story by Theodore Sturgeon.
Cast: Gert Froebe, Juliet Berto.
Story: A brilliant but lonely man repairs a female android.

L'Homme de la Nuit [*The Night Man*] (A2, col., four 60 min. episodes, 9-30 September 1983)

Dir: Juan Luis Buñuel; *Wri*: Jacques Armand, based on the novel by Gaston Leroux.
Cast: Georges Wilson (Maxime Broom), Bulle Ogier (Marthe), Claude Giraud (Franck), Véronique Delbourg (Maria), Mathieu Barbey, Corinne Le Poulain.
Story: In 1917 Russia, two lovers, Franck and Maria, get rid of her husband, Maxime) Twenty years later, he returns to revenge himself as a mysterious masked man.

L'Homme qui Revient de Loin [*The Man Who Returned from Far Away*] (A2, col., six 60 min. episodes, 18 September 1972-23 October 1972)
Dir: Michel Wyn; *Wri*: Marcel Desailly, based on a novel by Gaston Leroux
Cast: Alexandra Stewart (Fanny), Louis Velle (Jacques), Michel Vitold (André), Marie-Hélène Breillat, Roland Armontel, Pierre Leproux, Henri Crémieux, Martine de Breteuil, Claude Desailly, Patrice Lesieur, Patrick Préjean, Héléna Manson.
Story: A murder is revealed during a seance, and the victim appears to return to life.

L'Homme sans Visage [*The Faceless Man*] (TF1, col., eight 50 min. episodes, 1975)
Dir: Georges Franju; *Wri*: Jacques Champreux.
Cast: Jacques Champreux (The Faceless Man), Gayle Hunnicut (his girlfriend), Clément Harari (Dr. Dutreuil), Roberto Bruni (Maxime de Borrego), Gert Froebe (Commissioner Sorbier), Josephine Chaplin (Martine Leduc), Patrick Préjean (Séraphin Beauminou), Pierre Collet (Grandmaster of the Templars), Enzo Fisichella (Inspector Peclet), Henry Soskin (Prof. Petrie).
Story: Maxime and his girlfriend Martine fight a Fantômas-like villain, the Faceless Man, his girlfriend, and a

mad scientist who can turn people into zombies. Eventually, they find themselves competing to discover the Templars' treasure.
Episodes: 1. *La Nuit du Voleur de Cerveaux* [*The Night of the Brain Stealer*] (17/07/75); 2. *Le Masque de Plomb* [*The Lead Mask*] (24/07/75); 3. *Les Tueurs sans Âmes* [*The Soulless Killers*] (31/07/75); 4. *La Mort qui Rampait sur les Toits* [*Death Stalks the Rooftops*] (7/08/75) ; 5. *La Marche des Spectres* [*March of the Spectres*] (14/08/75); 6. *Le Sang Accusateur* [*The Accusatory Blood*] (21/08/75); 7. *Le Rapt* [*The Kidnapping*] (28/08/75); 8. *Le Secret des Templiers* [*The Templars' Secret*] (4/09/75).
Note: An edited version of this series was released as a feature film under the title *Nuits Rouges*.

Les Hordes [*The Hordes*] (Channel 5, col., four 90 min. episodes, 1991)
Dir: Jean-Claude Missiaen; *Wri*: Joël Houssin, Daniel Riche, Jean-Luc Fromental, Jean-Claude Missiaen, based on the novel by Jacques Zelde.
Cast: François Dunoyer, Corinne Touzet, Souad Amidou, Simon Eine, Jean-Pierre Kalfon, Philippe Lemaire, Féodor Atkine, Michel Peyrelon, Philippe Laudenbach, Jean-Claude Bouillaud, Bernard Freyd, Jean-Pierre Malo, Dominique Valera, Françoise Brion, Anouk Ferjac, Nils Tavernier, Jacques Ferrière, Pierre Londiche, Gérard Sergue, Louis Navarre.
Story: In a post-apocalyptic future, hordes of beggars spread chaos and violence. A policeman (Dunoyer) infiltrates the hordes to find their mysterious leader (Lemaire). A conflict erupts between the head of the military (Kalfon) and a demagogue (Eine) trying to use the hordes for political power. Eventually, the hordes win,

but the new regime is merely a screen for the establishment of a new totalitarian system.
Episodes: 1. *La Guerre des Gueux* [*The War of the Peasants*] (13/03/91); 2. *Les Hordes Noires* [*The Black Hordes*] (14/03/91); 3. *Les Hordes Blanches* [*The White Hordes*] (21/03/91); 4. *Les Hordes d'Acier* [*The Steel Hordes*] (27/03/91).

Il était une seconde fois [*Twice Upion a Time*] (Arte, col., four 52 min. episodes, August-September 2019).
Dir: Guillaume Nicloux; *Wri*: Guillaume Nicloux, Nathalie Leuthreau.
Cast: Gaspard Ulliel (Vincent), Freya Mavor (Louise), Patrick d'Assumçao, Jonathan Manzambi, Steve Tran, Esteban Carvajal-Alegria, Claire Sermonne, Sacha Canuyt, Jonathan Couzinié, Alaa Safi, Anne Cazenave, Richard Dillane, Anthony Paliotti.
Story: Vincent and Louise were once very much in love, but they split up some months ago. By chance, Vincent comes into possession of a box which allows him to revisit his time with Louise. Will he get a second chance?
Episodes: 1. *Ne me quitte pas* [*Don't Leave me*]; 2. *Reviens* [*Come back*]; 3. *Ti amo*; 4. *Hyme à l'Amour* [*Hymn to Love*].

L'Île Mystérieuse [*The Mysterious Island*] (RTF, B&W., two 60 min. episodes, 28 April & 5 May 1963)
Dir: Pierre Badel; *Wri*: Claude Santelli, based on the novel by Jules Verne.
Cast: René Arrieu (Nemo), Michel Etcheverry, Jacques Grello, Armand Meffre, Ibrahim Seck, Philippe Coussoneau.
Story: Castaways on a desert island are secretly aided by Captain Nemo.

L'Île Mystérieuse [*The Mysterious Island*] (ORTF 1, col., 40 min., 7 December 1969)
Dir/Wri: Claude Santelli, based on the novel by Jules Verne.
Cast: Pierre Dux (Nemo), Michel Etcheverry.
Story: Same as above.

L'Île Mystérieuse [*The Mysterious Island*] (ORTF 1, col., six 55 min. episodes, 1973)
Dir: Henri Colpi, Juan Antonio Bardem; *Wri*: Jacques Champreux, based on the novel by Jules Verne
Cast: Omar Sharif (Nemo), Gérard Tichy, Philippe Nicaud, Ambroise Bia, Jess Hahn, Rafaël Bardem, Gabriele Tinti, Vidal Molina, Rik Battaglia.
Episodes: 1. *L'Évasion* [*The Escape*] (17/12/73); 2. *Les Naufragés de l'Air* [*The Castaways of the Sky*] (19/12/73); 3. *Territoire Interdit* [*Forbidden Territory*] (21/12/73); 4. *L'Abandonné* [*The Forsaken One*] (24/12/73); 5. *Le Drapeau Noir* [*The Black Flag*] (26/12/73); 6. *Le Secret de l'Île* [*The Island's Secret*] (28/12/73).
Story: Same as above.
Note: An edited version was released as a feature film.

L'Île aux Trente Cercueils [*The Island of the Thirty Coffins*] (A2, col., six 60 min. episodes, 21 September-6 October 1979)
Dir: Marcel Cravenne; *Wri*: Robert Scipion, based on the novel by Maurice Leblanc.
Cast: Claude Jade (Véronique), Yves Beneyton (Philippe), Georges Marchal (M. d'Hergemont), Jean-Paul Zehnacker (Vorski), Julie Philippe (Elfide), Edith Perret (Gertrude), Pierrette Thévenon (Clémence), Peter Semler

(Otto), Armand Babel (Corréjou), Jean Le Mouel (Le-Goff), Jean-René Gossart (Conrad).
Story: In 1917, Véronique is stranded on the desolate island of Sarek off the coast of Britanny, when an ancient curse appears to be coming to life. In reality, her ex-husband, the villainous Vorski, who seeks revenge, is also using her to find a legendary miraculous radioactive stone.
Note: Based on an eponymous novel in the *Arsène Lupin* series, but the character of Lupin was removed from this version.

L'Île aux Trente Cercueils [*The Island of the Thirty Coffins*] (col., six 52 min. episodes, 22 February-8 March 2022)
Dir: Frédéric Mermoud; *Wri*: Elsa Marpeau, Florent Meyer, based on the novel by Maurice Leblanc.
Cast: Virginie Ledoyen (Christine), Charles Berling (Vorski), Jean-François Stévenin (M. Dormont), Jérémy Gillet (Paul), Anastasia Robin, Arthur Sénéchal, Stanley Weber, Martine Chevallier, Dominique Pinon, Noam Morgensztern, Maxime Bailleul, Nicky Marbot.
Story: Same as above, except the story now takes place today, and Virginie d'Hergemont has been rechristened Christine Dormont.

Intrusion (ARTE, three 45-mins. episodes, 28 May 2015).
Dir: Xavier Palud; *Wri*: Frédéric Azemar, Quoc Dang Tran, Florent Meyer, Xavier Palud.
Cast: Jonathan Zaccaï (Philippe/Marc), Judith El Zein, Marie Kremer, Éric Berger.
Story: Philippe, a concert pianist, has a breakdown during a recital. Afterwards, his brother, whom he believed

had died in childhood, appears and claims to be him. Is Philippe losing his mind or is there a conspiracy against him?

L'Italien, ou Le Confessionnal des Pénitents Noirs
[*The Italian, or The Confessional of the Black Penitents*]
(A2, col., six 60 min. episodes, 1977)
Dir: Alain Boudet; *Wri*: Marcel Moussy, based on the 1796 novel by Ann Radcliffe.
Cast: Pierre-François Pistorio, Aniouta Florent, Maurice Garrel, Odile Versois, Francis Claude, Marcel Imhof, Germaine Delbat.
Story: The gothic adventures of two star-crossed lovers in 18th century Italy.
Episodes: 1. *L'Italien* [*The Italian*] (1/07/77); 2. *L'Enlèvement* [*The Kidnapping*] (8/07/77); 3. *L'Évasion* [*The Escape*] (15/07/77); 4. *La Maison du Pêcheur* [*The Fisherman's House*] (22/07/77); 5. *Le Saint-Office* [*The Holy See*] (29/07/77); 6. *Révélations* (5/08/77).

Henry James (TF 1, col., two 55 min. episodes, 1976)
1. *De Grey* (20 /03/76)
Dir: Claude Chabrol; *Wri*: Roger Grenier.
Cast: Hélène Perdrière, Daniel Lecourtois, Catherine Jourdan, Yves Lefèvre.
Story: An ancient family curse plagues two young lovers.

2. *Owen Wingrave* (17 /04/76)
Dir/Wri: Paul Seban.
Cast: Mathieu Carrière, Bernard Giraudeau, Patrick Legal, Jean Boissery, Pierre Le Rumeur, Danièle Girard, Louise Conte.
Story: A young man dies of fright.

Joseph Balsamo (ORTF 1, col., seven 52-min. episodes, 8 January-19 February 1973)
Dir: André Hunebelle; *Wri*: Pierre Nivollet, based on the novel by Alexandre Dumas.
Cast: Jean Marais (Joseph Balsamo), Udo Kier (Gilbert), Henri Guisol (Taverney), Doris Kunstmann (Andrée), Bernard Alane (Philippe), Louise Marleau (Du Barry), Olympia Carlisi (Lorenza), Léonce Corne (Althotas), Guy Tréjean (Louis XV).
Story: Alchemist and fortune-teller Joseph Balsamo plots the downfall of the French monarchy in the days of Louis XV, using the mediumnic powers of his wife, Lorenza, and manipulating the greedy mistress of the King.

Kaamelott (M6, col., six seasons, 458 episodes, 2005-2009)
(Seasons 1 to 3: 100 eps of 3 min 30; Season 4: 98 eps. of 3 min 30 + 1 of 7 mins; Season 5: 50 eps. of 7 min, or 8 eps of 52 min dans le Director's Cut; Season 6: 9 eps. of 40 min).
Dir/Wri: Alexandre Astier.
Cast: Alexandre Astier (Arthur), Thomas Cousseau (Lancelot), Lionnel Astier (Léodagan), Anne Girouard (Guenièvre), Nicolas Gabion (Bohort), Frank Pitiot (Perceval), Jean-Christophe Hembert (Karadoc), Joëlle Sevilla (Dame Séli), Audrey Fleurot (Viviane the Lady of the Lake), Jacques Chambon (Merlin), Stéphane Margot (Calogrenant), Simon Astier (Yvain), Aurélien Portehaut (Gauvain), Alexis Hénon (Galessin), Josée Drevon (Ygerne), Tony Saba, Antoine de Caunes, Brice Fournier, Etienne Fague, Jean-Robert Lombard, Christian Bujeau, Caroline Ferrus, Bruno Fontaine, Thibault Roux, Vanessa Guedj, Valérie Kéruzoré, Caroline Pascal, Ma-

gali Saadoun, Alexandra Saadoun, Anne-Valérie Soler, Loïc Varraut, Alain Chapuis, Serge Papagalli, Gilles Graveleau, Bruno Salomone, Guillaume Briat, Bruno Boëglin, Truong Lan, François Rollin, Valentin Traversi, Eddy Letexier, Carlo Brandt, Alban Lenoir, Luc Chambon, Emmanuel Meirieu, Patrick Chesnais, François Levantal, Marion Creusvaux, Valeria Cavalli.
Story: French medieval fantasy comedy series based on the Arthurian legends. It follows the daily lives of King Arthur and his Knights of the Round Table in Camelot.
Note: The series was preceded in 2003 by a short film, *Dies iræ*, with mostly the same cast and concept, which was used to pitch the idea of the series to the network. *Kaamelott* is widely regarded as one of the best, most iconic, and most popular French TV series of all time. It has also been praised for its fidelity as, outside of comedic and linguistic liberties, it stays faithful to the mythology and historic context. While the series takes place in the 5th century, it uses modern language and situations to create a humorous view of the Arthurian legend. However, in latter seasons, the mood becomes darker and more dramatic as Arthur's kingdom begins to disintegrate. After the end of the series in 2009, Astier started working on a film trilogy meant to conclude the story of the series. First announced in 2012 and planned for a shooting on 2013, production for the first film, *Kaamelott: Le Premier Volet* (see previous section), was suspended and then repeatedly postponed due to various issues; filming eventually begun in January 2019, and it was released on July 21, 2021.
Episodes:
Pilot: Dies Irae (col., 14 mins., 2003)

Season 0: 1. *Le Duel* [*The Duel*]; 2. *L'Invasion Viking* [*The Viking Invasion*]; 3. *La Bataille rangée* [*The Pitched Battle*]; 4. *La Romance de Perceval* [*Perceval's Romance*]; 5. *Les Funérailles d'Ulfin* [*Ulfin's Funeral*]; 6. *Le Chevalier femme* [*The Female Knight*]; 7. *La Carte* [*The Map*]; 8. *Le Repas de famille* [*The Famuily Meal*]; 9. *Le Répurgateur* [*The Repurgator*]; 10. *Le Labyrinthe* [*The Maze*].

Season 1 (3/01/2005 to 03/2005): *1. Heat; 2. Les Tartes aux Myrtilles [The Blueberry Pies]; 3. La Table de Breccan [Breccan's Table]; 4. Le Chevalier Mystère [The Mystery Knight]; 5. Le Fléau de Dieu [The Scourge of God]; 6. Le Garde du Corps [The Bodyguard]; 7. Des Nouvelles Du Monde [World News]; 8. Codes et Strategies [Codes and Strategies]; 9. Le Maitre d'Armes [The Weapon Master]; 10. Le Négociateur [The Nergotiator]; 11. Dîner dansant [Dinner Dance]; 12. Le Sixième Sens [The Sixth Sense]; 13. Arthur et la Question [Arthur and the Question]; 14. Monogame [Monogamous]; 15. Les Défis de Merlin [Merlin's Challenges]; 16. Le Banquet des Chefs [The Chieftains' Banquet]; 17. Le Signe [The Sign]* (*Wri*: Fabien Rault)*; 18. En Forme de Graal [Shaped like a Grail]; 19. Le Repos du Guerrier [Warrior's Rest]; 20. La Dent de Requin [The Shark's Tooth]; 21. La Taxe Militaire [The Military Tax]; 22. La Queue du Scorpion [The Scorpion's Tail]; 23. La Potion de Fécondité [The Fertility Potion] 24. L'Interprète [The Interpréter]; 25. Le Sacrifuice [The Sacrifice]; 26. À la Volette [Lullaby]; 27. De Retour de Judée [Back From Judaea]; 28. La Botte Secrète [The Secret Trick]; 29. L'Assassin de Kaamelott [A Murderer in Kaamelott]; 30. Le Trois de Coeur [The Three of Hearts]; 31. Basidiomycètes [Basidiomycota];*

32. L'Imposteur [The Impostor]; 33. Compagnons de Chambrée [Roommates]; 34. La Grotte de Padraig [Padraig's Cavern]; 35. Ambidextrie [Ambidextrous]; 36. Raison d'Argent [Money Matters]; 37. La Romance de Lancelot [Lancelot's Romance]; 38. Merlin et les Loups [Merlin and the Wolves]; 39. Le Cas Yvain [The Case of Yvain]; 40. L'Adoubement [The Dubbing] (Wri: Fabien Rault)*; 41 Arthur et les Ténèbres [Arthur and the Darkness]; 42. Le Zoomorphe [The Zoomorph]; 43. La Coccinelle de Madenn [Madenn's Ladybug]; 44. Patience dans la Plaine [Patience in the Plains]; 45. Le Oud [The Oud]; 46. Le Code de Chevalerie [The Code of Chivalry]* (Wri: Fabien Rault)*; 47. Létal [Lethal]; 48. Azenor; 49. Le Sort de Rage [The Anger Sp[ell]; 50. Les Nouveaux Frères [The New Brothers]; 51. Enluminures [Engraviongs]; 52. Haunted; 53. Le Secret de Lancelot [Lancelot's Secret]; 54. Le Serpent géant [The Giant Snake]; 55. Guenièvre et les Oiseaux [Guenièvre and the Birds]; 56. Le Dernier Empereur [The Last Emperor]; 57. Perceval Relance de Quinze [Perceval Bids Fifteen]; 58. Le Coup d'épée [The Sword Blow]; 59. La Jupe de Calogrenant [Calogrenant's Skirt]; 60. Le Prodige du Fakir [The Fakir'sd Miracle]; 61. Un Bruit dans la Nuit [A Sou nd in the Night]; 62. Feu l'âne de Guethenoc [Guethenoc's Late Donkey]; 63. Goustan le Cruel [Goustan the Cruel]; 64. Le Chaudron Rutillant [The Shiny Cauldron]; 65. La Visite d'Ygerne [Ygerne's Visit]; 66. Les Clandestins [The Clandestines]; 67. Le Kleptomane [The Kleptomaniac]; 68. Le Pain [Bread]; 69. La Mort d'Arthur [The Death of Arthur]; 70. Le Problème du Chou [The Cabbage Problem]; 71. Un Roi à la Taverne [A King in the Tavern]; 72. Les Fesses de Guenièvre [Guenièvre's Behind]; 73. Le Billet Doux [The Love Letter]; 74. Guenièvre et l'Orage [Guenièvre* *and the Storm]*; 75. *Eunuque et Chauds Lapins [Ennuch and Hot Rabbits]*; 76. *Choc Frontal [Frontal Shock]*; 77. *Le Forgage [The Drilling]*; 78. *Le Discobole [The Discobolus]*; 79. *L'Expurgation de Merlin [Merlin's Expurgation]*; 80. *Les Volontaires [The Volunteers]*; 81. *Polymorphie [Polymorphy]*; 82. *Décibels Nocturnes [Nocturnal Decibels]*; 83. *La Fête de l'Hiver [Winter's Feast]*; 84. *Gladiateur [Gladiator]*; 85. *La Blessure Mortelle [The Fatal Wound]*; 86. *Le Dragon des Tunnels [The Dragon of the Tunnels]*; 87. *Retour de Campagne [Home from the Wars]*; 88. *L'Escote [The Escort]*; 89. *Tel un Chevalier [Like a Knight]*; 90. *La Pâte d'Amande [Almond Paste]*; 91. *La Fureur du Dragon [The Dragon's Fury]*; 92. *Vox Populi*; 93. *Unagi*; 94. *L'Éclaireur [The Scout]*; 95. *Lacrimosa*; 96. *La Quête des Deux Renards [The Quest of the Two Foxes]*; 97. *Agnus Dei*; 98. *Le Tourment [The Torment]*; 99. *La Retraite [Retirement]*; 100. *La Vraie Nature du Graal [The Grail's True Nature]*.

Season 2 (2/05/2005 to 7/10/2005, except for episodes 28, 45, 47, 52, 62, 68, 71, 80, 82, 98, 99, 100 broacast in 12/2005). 1. *Spangenhelm*; 2. *Les Alchimistes [The Alchemists]*; 3. *Le Dialogue de Paix [The Peace Talks]*; 4. *Le Portrait [The Portrait]* (*Wri*: Fabien Rault); 5. *Silbury Hill* (*Wri*: Joëlle Sevilla); 6. *Le Reclassement [Reclassification]*; 7. *Le Rassemblement du Corbeau [The Gathering of the Raven]*; 8. *Les Volontaires II [The Volunteers II]*; 9. *Le Terroriste [The Terrorist]*; 10. *La Chambre [The Bedroom]*; 11. *Le Message Codé [The Coded Message]*; 12. *La Délégation Maure [The Moorish Envoys]*; 13. *L'Enlèvement de Guenièvre [Guenièvre's Kidnapping]*; 14. *Les Classes de Bohort [Bohort's Classes]*; 15. *Le Monde d'Arthur [Arthur's*

World]; 16. Les Tuteurs [The Tutors]; 17. Les Jumelles du Pêcheur [The Fisherman's Twins]; 18. 744; 19. L'Absolution [The Absolution]; 20. Les Misanthropes [The Misanthropists]; 21. La Cassette [The Chest]; 22. Plus Près de Toi [Nearer to Thee]; 23. La Révolte [The Revolt]; 24. Sous les Verrous [Under Lock and Key]; 25. Séli et les Rongeurs [Séli and the Rodents]; 26. Un Roi A La Taverne II [A King in the Tavern II]; 27. L'Ancien Temps [The Olden Days]; 28. Le Passage Secret [The Secret Passage]; 29. Les Mauvaises Graines [The Bad Seeds]; 30. La Garde Royale [The Royal Guard]; 31. L'Ivresse [Drunkenness]; 32. Mater Dixit (*Wri*: Lionnel Astier & Alexandre Astier); *33. Spiritueux [Spirits]; 34. La Ronde [Circle Dance]; 35. Merlin l'Archaique [Archaic Merlin]; 36. Les Exploités [The Exploited]; 37. L'Escorte II [The Escort II]; 38. Le Larcin [The Theft]; 39. La Rencontre [The Meeting]; 40. Les Pigeons [ThePigeons]; 41. O, Brother; 42. La Fête du Printemps [The Feast of Spring]; 43. La Voix Céleste [The Heavenly Voice]; 44. L'Invincible [The Invincible]; 45. Amen; 46. Le Cadeau [The Gift]; 47. Le Complot [The Plot]; 48. La Vigilance d'Arthur [Arthur's Vigilance]; 49. Les Chiens de Guerre [The Dogs of War]; 50. Always; 51. Arthur in Love; 52. Excalibur et le Destin [Excalibur and Destiny]; 53. L'Absent [The Absentee]; 54. The Game; 55. La Quinte Juste [The Perfect Fifth]; 56 La Fumée Blanche [The White Smoke]; 57. Unagi II; 58. La Joute Ancillaire [The Battle of the Servants; 59. Le Donneur [The Informer]; 60. Le Jeu du Caillou [The Pebble Game]; 61. L'Alliance [The Alliance]; 62. Le Secret d'Arthur [Arthur's Secret]; 63. Aux Yeux de Tous [For All to See]; 64. Immaculé Karadoc [Immaculate Karadoc]; 65. La Morsure du Dace [The Dacian's Bite]; 66. Les Neiges Eternelles [The*

Eternal Snows]; 67. *Des Hommes d'Honneur [Men of Honor]*; 68. *Stargate;* 69. *Feue la Vache de Roparzh [Roparzh's Late Cow]*; 70. *Les Vœux [The Vows]*; 71. *Le Pédagogue [The Pedagogue]*; 72. *Perceval et le Contre Sirop [Perceval and the Counter-Syrup]*; 73. *L'Oubli [Forgetfulness]*; 74. *L'Ambition [Ambition]*; 75. *Le Poème [The Poem]*; 76. *Corpore Sano;* 77. *Le Havre de Paix [The Haven of Peace]*; 78. *L'Anniversaire de Guenièvre [Guenièvre's Birthday]*; 79. *La Botte Secrète II [The Secret Trick II]*; 80. *Les Parchemins Magiques [The Magic Scrolls]*; 81. *L'Enragé [The Furious One]*; 82. *Trois Cent Soixante Degrès [Three Hundred and Sixty Degrees]*; 83. *Pupi [Puppets]* (*Wri*: Joëlle Sevilla & Alexandre Astier); *84. Vox Populi II;* 85. *Le Rebelle [The Rebel]*; 86. *Les Félicitations [Congratulations]*; 87. *Les Paris [The Bets]*; 88. *Les Esclaves [The Slaves]*; 89. *Les Drapeaux [The Flags]*; 90. *Le Guêt [The Lookout]*; 91. *Le Sort Perdu [The Lost Spell]*; 92. *La Restriction [The Restriction]*; 93. *La Corde [The Rope]*; 94. *Tourment II [Torment II]*; 95. *Le Plat National [The National Dish]*; 96. *Le Temps des Secrets [The Time of Secrets]*; 97. *La Conscience d'Arthur [Arthur'ms Conscience]*; 98. *La Frange Romaine [The Roman Fringe]*; 99. *L'Orateur [The Speaker]*; 100. *Les Comptes [The Accounts]*.

Season 3 (9/01/2006 to 22/03/2006): *1. Le Chevalier Errant [The Knight Errant]*; 2. *L'Aveu de Bohort [Bohort's Confession]*; 3. *Le Magnanime [The Magnanimous One]*; 4. *Le Porte-Bonheur [The Good-Luck Charm]*; 5. *Séfriane d'Aquitaine [Séfriane of Aquitaine]*; 6. *Le Combat des Chefs [The Battle of the Chieftains]*; 7. *Le Déserteur [The Deserter]*; 8. *La Potion de Vivacité [The Life Potion]*; 9. *Le Sanglier de Cor-*

nouailles [The Boar of Cornwall]; 10. L'Ankou [The Ankou]; 11. Ablutions; 12. La Poétique 1 [Poetics 1]; 13. La Poétique 2 [Poetics 2]; 14. Les Derniers Outrages [The Last Insults]; 15. Guenièvre et Euripide [Guenièvre and Euripides]; 16. Unagi III; 17. Le Fléau de Dieu II [The Scourge of God II]; 18. Cryda de Tintagel [Cryda of Tintagel]; 19. L'Ivresse II [Drunkenness II]; 20. Legenda; 21. Le Renfort Magique [Magical Reinforcements]; 22. Silbury Hill II; 23. Le Professionnel [The Professional]; 24. Les Suppléants [The Replacements]; 25. La Nuit du Nomade [Nomad's Night]; 26. L'Assemblée des Rois 1 [The Kings' Gathering 1]; 27. L'Assemblée des Rois 2 [The Kings' Gathering 2]; 28. L'Arche de Transport [The Transport Arch]; 29. Les Cousins [The Cousins]; 30. Le Trouble [The Trouble]; 31. Le Tournoi [The Tournament]; 32. La Pierre de Lune [The Moonstone]; 33. La Pythie [The Pythia]; 34. Les Cheveux Noirs [The Black Hair]; 35. Dream On; 36. Feue la Poule de Guethenoc [Guethenoc's Late Hen]; 37. Le Repos Du Guerrier II [Warrior's Rest II]; 38. Les Affranchis [The Emancipated Slaves]; 39. Les Clous de la Sainte Croix [The Nails of the Holy Cross]; 40. La Corne d'Abondance [The Cornucopia]; 41. Morituri; 42. Le Dialogue de Paix II [The Peace Talks II]; 43. Stargate II; 44. L'Abstinent [The Abstinent One]; 45. Aux Yeux De Tous II [For All to See II]; 46. La Potion de Vérité [The Truth Potion]; 47. Le Petit Poucet [Hop O'my Thumb]; 48. Haunted II; 49. La Révolte II [The Revolt II]; 50. Perceval Chante Sloubi [Perceval Sings Sloubi]; 51. Le Jour d'Alexandre [Alexander's Day]; 52. La Cassette II [The Chest II]; 53. Poltergeist; 54. Les Paris II [The Bets II]; 55. Au Bonheur des Dames [Ladies' Delight]; 56. Les Tourelles [The Towers]; 57. Cuisine et Dépendances [Kitchen and Additions]; 58.

Arthur Sensei; 59. *Le Solitaire [The Loner];* 60. *Les Festivités [The Festivities];* 61. *La Menace Fantôme [The Phantom Menace];* 62. *La Coopération [Cooperation];* 63. *L'Empressée [Woman in a Hurry];* 64. *La Ronde II [The Round Dance II];* 65. *Mission;* 66. *La Baliste [The Catapult];* 67. *La Baraka;* 68. *La Veillée [The Watch];* 69. *Le Tourment III [The Torment III];* 70. *La Potion de Fécondité II [The Fertility Potion II];* 71. *L'Attaque Nocturne [The Night Attack];* 72. *La Restriction II [The Restriction II];* 73. *Les Défis de Merlin II [Merlin's Challenges II];* 74. *Saponides et Detergents [Soap and Detergents];* 75. *Le Justicier [The Avenger];* 76. *La Crypte Maléfique [The Evil Crypt];* 77. *Arthur in Love II;* 78. *La Grande Bataille [The Great Battle];* 79. *La Fête de l'Hiver II [The Feast of Winter II];* 80. *Sous Les Verrous II [Under Lock and Key II];* 81. *Le Vulgarisateur [The Popularizer];* 82. *Witness;* 83. *Le Tribut [The Tribute];* 84. *Le Culte Secret [The Secret Cult];* 85. *Le Mangonneau [The Mangonel];* 86. *La Chevalerie [The Chivalry];* 87. *Le Mauvais Augure [The Bad Omen];* 88. *Raison d'Argent II [Money Matters II];* 89. *Les Auditeurs Libres [The Free Auditors];* 90. *Le Baiser Romain [The Roman Kiss];* 91. *L'Espion [The Spy];* 92. *Alone in the Dark;* 93. *Le Législateur [The Legislator];* 94. *L'Insomniaque [The Insomniac];* 95. *L'Étudiant [The Student];* 96. *Le Médiateur [The Mediator];* 97. *Le Trophée [The Trophy];* 98. *Hollow Man;* 99. *La Dispute I [The Quarrel I];* 100. *La Dispute II [The Quarrel II].*

Season 4 (18/09/2006 to 24/11/2006) (the final episode being a double one with no pause): *1. Tous les Matins du Monde I [All the Mornings of the World I]; 2. Tous les Matins du Monde II [All the Mornings of the World II]; 3. Raison et Sentiments [Sense and Sensibility]; 4. Le*

Dédale [The Labyrinth]; 5. *Les Tartes aux Fraises [The Strawberry Pies]*; 6. *Les Pisteurs [The Trackers]*; 7. *Le Traître [The Traitor]*; 8. *La Faute I [The Fault I]*; 9. *La Faute II [The Fault II]*; 10. *L'Ascension du Lion [The Rise of the Lion]*; 11. *Une Vie Simple [A Simple Life]*; 12. *Le Privilégié [The Privileged Man]*; 13. *Le Bouleversé [The Upset Man]*; 14. *Les Liaisons Dangereuses [Dangerous Liaisons]*; 15. *Les Exploités II [The Exploited II]*; 16. *Dagonnet Et le Cadastre [Dagonnet and the Land Register]*; 17. *Duel I*; 18, *Duel II*; 19. *La Foi Bretonne [The Breton Faith]*; 20. *Au Service Secret de Sa Majesté [On His Majesty's Secret Service]*; 21. *La Parade [The Parade]*; 22, *Seigneur Caius [Lord Caius]*; 23. *L'Échange I [The Exchange I]*; 24. *L'Échange II [The Exchange II]*; 25. *L'Échelle de Perceval [Perceval's Ladder]*; 26. *La Chambre de la Reine [The Queen's Bedroom]*; 27. *Les Émancipés [The Emancipated Ones]*; 28. *La Révoquée [A Woman Fired]*; 29. *La Baliste II [The Catapult II]*; 30. *Les Bonnes [The Maids]*; 31. *La Révolte III [The Revolt III]*; 32. *Le Rapport [The Report]*; 33. *L'Art de la Table [The Art of Cooking]*; 34. *Les Novices [The Novices]*; 35. *Les Refoulés [The Repressed]*; 36. *Les Tuteurs II [The Tutors II]*; 37. *Le Tourment IV [The Torment IV]*; 38. *Le Rassemblement du Corbeau II [The Gathering of the Raven II]*; 39. *Le Grand Départ [The Great Departure]*; 40. *L'Auberge Rouge [The Red Inn]*; 41. *Les Curieux I [The Curious I]*; 42. *Les Curieux II [The Curious II]*; 43. *La Clandestine [The Clandestine]*; 44. *Les Envahisseurs [The Invaders]*; 45. *La Vie est Belle [Life is Beautiful]*; 46. *La Relève [The Replacements]*; 47. *Les Tacticiens I [The Tacticians I]*; 48. *Les Tacticiens II [The Tacticians II]*; 49. *Drakkars!*; 50. *La Réponse [The Answer]*; 51. *Unagi IV*; 52. *La Permission [The Leave]*; 53. *Anges et*

Démons [Angels and Demons]; 54. *La Rémanence [The Remanence]*; 55. *Le Refuge [The Shelter]*; 56. *Le Dragon Gris [The Gray Dragon]*; 57. *La Potion de Vivacité II [The Life Potion II]*; 58. *Vox Populi III*; 59. *La Sonde [The Probe]*; 60. *La Réaffectation [The Reassignment]*; 61. *La Poétique II-1 [Poetics II-1]*; 62. *La Poétique II-2 [Poetics II-2]*; 63. *Le Jeu de la Guerre [The War Game]*; 64. *Le Rêve d'Ygerne [Ygerne's Dream]*; 65. *Les Chaperons [The Chaperones]* 66. *L'Habitu é [The Regular]* 67. *Le Camp Romain [The Roman Camp]*; 68. *L'Usurpateur [The Usurper]*; 69. *Loth et le Graal [Lot'h and the Grail]*; 70. *Le Paladin [The Paladin]*; 71. *Perceval fait ritournelle [Perceval Plays a Ritournelle]*; 72. *La Dame et le Lac [The Lady and the Lake]*; 73. *Beaucoup de Bruit pour Rien [Much Ado About Nothing]*; 74. *L'Ultimatum [The Ultimatum]*; 75. *Le Oud II [The Oud II]*; 76. *La Répétition [The Rehearsal]*; 77. *Le Discours [The Speech]*; 78. *Le Choix de Gauvain [Gauvain's Choice]*; 79. *Fluctuat nec mergitur]*; 80. *Le Face-à-Face 1 [Face to Face 1]*; 81. *Le Face-à-Face II [Face to Face II]*; 82. *Entente Cordiale [Cordial Alliance]*; 83. *L'Approbation [The Approval]*; 84. *Alone in the Dark II*; 85. *La Blessure d'Yvain [Yvain's Wound]*; 86. *Corpore Sano II*; 87 *L'Enchanteur [The Enchanter]*; 88. *Les Bien Nommés [The Well-Named]*; 89. *La Prisonnière [The Woman Prisoner]*; 90. *Les Paris III [The Bets III]*; 91. *Les Plaques de Dissimulation [The Camouflage Shields]*; 92. *Le Vice de Forme [The Technicality]*; 93. *Le Renoncement I [The Renunciation I]*; 94. *Le Renoncement II [The Renunciation II]*; 95. *L'Inspiration [The Inspiration]*; 96. *Les Endettés [The Debtors]*; 97. *Double Dragon*; 98. *Le Sauvetage [The Rescue]*; 99 & 100. *Le Désordre et la Nuit [Disorder and Night]*.

Season 5 (two 50-minute episodes on 1 May 2007, followed by twenty-five 7-minute episodes and one 50-minute episode on 5 November 2007, followed by twenty-five 7-minute episodes): *1. Les Repentants [The Penitents]; 2. Miserere Nobis; 3. Le Dernier Recours [The Last Resort]; 4 Les Nouveaux Clans [The New Clans]; 5. La Sorcière [The Witch];6. L'Épée des Rois [The Sword of the Kings]; 7. Corvus Corone; 8. Le Périple [The Journey]; 9. La Démission [The Resignation] ; 10. Les Recruteurs [The Recruiters]; 11. Hurlements [Howls]; 12. La Roche et le Fer [The Stone and the Sword]; 13. Les Dauphins [The Crown Princes]; 14. Vae Soli!; 15. Les Aquitains [The Aquitanians]; 16. Les Fruits d'Hiver [Winter Fruits]; 17. Les Exilés [The Exiles]; 18. Perceval de Sinope; 19. Les Nocturnales [The Nocturnals]; 20 Les Rivales [The Rivals]; 21. Aux Yeux de Tous III [For All To See III]; 22. La Promesse [The Promise]; 23. Le Forfait [The Forfeit]; 24. Le Dernier Jour [The Last Day]; 25, L'Élu [The Elected One]; 26. Le Royaume sans tête [The Kingdom Without a Head]; 27. Le Jurisconsulte [The Legal Adviser]; 28. Executor; 29. Le Substitut [The Substitute]; 30. L'Avènement du Sanguinaire [The Rise of the Blood-Thirsty]; 31. Les Sentinelles [The Sentinels]; 32. L'Odyssée d'Arthur [Arthur's Odyssey]; 33. Domi Nostrae; 34. La Supplique [The Supplicant]; 35. Les Embusqués [The Ambushed]; 36. La Nourrice [The Nanny]; 37. Les Transhumants; 38. Jizo; 39. Unagi V; 40. Les Pionniers [The Pioneers]; 41. La Conspiratrice [The Scheming Woman]; 42. Le Destitué [The Destitute Man]; 43. Le Phare [The Lighthouse]; 44. Le Guide [The Guide]; 45. Anton; 46. Les Itinérants [The Wanderers]; 47. Le Garçon qui criait au loup [The Boy Who Cried Wolf]; 48. Le Théâtre Fantôme [The Phantom*

Theater]; 49. Le Retour du Roi [The Return of the King]; 50. La Rivière Souterraine [The Underground River].

Season 6 (nine episodes of 40 minutes broadcast as follows: the first three on 17 October 2009, the next six on 24 and 31 October 2009. The titles are all in Latin): 1. *Miles Ignotus [The Unknown Soldier]*; 2. *Centurio [The Centurion]*; 3. *Praeceptores [The Teachers]*; 4. *Arturi Inquisitio [In Search of Arthur]*; 5. *Dux Bellorum [Battle Leader]*; 6. *Nuptiae [The Wedding]*; 7. *Arturus Rex [King Arthur]*; 8. *Lacrimosa [The Tears]*; 9. *Dies Irae [Day of Wrath]*.
Note: This season is not a sequel to Season 5, but a prequel. The first eight episodes will retrace Arthur's youth. The last episode, however, is a direct continuation of Season 5, concluding the series and announcing the first feature film (see previous section).

La Lance de la Destinée [*The Spear of Destiny*] (M6, col., six 52 min. episodes, 20-27 December 2008)
Dir: Dennis Berry; *Wri*: Anthony Maugendre.
Cast: Hélène Seuzaret (Sofia Béranger), Max Von Thun, Jacques Weber, Jacques Perrin, Natacha Lindinger, Michaël Cohen.
Story: Sophia, a young archaeologist, finds the trace of the famous Spear of Destiny, which would allow its possessor to become immortal. But her discovery attracts the attention of two powerful secret societies who want to seize the Spear.

La Légende des Trois Clefs [*The Legend of the Three Keys*] (M6, col., three 90 min. episodes, 20 December 2007-2 January 2008)

Dir: Gilbert Sinoué, Julien Sarfati, Patrick Dewolf; *Wri*: Gilbert Sinoué, Julien Sarfati, Jean-Vincent Fournier, Michel Alexandre, Patrick Dewolf.
Cast: Julien Crampon (Jimmy), Manon Gaurin (Juliette), Paul Blaise (Damien), Julie de Bona, Julie Gayet, Thierry Neuvic, Michel Duchaussoy, Danièle Lebrun, Jean-Pierre Lorit.
Story: Damien, who has a gift for mathematics, Juliette, who speaks several languages, and Jimmy, a gifted artist, are three 13 years-old born on the same day. They are hunted down by a mysterious organization and embark on an adventure that leads them to discover a secret dating back to the dawn of time.

Le Loup Blanc [*The White Wolf*] (FR 3, col., three 55 min. episodes, 1977)
Dir: Jean-Pierre Decourt; *Wri*: J.-P. Decourt, Henri de Turenne, based on the novel by Paul Féval.
Cast: Jacques Rosny (Jean Blanc/Loup Blanc), Henri Lambert, Michel Vitold, Claude Giraud, Maryvonne Schiltz, Jean Leuvrais, Sébastien Foure.
Episodes: *1. L'Albinos* [*The Albino*] (30/12/77); *2. La Forêt de Rennes* [*The Forest of Rennes*] (31/12/77); *3. Jean Blanc* (1/1/78).
Story: In 18th century Britanny, the peasants revolt against the Regency, led by a mysterious Robin Hood-like figure hiding behind the mask of a white wolf.

Marianne (Netflix, eight 50-mins. episodes, 13 September 2019)
Dir: Samuel Bodin; *Wri*: Samuel Bodin, Quoc Dang Tran.
Cast: Victoire Du Bois (Emma), Lucie Boujenah, Tiphaine Daviot.

Story: When Emma, a famous horror writer, goes back to her hometown, she finds out that the evil spirit that plagues her dreams is also there in real life.

Mes Chers Disparus [*My Dearly Departed*] (France 2, col., six 52 min. episodes, 23-30 December 2015)
Dir: Stéphane Kappes; *Wri*: Barbara Grinberg, Philippe Mari, Hélène Cohen
Cast: Sophie Le Tellier (Marianne), Arnaud Lechien (José), Sandra Nkake, Loup-Denis Elion, Francis Perrin, Jean-Baptiste Maunier, Hubert Saint-Macary.
Story: Marianne Elbert, puts her house up for sale against the will of her husband José, her children and her godfather. Soon, her dead ancestors reappear return as ghosts.

Métal Hurlant Chronicles [*Heavy Metal Chronicles*] (France 4, col., twelve 26 min. episodes, 27 October 2012-12 May 2014)
Dir: Guillaume Lubrano; *Wri*: Guillaume Lubrano, Justine Veillot, Dan Wickline.
Cast: Scott Adkins, Karl E. Landler, Michael Jai White, James Marsters, Michelle Ryan, David Belle, Dominique Pinon, Kelly Brook, Joe Flanigan, Frédérique Bel, Rutger Hauer.
Story: Anthology of stories having appeared in the French science fiction comic magazine *Métal hurlant*. Each episode is a different story, having only in common the Loc-Nar, a meteorite crossing space and time to change the lives of the protagonists. However, some episodes are connected, e.g.: in *Oxygen* and *The Masters of Destiny*, a character recounts an event occurring in the other story.

Season 1 (2012): *1. La Couronne du roi [The King's Crown]; 2. Protège-moi [Protect me]; 3. Lumière rouge / Réalité glaçante [Red Light / Icy Reality]; 4. Oxygène [Oxygen]; 5. Les Maîtres du destin [The Masters of Destiny]; 6. Le Serment d'Anya [Anya's Oath].*
Season 2 (2014): *1. L'Endomorphe [The Endomorph]; 2. Whisky; 3. Seconde chance [Second Chance]; 4. Le Dernier Khondor [The Last Khondor]; 5. Le Second fils [The Second Son]; 6. Retour à la réalité [Return to Reality].*

Missions (OCS, col., twenty-five episodes of 26 to 50 min., 1 June 2017-23 December 2021)
Dir: Julien Lacombe; *Wri*: Ami Cohen, Henri Debeurme, Julien Lacombe.
Cast: Mathias Mlekuz (Meyer), Hélène Viviès (Jeanne), Clément Aubert, (Simon) Jean-Toussaint Bernard, Giorgia Sinicorni, Côme Levin, Adrianna Gradziel, Christophe Vandevelde, Arben Bajraktaraj (Komarov), Ralph Amoussou (Samuel Becker), Natasha Andrews, Ben Homewood, Nathan Willcocks, Shane Woodward, Vincent Londez, Lucas Englander.
Season 1 (2017): *1. Ulysse; 2. Mars; 3. Survivant [Survivor]; 4. Pierre [Stone]; 5. Alliance; 6. Irène; 7. Faute [Fault]; 8. Phenix; 9. Volodia. 10. Orage [Storm].*
Story: In the near future, the first manned mission to Mars, *Ulysses 1*, is a European mission funded by the European Space Agency and William Meyer, a Swiss billionaire. The crew is made up of the best European astronauts and scientists. They eventually discover they were preceded by an American mission which has mysteriously vanished. Once on Mars, the European astronauts find a dead Russian cosmonaut who arrived there in 1967.

Season 2 (2019): *1. Aube [Dawn]; 2. Retours [Returns]; 3. Évolution; 4. Passage; 5. Réplique; 6. Alice; 7. Furie [Fury]; 8. Autres [Others]; 9. Architectes [Architects]; 10. Singularité [Singularity].*
Story: Five years later, Jeanne appears to be living in a strange society in a forest in symbiosis with nature. Realizing that she is still alive, Simon discovers that all the other members of the mission have seen her in their dreams. So they decide to return to Mars to look for her. There, they discover a portal leading to another planet.

Season 3 (2021): *1. Le Rasoir d'Ockham [Ockham's Razor]; 2. La Clé [The Key; 3. Les Mains vides [Empty Hands]; 4. Le Sanctuaire [Sanctuary]; 5. Théogonie.*
Story: Samuel Becker is the only astronaut to return to Earth. When he arrives, he discovers that no one is waiting for him. He finds himself in a world where another version of himself lives a different life. An empathetic interrogator believes his story. Something or someone has created two different timelines. But who and how?

Moloch (ARTE, six 52-mins. episodes, 22-29 October 2020)
Dir: Arnaud Malherbe; *Wri*: Arnaud Malherbe, Marion Festraëts.
Cast: Marine Vacth (Louise), Olivier Gourmet (Gabriel), Arnaud Valois, Marc Zinga, Alice Verset, Soufiane Guerrab, Babetida Sadjo, Laurent Capelluto, Julie-Anne Roth, Jan Hammenecker.
Story: In a coastal town, people mysteriously and spontaneously combust. Louise, journalist and Gabriel, psychiatrist, investigate.

Le Monde Enchanté d'Isabelle [*Isabelle's Enchanted World*] (ORTF 1, col., thirteen 30 min. episodes, Avril-June 1973)
Dir/Wri: Jean-Claude Youri.
Cast: Isabelle Youri (Isabelle), Jean Topart, Laurence Badie, Léo Campion, Fabrice Bruno.
Story: A little girl explores a fantasy world.

Mortel [*Mortal*] (Netflix, twelve 45-to-54 mins. episodes, 21 November 2019-2 July 2021)
Dir: Edouard Salier, Simon Astier, Xavier Gens; *Wri*: Frédéric Garcia (creator), Virginie Brac, Yann Le Gal, Lola Roqueplo, Fanny Talmone.
Cast: Carl Malapa (Sofiane), Némo Schiffman (Victor), Manon Bresch (Luisa), Corentin Fila (Obé), Sami Outalbali (Reda), Firmine Richard, Anaïs Thomas, Raphaëlle Agogué, Marvin Dubart, Léa Léviant, Assa Sylla, Stéphane Brel, Daouda Keita.
Story: Two teenagers, Sofiane and Victor, make a pact with a voodoo god Obé to allow them to solve and avenge the apparent murder of Sofiane's brother, Reda. Sofiane is given the power by Obé to manipulate other people's actions, while Victor can read their minds. Both however must be present near each other for their powers to work. They then enlist the help of Luisa, who practices voodoo with her grandmother, so they may be free of the grip that Obé has on them and banish Obé from the world.
Season 1 (2019): *1. Archi Dead; 2. Flammes. Flammes. Flammes; 3. Mise à Nudes; 4. Un Mec toxique [A Toxic Guy]; 5. La Solitudine; 6. L'Ensecrètement.*

Season 2 (2021): *1. Archi pas dead; 2. Ancré a ton corps [Anchored to Youir Body]; 3. Je ne peux plus me décol-*

ler [I Can't Get unstuck]; 4. Le mariage d'Obé [Obé's Wedding]; 5. Qumra ; 6. Aprézan nou Lyanné.

Le Mutant [*The Mutant*] (TF1, col., six 60 min. episodes, 15 June-20 July 1978)
Dir: Bernard Toublanc-Michel; *Wri*: Alain Page.
Cast: Fanny Ardant (Jeanne Laurent), Bernard Woringer (Walter), Jacques Dacqmine (Prof. Masson), Nicolas Pignon (Saül Masson), Idwig Stephane (Henri Muller), Anton Diffring (Martin O'Brien), Haydée Politoff (Marie Morand), Stéphane Bouy, Philippe Forquet, Gilles Kohler, Barbara Sommers, Laure Moutoussamy, Rudolph Gessler, Matt Carney, Billy Kearns.
Story: The mysterious head of an equally mysterious organisation hires Walter to research the life of a mutant boy, Saül Masson, who grew up to become a genius. Eventually, the "head" is revealed to be Saül himself, who is plotting to take over mankind with mind-controlling implants.

Mystère [*Mystery*] (TSR, col., twelve 52 min. episodes, 13 June-12 August 2007)
Dir: Didier Albert; *Wri*: Malina Detcheva, Franck Ollivier.
Cast: Toinette Laquière (Laure), Arnaud Binard, Patrick Bauchau, Babsie Steger, Marisa Berenson, Fanny Cottençon, Yann Sundberg, Jean-Philippe Écoffey, Xavier Lafitte, Antoine De Prekel.
Story: A young woman whose mother was once abducted by aliens try to solver the mystery of her disdappearance.

Le Mystérieux Docteur Cornelius [*The Mysterious Dr. Cornelius*] (A2, col., six 60 min. episodes, 16 September-21 October 1984)
Dir: Maurice Frydland; *Wri*: Jean-Pierre Petrolacci, Jean-Daniel Simon, Pierre Nivollet, based on the novel by Gustave Le Rouge.
Cast: Gérard Desarthe (Cornelius Kramm), Jean Bouise (Fritz Kramm), François-Eric Gendron (Harry Dorgan), Hugues Quester (Barruch Jorgel), Renzo Palmer (William Dorgan), Robert Rimbaud (Bondonnat), Caroline Sihol (Isadora Jorgel), Georges Géret (Fred Jorgel), Maurice Vaudaux (Joe Dorgan), Maria Blanco (Frédéricque Bondonnat), Anne Fontaine (Andrée de Maubreuil), Enzo Robutti (M. de Maubreuil), Jacques François (Lord Burydan).
Story: Two millionaires, their families and friends, fight the evil schemes of the mad scientist Dr. Cornelius Kramm, his brother Fritz, and their secret organisation, the Red Hand, in a series of globe-spanning adventures.

Mycènes, Celui Qui Vient Du Futur [*Mycenes, He Who Comes From The Future*] (ORTF 1, col., two 90 min., episodes, 1972)
Dir: François Chatel, Pierre Neel; *Wri*: Aimé Michel, Stéfan Wul, Louis Rognoni.
Cast: Armand Ablanalp (Mycènes), Dominique Leverd, Catherine Ciriez, Jean Coste, Frédéric Lambre.
Story: Mycènes, an android from the future, travels to the present to learn about our era.
1. *La Planète Fermée* [*The Closed Planet*] (29 January);
2. *La Piste Sans Étoiles* [*The Starless Arena*] (19 February).

Note: Originally slated for thirteen episodes, this series was cancelled after only two because of its low ratings and viewers' negative reactions.

Noires Sont Les Galaxies [*Dark Are The Galaxies*] (A2, col., four 60 min. episodes, April 1981)
Dir: Daniel Moosmann; *Wri*: Jacques Armand.
Cast: Richard Fontana, Catherine Leprince, François Perrot, Catriona McCall, Stéphane Bouy, Maryvonne Schiltz, Raoul Guillet, Roger Riffard.
Story: A young doctor discovers that alien exiles have been stealing human corpses to inhabit them. But the exiles are themselves hunted by hostile aliens from their homeworld.

Nox (Canal+, six 52 mins. episodes, 2018)
Dir: Mabrouk El Mechri; *Wri*: Fred Cavayé, Quoc Dang Tran, Jérôme Fansten.
Cast: Nathalie Baye (Catherine), Malik Zidi, Maïwenn (Julie), Frédéric Pierrot, Lubna Azabal, Valérie Donzelli, Sophie Cattani.
Story: When her daughter Julie disappears in the Underground under Paris, Catherine is convinced that she alone can find her. A former cop, she teams up with Raphael, her daughter's friend, and leave the surface to explore the depths of Paris…

Nu [*Naked*] (OCS Max, ten 22-mins. episodes, 7 June-6 July 2018)
Dir: Olivier Fox; *Wri*: Olivier Fox, Olivier de Plas, Judith Godinot.
Cast: Satya Dusaugey (Franck), Malya Roman (Lucie), Brigitte Faure, Sebastian Barrio.

Story: In 2026, after the passing of the "transparency law", everyone lives naked in France. But the murder of the lawmaker, found fully dressed, revives tensions. Inspector Lucie and her ex-partner Franck, who has just awakened from an 8-year coma, investigate.

Objectif Nul (Canal+, col., forty-three 7 min. episodes, 2 February-20 April 1987)
Dir: Christine Bertholier Jean-Louis Cap, Gilles Daude, Myriam Isker, Mathias Ledoux, Jean-Pierre Moscardo;
Wri: Alain Chabat, Bruno Carette, Chantal Lauby, Dominique Farrugia
Cast: Alain Chabat, Bruno Carette, Chantal Lauby, Alexandre Pottier, Dominique Farrugia.
Story: Comedy sketches with frequent sci-fi content.

L'Oeil de la Nuit [*The Eye of Night*] (A2, col., eight 30 min. episodes, 1979, 1981)
Wri/Dir: Jean-Pierre Richard.
Regular Cast: Gérard Séty, Fred Personne, Maurice Bourbon, Jean Bollery.
Story: Four men meet at the Inn of Legends to tell stories.

1. *Le Ballet Inachevé* [*The Unfinished Ballet*] (8 October 1979)
Story: A poor musician hears a man whistling the music he has just composed.

2. *Le Chien de la Colonelle* [*The Colonel's Wife's Dog*] (13 October 1979)
Story: A colonel is addicted to gambling, much to his wife's dismay.

3. *Le Vin des Carpates* [*The Wine From The Carpathians*] (20 October 1979)
Story: A man visits a haunted castle.

4. *La Locataire des Bois* [*The Tenant in the Woods*] (27 October 1979) (previously aired on 23 July 1978 as *La Rose Impossible* [*The Impossible Rose*])
Guest Cast: Benoist Brione, Jenny Arasse, Maurice Jaquemont.
Story: A young biker picks up a mysterious female hitchhiker.

5. *On l'appellait l'Américain* [*They Called Him The American*] (17 December 1981)
Guest Cast: Raymond Bussières, Jérôme Zucca.
Story: A strange friendship develops between a young sailor and an old tramp.

6. *Le Fantôme est Amoureux* [*The Ghost Is In Love*] (18 December 1981)
Guest Cast: Jean Bouise, Thérèse Liotard.
Story: A down on his luck comedian, hired to play a ghost, meets a real ghost.

7. *La Fin d'un Cauchemar* [*The End of a Nightmare*] (21 December 1981)
Guest Cast: Jacques Duby, Pascale Roberts, Robert Rimbaud.
Story: A travel agent is plagued by a recurring nightmare.

8. *Le Syndrome de Cendrillon* [*The Cinderella Syndrome*] (22 December 1981)
Guest Cast: Guy Marchand.

Story: A traveling salesman accepts the hospitality of two strange sisters.

Les Oraliens (Télévision de Radio-Canada, col., 125 13 min. episodes, 20 October 1969-5 June 1970)
Dir/Wri: Laurent Lachance.
Cast: Hubert Gagnon, Lisette Anfousse, Serge L'Italien, Gaétane Laniel.
Story: The adventures of two tiny extra-terrestrials from the planet Oralie Kalinelle (Lisette Anfousse) and Picabo (Hubert Gagnon), who discover, as all children would, the world around them.

Osmosis (Netflix, eight 40-moins. episodes, 29 March 2019)
Dir: Pierre Aknine (eps. 3, 4, 7, 8), Mona Achache (eps. 5, 6), Julius Berg (eps 1, 2); *Wri*: Audrey Fouché, based on the eponymous web-serie by Louis Chiche, William Chiche & Gabriel Chiche, Anne Badel, Aurélie Belko, José Caltagirone, Sylvie Chanteux, Thomas Finkielkraut, Éric Forestier, Olivier Fox, Simon Jablonka, Anne Rambach, Marine Rambach.
Cast: Agathe Bonitzer (Esther), Hugo Becker (Paul), Gaël Kamilindi, Yuming Hey, Manoël Dupont, Stéphane Pitti, Luna Silva, Philypa Phoenix, Fabien Ducommun, Lena Laprès, Vincent Renaudet, Jeremy Lewin,
Story: In near-future Paris, a new dating app called Osmosis can decode true love, dig deep into its users' brain data to find a perfect match with 100% accuracy. But is there a price to pay when letting an algorithm decide whom you will love, using technology that can access the innermost recesses of your mind and your best-kept secrets.

OVNI(s) [*UFOs*] (Canal+, twenty-four 30 mins. episodes, 11 January 2021-14 March 2022)
Dir: Antony Cordier; *Wri*: Clémence Dargent, Martin Douaire, Julien Anscutter, Marie Eynard, Clémence Madeleine-Perdrillat, Raphaëlle Richet.
Cast: Melvil Poupaud (Didier Mathure), Michel Vuillermoz (Marcel), Géraldine Pailhas (Elise), Quentin Dolmaire (Remy), Daphné Patakia (Vera), Nicole Garcia, Alice Taglioni, Capucine Valmary, Alessandro Mancuso, Olivier Broche.
Story: In 1978, Didier Mathure, a brilliant space engineer working for the French National Center for Space Studies (CNES), sees his career wrecked when the rocket he's spent a decade building explodes on take-off. He is demoted and pout in charge of the Group for the Study of Unidentified Aerospace Phenomena (GEPAN), an organization responsible for studying UFOs.

Parallèles [*Parallels*] (Disney+, six 34-to-42 mins. episodes, 23 mars 2022)
Dir: Benjamin Rocher, Jean-Baptiste Saurel; *Wri*: Quoc Dang Tran, Anastasia Heinzl.
Cast: Thomas Chomel (Sam), Jules Houplain (Victor), Omar Mebrouk (Bilal), Jade Pedri (Romane), Maxime Bergeron, Timoté Rigault, Victoria Eber, Naidra Ayadi, Guillaume Labbé, Gil Alma, Elise Diamant, Dimitri Storoge, Agnès Miguras.
Story: Four lifelong friends preparing to start high school – Bilal, Romane, and brothers Sam and Victor – find their reality disrupted when the test of an experimental particle collider sends them into parallel worlds.
Episodes: *1. Le Monde dans ta face [Hard Awakening]; 2. Contre toute attente [Against All Odds]; 3. Le Temps*

perdu [Lost Time]; 4. *Innocence révolue [Bygone Innocence]*; 5. *Un plan simple [A Simple Plan]*; 6. *H-4*.

La Poupée Sanglante [*The Bloody Puppet*] (A2, col., six 60 min. episodes, 17 September-22 October 1976)
Dir: Marcel Cravenne; *Wri*: Robert Scipion.
Cast: Jean-Paul Zehnacker (Benedict Masson), Yolande Folliot (Christine), Ludwig Gaum (Gabriel), Georges Wod (Marquis), Édith Scob (Marquise), Dominique Leverd (Jacques), Julien Verdier (Gaillard), Sacha Pitoëff (Sahib Khan), Cathy Rosier, Georges Lycan, Gabriel Gobin, Germaine Delbat, Florence Brière, Jacqueline Rouillard, Roland Armontel, Jean Rupert.
Story: The brain of Benedict Masson, a man unjustly guillotined, is transplanted into an android body. He later helps expose and defeat a vampiric cult led by a depraved nobleman.

La Prophétie d'Avignon [*The Avignon Prophecy*] (TSR, col., eight 52 min. episodes, 8 August 2007)
Dir: David Delrieux; *Wri*: Emmanuelle Rey-Magnan, Pascal Fontanille.
Cast: Louise Monot , François Perrot, Claude Gensac , François Dunoyer, Gonzague Montuel, Jean-Marie Winling, Élise Tielrooy, Valeria Cavalli, Isabelle Tanakil, Guillaume Cramoisan, Bruno Madinier, Annie Grégorio, Salem Kali, Serge Gisquière, Emmanuelle Boidron, Marthe Keller.
Story: Esoteric mini-series centered around an investigation that resembles an initiatory quest whose key lies in the past of the Esperanza family. A puzzling secret is known to only a few insiders.

Reboot (France 4, col., fourteen 10 min. episodes, 10 November 2015-15 December 2017)
Dir: Davy Mourier; *Wri*: Davy Mourier, Lewis Trondheim.
Cast: Sébastien Lalanne (Oscar), Davy Mourier, Lénie Chérino, Aurélia Poirier.
Story: Oscar is a happy greengrocer until he discovers that he and all his colleagues are robots.

Les Revenants [*The Returned*] (Canal+, col., sixteen 52 min. episodes, 26 November 2012-19 October 2015)
Dir: Fabrice Gobert, Frédéric Mermoud, Frédéric Goupil; *Wri*: Fabrice Gobert, Emmanuel Carrère, Fabien Adda, Céline Sciamma, Nicolas Peufaillit, Catherine Hoffmann, based on the 2004 film by Robin Campillo.
Cast: Swann Nambotin (Victor), Yara Pilartz (Camille), Guillaume Gouix (Serge), Pierre Perrier (Simon), Laetitia de Fombelle (Viviane), Ana Girardot (Lucy), Armande Boulanger (Audrey), Jenna Thiam (Léna), Anne Consigny (Claire), Frédéric Pierrot (Jérome), Jean-François Sivadier (Pierre), Matila Malliarakis (Frédéric) , Clotilde Hesme (Adèle), Samir Guesmi (Thomas), Céline Sallette (Julie) , Alix Poisson (Laure), Grégory Gadebois (Toni) , Michaël Abiteboul (Milan), Laurent Lucas (Berg).
Story: The series takes place in a small French mountain town dominated by an artificial lake, held back by a huge dam. Several people who had been dead for years came back to life at the same time: Camille, a young teenager who died in a bus accident in 2008; Simon, a young man who committed suicide in 2002; Victor, a little boy who was murdered by burglars in 1977; and Serge, a serial killer murdered by his brother in 2005. They try to resume the course of their lives when strange

phenomena begin to appear: power cuts, drop in the water level of the dam, bedsores on the body the living and the dead...
Season 1 (11/26/2012 to 12/17/2012): *1. Camille ; 2. Simon ; 3. Julie ; 4. Victor ; 5. Serge et Toni ; 6. Lucy ; 7. Adèle ; 8. La Horde*.

Season 2 (9/28/2015 to 10/19/2015) : *1. L'Enfant [The Child] ; 2. Milan ; 3. Morgane ; 4. Virgil ; 5. Madame Costa ; 6. Esther ; 7. Étienne; 8. Les Revenants [The Returned]*.
Note: Remade in the U.S. in 2015 as *The Returned* by Carlton Cuse.

Le Roi Mystère [*King Mystery*] (FR 3, col., four 90 min. episodes, 1991)
Dir: Paul Planchon; *Wri*: Marcel Jullian.
Cast: Christopher Bowen (King Mystery/Robert Pascal), Philippe Bouclet (Sinnimari), Pierre Piéral (Mac Callan), Aurelle Doazan (Gabrielle), Éva Mazauric (Liliane), Patrick Polvey, Dominique Pinon, Patrick Burgel, Carina Barone, Yan Epstein, Fred Ulysse, Amadeus August, Gaby Fuchs.
Story: In this story inspirfed by *The Count of Monte-Cristo*, the mysterious King of the Parisian Underworld challenges the evil schemes of the corrupt Imperial Prosecutor Sinnimari.
Episodes: 1. *La Guillotine* (23 April 1991); 2. *Le Perroquet [The Parrakeet]* (30 April 1991); 3. *La Dent Creuse [The Hollow Tooth]* (7 May 1991); 4. *Le Châtiment [The Punishment]* (14 May 1991)

Rocambole (ORTF 2, B&W., three seasons of twenty-xix 15-min. episodes, 1964-65)

Dir: Jean-Pierre Decourt; *Wri*: Jean-Pierre Decourt, Anne-Marie Salerne, Louis Falavigna, based on the novels by Pierre-Alexis Ponson du Terrail.
Cast: Pierre Vernier (Rocambole), Jean Topart (Sir Williams), Marianne Girard (Baccarat), René Clermont (Beaupréau), Alain Dekock (Marmouset), Jean Heynau (Mourax), Paul Bisciglia (Bistoquet), Michel Puterflam (Mort-des-Braves), Jeanne Herviale (Maman Fipart), Michel Beaune (de Kergaz), Jacques Dynam (Bastien), Cécile Vassort (Cerise), Raoul Curet (Colar), Henri Piégay (Fernand), Jacqueline Corot (Jeanne), Marie-France Boyer (Hermine), Jean-Paul Moulinot (Lord Charring), Hubert Deschamps (Murph), Jean Negroni (Guhri), Mario Pilar (Nively), Raoul Curet (Le Patissier), Elisabeth Wiener (Gipsy), Nadine Alari (Milady), Francine Bergé (Belle Jardinière), Michel Ruhl (Volovodine), Julien Guiomar (Capendoc), Jacques Seiler (Artoff), Bernard Ceyleron (Serguei), Jean Degrave (Illyne).
Story: Taking place in the mid-19th century, this serial-like series narrates the adventures of gentleman-burglar Rocambole against his former master and enemy, the arch-villain Sir Williams and his adversary-turned-lover, Baccarat. In the first season, Rocambole rescues a young heiress. In the second season, he thwarts a gang of Thugees. In the third season, he becomes involved in a war between two Russian secret societies.
Seasons: 1. *L'Héritage Mystérieux* [*The Mysterious Inheritance*] (18 April-7 May 1964); 2. *Les Étrangleurs* [*The Stranglers*] (8 May-9 June 1964); 3. La Belle Jardinière [*The Beautiful Gardener*] (15 April-10 May 1965).

Rouletabille
Story: Young journalist Joseph Joséphin, a.k.a. Rouletabille, investigates murders committed in mysterious, of-

ten uncanny, circumstances. Based on the niovels by Gaston Leroux.

1. *Le Mystère de la Chambre Jaune* [*The Mystery of the Yellow Room*] (ORTF 1, B&W., 90 min., 27 November 1965)
Dir: Jean Kerchbron; *Wri*: Jean Gruault, Jean Kerchbron.
<u>Cast</u>: Claude Brasseur (Rouletabille), François Maistre (Larsan), Marika Green (Mathilde), Lucien Nat, Géo Wallery, Jean Champion.

2. *Le Parfum de la Dame En Noir* [*The Scent of the Lady in Black*] (ORTF 1, B&W., ten 15 min. episodes, 3-14 March 1966)
Dir: Yves Boisset; *Wri*: Bernard Dabry, Guy Jorré.
Cast: Philippe Ogouz (Rouletabille), Raymond Loyer (Darzac), Nicole Maurey (Mathilde), Aimé Demarch, Lucien Raimbourg, Tania Lopert, René Lefèvre.

3. *Rouletabille chez le Tsar* [*Rouletabille at the Tsar's*] (ORTF 1, B&W., ten 15 min. episodes, 17-30 March 1966)
Dir: Jean-Charles Lagneau; *Wri*: Bernard Dabry, Guy Jorré.
Cast: Philippe Ogouz (Rouletabille), Maria Meriko (Matrena), Julien Guiomar (Trebassof), Paloma Matta, Georges Claisse, Pierre Tornade.

4. *Rouletabille chez les Bohémiens* [*Rouletabille and the Gypsies*] (ORTF 1, B&W., ten 15 min. episodes, 31 March - 13 April 1966)
Dir: Robert Mazoyer; *Wri*: Bernard Dabry, Guy Jorré.

Cast: Philippe Ogouz (Rouletabille), Tania Balachova (Zina), Judith Magre (Calista), Caroline Cellier, Annie Savarin, Henri Piégay, Henri Virlojeux, Jacques Robiolles.

Section Zéro (Canal+, col., eight 52-min. episodes, 4 April-23 May 2016).
Dirs: Olivier Marchal (eps. 1-7), Ivan Fegyvères (ep. 8); *Wri*: Olivier Marchal, Laurent Guillaume, Franck Philippon, David Martinez.
Cast: Ola Rapace (Sirius), Pascal Greggory, Tchéky Karyo, Catherine Marchal, Francis Renaud, Laurent Malet, Juliette Dol, Hilde De Baerdemaeker, Marc Barbé.
Story: In 2024, in a Europe ruled by multinational corporations, the Prometheus Conglomerate wants to generalize the use of the Black Squad, a robotic police officers. Faced with this threat, Commander Sirius Becker wants to resist by leading Section Zero, an elite group.

Les Sept Vies de Léa [*The Seven Lives of Lea*] (Netflix, seven 32-to-42 mins. episodes, 28 April 2022)
Dir: Julien Despaux, Émilie Noblet; *Wri*: Charlotte Sanson based on a novel by Nataël Trapp, Frédéric Rosset, Camille Rosset, Dorothée Lachaud, Alice Vial, Deborah Hassoun.
Cast: Raïka Hazanavicius (Lea), Khalil Ben Gharbia, Mélanie Doutey, Samuel Benchetrit.
Story: Léa discovers the dead body of Ishmael and finds herself thirty years earlier in his body. Every day she finds herself in the body of another character from the past, while trying to solve Ishmael's death.

Le Sérum de Bonté [*The Happiness Serum*] (RTF 1, B&W., thirteen 30-min. episodes, October-December 1960)
Dir: Jean-Daniel Norman; *Wri*: Pierre Armand.
Cast: Jean Richard (Dupont), Paulette Dubost, Evelyne Ker, Nicolas Ray, Hélène Vallier.
Story: In this sitcom, the French Government tests on an average family a new drug that is intended to improve people.

Si Perrault m'était conté [*If Perrault Was Retold*] (ORTF, col., four 55-min. episodes, 3-24 January 1966)
Dir/Wri: Anne Béranger, Jacques Charon.
Cast: Pierre Tchernia (Host), Jacques Charon (Puss in Boots), Perrette Pradier, Laurence Badie, Christine Delaroche, Jean-Claude Drouot, Michel Duchaussoy, Claude François, Geneviève Grad, Maria Pacôme.
Story: The fairy tales of Charles Perrault are adapted in a modern urban setting in a comical tone, with song and dance numbers.
Episodes: *1. Le Petit Chaperon Rouge [Little Red Riding Hood]; 2. Cendrillon [Cinderella]; 3. Le Chat Botté [Puss-in-Boots]; 4. Riquet à la Houppe [Ricky with a tuff].*

Siocnarf (Radio-Canada Television, col., 30 min. episodes, 1981)
Dir/Wri: Hélène Roberge
Siocnarf (François spelled backwards) is an alien prince from a far-away galaxy. His two friends are Evelyna and Theodore.

Les Soirées du Bungalow [*Evenings at the Bungalow*] (ORTF 1, col., four 60-min. episodes, 1969)

Dir/Wri: Roger Iglésis; *Wri*: Louis Pauwels.
Regular Cast: Tom Duggan, Gianni Esposito, François Maistre, Jean-Roger Caussimon, Olivier Hussenot, Muse d'Albray.
Story: Guests at a bungalow tell each other fantasy stories.

1. *La Merveilleuse Histoire du Major Brown* [*The Marvellous Story of Major Brown*] (26 April 1969)
Story: based on a story by G. K. Chesterton.
Guest Cast: Vytte Pedersen, Robert Le Beal, Sacha Pitoëff, Dominique Bernard.
Story: A doctor meets a ghost.

2. *Histoire d'une Famille de Tyrone* [*The Story of a Family From Tyrone*] (26 April 1969)
Story: based on a story by Sheridan Le Fanu.
Guest Cast: Marika Green, François Perrot, Katharina Reen.
Story: An Irish castle is haunted.

3. *Le Coeur Cambriolé* [*The Stolen Heart*] (7 September 1969)
Story: based on the novel by Gaston Leroux.
Guest Cast: Giani Esposito, Juliette Villard, Jean-Pierre Jorris, Raymond Meunier.
Story: A painter uses his psychic powers to steal a young man's bride.

4. *L'Homme Hanté* [*The Haunted Man*] (22 December 1969)
Wri: Paule de Beaumont, based on a story by Charles Dickens.

Guest Cast: Jean-Roger Caussimon, Edith Scob, Etienne Bierry, Colette Ripert, Henri Poirier, Yves-Marie Maurin.
Story: A chemist haunted by his memories, discovers that forgetting the past comes at a price.

La Sorcellerie [*Witchcraft*] (FR 3, col., three 90-min. episodes, October-November 1985)

1. *Un Jour entre Chien et Loups* [*One Day, Between Dogs and Wolves*]
Dir: Patrick Saglio; *Wri*: Michel Picard, Alain Doutey.
Cast: Valérie Popesco, Xavier Gélin, Vanessa Vaylord.
Story: After a car accident in the country, a man's wife disappears.

2. *L'Enfant et les Magiciens* [*The Child and the Magicians*]
Dir: Philippe Arnal; *Wri*: Paul Wagner, Philippe Arnal.
Cast: Magali Noël, Etienne Berry, Alexandre Sterling, Alain Libolt.
Story: A warlock and a witch try to teach their trade to their nephew.

3. *L'Oeil du Sorcier* [*The Wizard's Eye*] (previously aired on 26 September 1979)
Dir: Alain Dhénault; *Wri*: Patrick Pesnot, Philippe Alfonsi.
Cast: Christian Barbier, Elina Labourdette, Lucienne Lemarchand, Catherine Lafond, Marie Delarue, Edmond Beauchamps, Roger Riffard.

Story: A medical doctor who has returned to the country to live, is threatened by local witchcraft.

S.O.S. Terre [*SOS Earth*] (Television Romande, B&W., 8 episodes, 1966)
Dir: Roger Gillioz ; *Wri*: Germaine Epiere.
<u>*Cast*</u>: Jean Bruno (Louvier), Gilbert Divorne (Clarière). André Faure (Franke), Jean Vigny (Ventermne), Edouard Nervbazl, Pierre Holdener, Michel Cassagne, Bernard Heymann, Maurice Auclair, Pierre Boulanger, Adrien Nicati, Michel Corod, Jacqueline Burnand.
Story: Captain Louvier is appointed to the Corsair space base to watch over the *Célestine* rocket. As he visits the rocket with his two lieutenants, the clumsiness of a painter gives the starting signal...

Sueurs Froides [*Cold Sweat*] (Canal Plus, col., eighteen 30-min. episodes, 1988)
This anthology series of crime thrillers, hosted by director Claude Chabrol, included three genre episodes:

2. *La Sublime Aventure* [*The Sublime Adventure*] (6 February 1988)
Dir/Wri: René Manzor, based on a story by Louis C. Thomas.
Cast: Guy Marchand, Frédéric Mitterand, Anne Zamberlan.
Story: People turn into gasses and vanish into thin air.

4. *Toi Si Je Voulais* [*You If I Wanted*] (5 March 1988)
Dir/Wri: Patrice Leconte, based on a story by Louis C. Thomas.
Cast: Gérard Jugnot, Julie Jezequel, Christine Amat, Patrick Baroude, Etienne Fernagut.
Story: A man discovers that he can wish people dead.

8. *Mise à l'Index* [*Put on the Black List*] (2 April 1988)
Dir: Bernard Nauer; *Wri*: Philippe de Chauveron, Bernard Nauer, based on a story by Bruno Léandri.
Cast: Jean Carmet, Eva Darlan, Jean Rougerie, Marc Berman, Ticky Holgado.
Story: A journalist accidentally uncovers the trafficking of human flesh.

Tang (ORTF 2, col., thirteen 26 min. episodes, June 1971)
Dir: André Michel; *Wri*: Jacques Faurie.
Cast: Valery Inkijinoff (Tang), Abbie Kerani (Kyoo), Xavier Gélin (André), Catherine Samie (Léna), Patrick Préjean (Marcel), Jacques Galipeau (Carteau).
Story: A secret organization, led by the evil Tang, schemes control an all-powerful weapon dubbed 327 and take over the world.

La Tante de Frankenstein [*Frankenstein's Aunt*] (FR3, col., thirteen 30 min. episodes, February-April 1990)
Dir: Jurad Jakubisko; *Wri*: Jurad Jakubisko, Jurad Dietl, Allan Rune Petterson.
Cast: Viveca Kindfors (Aunt Frankenstein), Ferdy Mayne (Dracula), Eddie Constantine, Flavio Bucci, Jacques Herlin, Gail Gatterburg.
Story: The descendents of Frankenstein attempt to carry on his dream in this satirical series of fantastic adventures.
Note: International co-production between Austria, the then-Czechoslovakia, the then-West Germany, and France.

Temps Mort [*Dead Time*] (13ᵉ rue, six 15 mins episodes, 16 July 2008)
Dir: James L. Frachon; *Wri*: James L. Frachon, Guy Giraud, from a concept by Thibault Poulain de Saint Père and Alain Robak.
Cast: Jean Rieffel (Jean), Marie-France Santon, Charles Schneider, Frédérique Bel, Caroline Beaune, Philippe du Janerand, Karen Alyx, Eric Mariotto, Karina Testa.
Story: Jean, an embalmer in his thirties working in a funeral home, discovers that he is able to see and speak with the dead.

Le Tour du Monde en 80 Jours [*Around The World In 80 Days*]
Based on the novel by Jules Verne.
   1. (A2, col., two 90 min. episodes, 29-30 December 1975)
Dir: Pierre Nivollet; *Wri*: Jean Marsan, Jean Le Poulain.
Music: Gérard Calvi; *Chroreography*: Jean Guélis.
Cast: Jean Le Poulain (Fogg), Pierre Trabaud (Passepartout), Roger Carel.
Note: Musical comedy.

   2. (A2, col., 25 December 1979)
Dir: André Frédérick; *Wri*: Pavel Kohout.
Cast: Daniel Ceccaldi (Fogg), Roger Pierre (Passepartout), Jean-Pierre Darras.

   3. (FR3, col., twelve 5 min., episodes, 22 December 1980-3 January 1981)
Dir/Wri: Serge Danot.

Cast: Jean Pellotier (Fogg), Charles Caunant (Passepartout), Christian Duc, Paul Bisciglia, Michel Bruzat.
Note: Serge Danot is the creator of *Le Manège Enchanté* [The Magic Roundabout].

Transferts (Arte, col., six 58 min. episodes, 16-23 November 2017)
Dir: Olivier Guignard, Antoine Charreyron; *Wri*: Claude Scasso, Patrick Benedek.
Cast: Arieh Worthalter (Florian), Brune Renault, Toinette Laquière, Steve Tientcheu, Pili Groyne, Patrick Descamps, Patrick Raynal, Xavier Lafitte, Juliette Plumecocq-Mech, Aïssatou Diop.
Story: In the near future, Florian, an ordinary cabinetmaker, wakes up after five years of coma in the body of Sylvain, a police captain at a brigade that tracks "transferred" people, people whosae minds have been transferred from one body to another. Once legalized, "transferences" have been prohibited after rejections called "countertransferences" comparable to dementia.

Traquenards [*Traps*] (FR3, col., thirteen 30 min. episodes, December 1987-January 1988)
Story: Thirteen adolescents manage to extricate themselves from seemingly inescapable traps. Many situations contain genre elements (either fantastic or horrific).
Note: French-Canadian co-production.

    1. *Le Chevalier de Passignac* [*The Knight of Passignac*] (12/21/1987)
    Dir: François Labonté; *Wri*: François Labonté, Roland Paret, Raymond Plante.
    Cast: Ginette Boivin, Jo Doumerg, Sophie Léger, Guy Louret, Jacques Serres

Story: An armored knight is hauting a village.

2. *La Bibliothèque oubliée* [*The Forgotten Library*] (12/22/1987)
Dir: Bruno Carrière; *Wri*: Roger Cantin.
Cast: Claude Gai, Yvon Bouchard, Marcel Girard, Pierre Le Gardeur, Vincent Legault, Patrick Marchesson, Sébastien Tougas, Mathieu Vézina.
Story: A strange man hides in a long forgotten library.

3. *Les Mannequins de la forteresse* [*The Mannikins from the Fortress*] (12/23/1987)
Dir: Bruno Carrière; *Wri*: Gilles Parent.
Cast: Stéphan Côté, Isabelle Cyr, Paul Dion, Pascale Dupont, Réjean Gauvin, Dedan Hill, Charles Migueault, Diane St-Jacques.

4. *La Caverne des disparus* [*The Cave of the Disappeared*] (12/24/1987)
Dir: Bruno Carrière; *Wri*: Gilles Parent, Bruno Carrière.
Cast: Pierre Curzi, Robert Gauvin, Jacques Godin, Cédric Jourde, Michel Mailhot, Jacques Paris, Bruno Rouyère, Patricia Tulasne.

5. *Murée vive* [*Buried Alive*] (12/27/1987)
Dir: Bruno Carrière; *Wri*: Bruno Carrière, Jacques Jacob, G. Lenôtre.
Cast: Francis Facon, Jean-François Guemy, Alexis Martin, Xavier Mienniel, Sylvie Pascaud.

6. *Quasimodo* (12/28/1987)

Dir: François Labonté; *Wri*: François Labonté, Raymond Plante, based on Victor Hugo.
Cast: Daniel Benoît, Eric Brisebois, Jacques Charby, André Chaumeau, Eric Del, Pierre Dumur, Didier Garry, Macha Grenon.
Story: The story of the Hunchback of Notre-Dame recast in modern times.

7. *Le Bonsaï millénaire* [*The Thousand Year-Old Bonsaï*] (12/29/1987)
Dir: Bruno Carrière; *Wri*: Roger Cantin.
Cast: Serge Christianssens, Marie-Andrée Courchesne, Khan Hua, Michel Labelle.

8. *Mort à minuit* [*Death at Midnight*] (12/30/1987)
Dir: Raoul Held; *Wri*: Nacer Mazani.
Cast: André Morissette, Anna Gianotti, J.-P. Scantanburlo, Jacques Rossi, Janine Sutto, Renato Trujitto, Richard Groulx, Thomas Heliman.
Story: A young pizza delivery man is trapped in a house identical to that featured in a horror film he saw earlier.

9. *La Cage de fer* [*The Iron Cage*] (01/04/1988)
Dir: Jean-Claude Charnay; *Wri*: Claude Main Arnaud, Gilles Parent.
Cast: Claire Magnin, Gilbert Turp, Jean-Claude Sachot, Jean-Luc Gonsalez, Michel Larivière, Olivier Proust.

10. *La Source du mal* [*The Source of Evil*] (01/05/1988)
Dir: Bruno Carrière; *Wri*: Louise Anne Bouchard.

Cast: Mireille Bergeron, Mine Caron, Sophie Dansereau, Gilbert Delasoie, Marie-Chantal Labelle, Pierre Legris, Louise Marleau, Julie Morrissette, Marc Proulx.
Story: The water from a spring confers eternal youth.

11. *L'Héritage maudit* [*The Cursed Inheritance*] (01/06/1988)
Dir: Raoul Held; *Wri*: Raoul Held, Pierre Larry.
Cast: Jean-Yves Crochemore, Maripierre A. D'Amour, Sophie Faucher, Alain Françoise, Michel Hart, Frédérique Jamet, Michel Vitold.

12. *Le Trésor de feu* [*TheTreasure of Fire*] (01/07/1988)
Dir: Christian Alba; *Wri*: Gilles Parent, Christian Alba.
Cast: Jean-Marie Balembois, Jacques Bérard, Marc Bessou, Dominique Cornet, Antoine Corsales, René Gouzenne, Richard Guèvremont, Daniel Langlet, Maurice Mons, Yvon Palec, Hélène Surgère, Georges Vaur, Jacques Vogel.

13. *Les Tableaux qui parlent* [*The Talking Paintings*] (01/08/1988)
Dir: Marianne Lamour; *Wri*: Jean-Pierre Enard.
Cast: Chantal Neuwirth, Denise Boulet, Françoise Dorysse, Mélanie Marchand, Roch Leibovici, Roger Souza, Suzy Delair.

Treize Contes Fantastiques [*Thirteen Fantastic Tales*] (aka *Une École Belge de l'Étrange* [*A Belgian School of*

the Strange]) (Radio-Television Belge, B&W, thirteen 26 min. episodes, November 1967-1968)
Prod: Pierre Levie.
Story: TV adaptation of stories by the Belgian masters of horror.

1. *L'homme qui osa* [*The Man Who Dared*]
Dir/Wri: Jean Delire, based on a story by Jean Ray.
Host: Jacques Brel.
Cast: Danièle Denie, Christian Barbier, Quentin Milo.
Story: Animals and people vanish in an area known as the Black Lakes.

2. *Noces de plumes* [*Feather Wedding*]
Dir/Wri: Patrick Ledoux, based on a story by Eric Uytbrock.
Host: Maurice Béjart.
Cast: Edmond Bernhard, Laetitia Dufer, Kupissonoff, Max Renard, Emile Verhoeren.
Story: In a ruined abbey, a man attends a strange wedding.

3. *Le Gardien* [*The Caretaker*]
Dir/Wri: Christian Mesnil, based on a story by Jean Ray.
Cast: Lucien Froidebise, Claude Grandclaude, Guy Leclerc.
Story: A caretaker is the victim of a vampire.

4. *Non lieu* [*Case Withdrawn*]
Dir/Wri: Michel Stameschkine, based on a story by Thomas Owen.
Cast: Georges Randax, Lucien Salkin, Georges Bossair, Piroska Muharay.

Story: A doctor is haunted by war time memories.

5. *Simple alerte* [*Simple Alert*]
Dir/Wri: Jean Delire, based on a story by Marcel Thiry.
Host: Maurice Béjart.
Cast: Jean-Marie Deblin, Marc Audier, Irène Vernal, Yvan Fadel.
Story: A man in prey to despair finds an unexpected way out.

6. *Ultra, je t'aime* [*Ultra, I love you*]
Dir/Wri: Patrick Ledoux, based on a story by Jean Ray.
Host: Jacques Brel.
Cast: Nadia Gary, Paul Louka, Suzy Falk, Frédéric Latin, Georges Mony.
Story: A man suffers from a recurring dream in which he sees his dead mother and sister.

7. *Pitié pour une ombre* [*Mercy for a Shadow*]
Dir/Wri: Lucien Deroisy, based on a story by Thomas Owen.
Host: Jacques Brel.
Cast: Nadine Forster, Gysèle Oudart, Lucien Salkin, Yves Larec.
Story: A recumbent statue comes to life in a ruined castle.

8. *La Choucroute* [*The Sauerkraut*]
Dir/Wri: Jean Delire, based on a story by Jean Ray.
Host: Maurice Béjart.
Cast: Fernand Léane, Maurice Schwilden, Jacques Lippe

Story: A bookseller travels to a parallel world.

9. *La Princesse vous demande* [*The Princess Wishes To See You*]
Dir/Wri: Jean Delire, Jean-Louis Roncoroni, based on a story by Thomas Owen.
Host: Maurice Béjart.
Cast: Gianni Esposito, Danièle Denie, Claude Etienne, Amédée.
Story: A famous violonist is haunted by the thought he might lose his hands.

10. *La Maison des Cigognes* [*The House of Storks*]
Dir/Wri: Émile-Georges De Meyst, Louis Verlant, based on a story by Jean Ray.
Host: Jacques Brel.
Cast: Louis Verlant, Gil Lagay, Monique Verley, Nadia Gary.
Story: A mysterious house feeds on human flesh.

11. *Futur antérieur* [*Future Past*]
Dir/Wri: Jean-Jacques Péché, based on a story by Jean le Paillot.
Host: Maurice Béjart.
Cast: Nena Novovitch, Andy Van Ghendt, Martine Bertrand, Bernard Graczyk, Gilbert Bremans.
Story: A TV director finds he can kill people by tearing up their photos.

12. *Le Testament de Mr Breggins* [*The Testament of Mr. Breggins*]
Dir/Wri: Jean-Louis Colmant, based on a story by Thomas Owen

Cast: Françoise Oriane, Nelly Corbusier, Jane Max, Pierre Dermo, Georges Lambert.
Story: Mr. Breggins witnesses his own death.

13. *Le Voyageur* [*The Traveller*]
Dir/Wri: Françoise Levie, based on a story by Thomas Owen.
Host: Maurice Béjart.
Cast: Sonia Servais, André Ernotte, Louis Mercy, Olivier de Saedeleer.
Story: A train never stops at a tiny station.

Trepalium (ARTE, six 52 mins. episodes, 11-18 February 2016)
Dir: Vincent Lannoo; *Wri*: Antarès Bassis, Sophie Hiet, Thomas Cailley, Sébastien Mounier.
Cast: Léonie Simaga (Izia/Thaïs), Pierre Deladonchamps (Ruben), Ronit Elkabetz, Sarah Stern, Arauna Bernheim-Dennery, Grégoire Monsaingeon, Aurélien Recoing, Charles Berling, Lubna Azabal, Olivier Rabourdin.
Story: In the near future, the population is separated in two by a wall. On one side, the Zone, with the 80% of unemployed, on the other, the City, hosting the other 20%. Izia lives in the Zone where she raises her son alone. She is selected by the government to become a "solidarity worker" at Aquaville. She goes to work with Ruben, a depollution engineer devoted to his work, who lives with his wife Thaïs and his mute daughter.

Le Tribunal de l'Impossible [*The Tribunal of the Impossible*] (ORTF 1, col., fourteen 90 min. episodes, 1967-74)
Prod: Michel Subiela.

Note: This anthology of telefilms focused on the uncanny, the paranormal and the unexplained. It was followed by a round table discussion between a panel of experts, some "believers," others skeptics.

1. *La Bête du Gévaudan* [*The Beast of Gevaudan*] (3 October 1967)
Dir: Yves-André Hubert; *Wri*: Michel Subiela.
Cast: André Valmy, Georges Chamarat, Pierre Hatet, Guy Tréjean, Maria Meriko, Yvon Sarray, Jean Violette, Bernadette Lange, André Falcon, Marcel Champel, Claude Richard, Patrick Préjean.
Story: A legendary wolf-like creature plagues the Gevaudan countryside in 18th century France.

2. *Le Fabuleux Grimoire de Nicolas Flamel* [*The Fabulous Grimoir of Nicolas Flamel*] (25 November 1967)
Dir: Guy Lessertisseur; *Wri*: Alain Decaux.
Cast: Paul Crauchet (Flamel), Ariette Gilbert, Roger Crouzet, Lucien Nat, Maurice Bourbon, Georges Riquier, Jacques Lalande, Françoise Dorner, Maurice Garrel, Frank Estange, François Dyrek.
Story: Cardinal de Richelieu orders the arrest of the grand-nephew of notorious 14th century alchemist Nicolas Flamel, who may have inherited his ancestor's secrets.

3. *Les Rencontres du Trianon, ou La Dernière Rose* [*The Trianon Encounters, or The Last Rose*] (10 February 1968)
Dir: Roger Kahane; *Wri*: Francis Lacassin.
Cast: Louise Conte, Jacqueline Jefford, Jacques Alric, Jean Calve, Denise Benoit, Sylvie Vaneck.

Story: Two English tourists appear to have mysteriously been transported back through time for an hour at Versailles Castle.

4. *Nostradamus, ou Le Prophète en son Pays* [*Nostradamus, or A Prophet In His Own Land*] (11 May 1968)
Dir: Pierre Badel; *Wri*: Michel Subiela.
Cast: Jean Topart (Nostradamus), Rosy Varte, Jean Leuvrais, François Maistre, Catherine Le Couey, Robert Murzeau, Lucien Nat.
Story: Was the famous seer only a charlatan?

5. *Qui Hantait le Presbytère de Borley ?* [*Who Haunted the Borley Presbytery?*] (30 November 1968)
Dir: Alain Boudet; *Wri*: Michel Subiela.
Cast: Guy Tréjean, Catherine Rich, Jean Obé, Bernadette Lange, Jean Martin, Juliette Mills, Guy Pierauld, Hélène Dieudonné, Madeleine Damiens, Catherine Lafond, Sylvain Joubert.
Story: A haunted house case from the late 1920s.

6. *Le Sabbat du Mont d'Etenclin* [*The Sabbath of Mount Etenclin*] (1st March 1969)
Dir: Michel Subiela; *Wri*: André Desvallées.
Cast: Edith Garnier, Charles Moulin, Serge Duchez, Roger Guillo, Jean-Pierre Herce, Renée Gardes, Marc de Georgi, Frédérique Ruchaud, André Valmy, Jean Vinci.
Story: The last witch trial held in France in 1668.

7. *La Passion d'Anne-Catherine Emmerich* [*The Passion of Anne-Catherine Emmerich*] (29 November 1969)
Dir: Michel Subiela; *Wri*: Marcelle Maurette.
Cast: Anouk Ferjac, Claude Titre, Bernard Verley, Jacques Monod, Sylvie Bourgoin, Gérard Denizot, Maike Jansen, Erwan Kerne.
Story: An 18th century German girl experiences visions of Christ, and bears stigmata of his crucifixion.

8. *Un Esprit Nommé Katie King* [*A Spirit Called Katie King*] (24 January 1970)
Dir: Pierre Badel; *Wri*: Hélène Misserly.
Cast: Bulle Ogier, Michel Vitold, Loleh Bellon, Robert Party, Maurice Teynac, Hélène Duc, Raymond Pélissier, Clément Bairam.
Story: In 1874 London, young medium Florence Cook summons the spirit of Katie King, a girl who died under Cromwell.

9. *Un Mystère Contemporain* [*A Contemporary Mystery*] (14 March 1970)
Dir: Alain Boudet; *Wri*: Albert Husson.
Cast: Claude Vernier, Dominique Leverd, Marika Green, Christine Audhuy, Arch Taylor, Jacques Riberolles, Jacques Debary, Martine Ferrière.
Story: A contemporary Belgian medium helps solve a case of kidnapping and a case of murder.

10. *La Cité d'Is* [*The City of Ys*] (30 May 1970)
Dir/Wri: Michel Subiela.
Cast: André Valmy, Isa Mercure, Jean-Pierre Herce, Roland Monod, Yvon Sarray, Raoul Guillet, Pierre Rich, Mirès Vincent, Eva Simmonet.

Story: The legendary city of Ys in Britanny is cursed to be swallowed by the ocean because of the sins of its evil queen, Dahuse.

11. *Le Voleur de Cerveau* [*The Mind Stealer*] (6 February 1971)
Dir: Alain Boudet; *Wri*: Francis Lacassin.
Cast: Marcel Cuvelier, Gérard Berner, Geneviève Bray, Nita Klein, Jean Barney, Elisabeth Hary.
Story: Did a murderer act under someone else's hypnotic control?

12. *La Double Vie de Mademoiselle de la Faille* [*The Two Lives of Mademoiselle de la Faille*] (9 February 1974)
Dir: Michel Subiela; *Wri*: André Desvallées.
Cast: Muriel Baptiste, Pierre Le Rumeur, Joël Bion, Mirès Vincent, Pascale Berger, Marcel Champel, Serge Merlin, Régis Outin.
Story: The young bride of an 18th century nobleman looks uncannily like his former lover, who died several years earlier. Is she merely a look-alike or the reincarnation of the dead girl?

13. *Agathe, ou l'Avenir Rêvé* [*Agatha, or Dreams of the Future*] (24 August 1974)
Dir: Yves-André Hubert; *Wri*: Hélène Misserly.
Cast: Douchka, Maud Rayer, Janine Souchon, Van Doude, Guy Gerbaud, Christian de Tilière, Marc Cassot, Patrick Guillaumin, Jean-Pierre Moreux, Simone Landry.
Story: In 19th century Nîmes, a young girl experiences dreams that uncannily come true.

14. *Le Baquet de Frédéric-Antoine Messmer* [*Messmer's Bucket*] (7 September 1974)
Dir: Michel Subiela; *Wri*: Daniel Heran, Michel Berthier.
Cast: Bernard Verley, Nicole Hiss, Roger Crouzet, Olivier Nolin, Philippe Kellerson, Teddy Bilis, Jean Lescot, Gérald Denizot, André Valtier, Gilbert Damien, Georges Aubert.
Story: The biography of the man who pioneered hypnotism.

Note: A fifteenth episode, *Enquête Posthume sur un Vaisseau Fantôme* [*Posthumous Investigation of a Ghost Ship*], devoted to the mystery of the *Mary-Celeste*, was shot but not broadcast, due to a management change in French television. It starred Diane Kurys, who went on to become a famous director.

Vampires (Netflix, six 40-mins. episodes, 20 March 2020)
Dir: Vladimir de Fontenay, Marie Monge; *Wri*: Benjamin Dupas, Isaure Pisani-Ferry, Anne Cissé, Charlotte Sanson, Sylvie Chanteux.
Cast: Oulaya Amamra (Doïna), Suzanne Clément (Martha), Aliocha Schneider, Kate Moran, Mounir Amamra, Juliette Cardinski.
Story: Vampires exist among us. The Radescu lives clandestinely in Paris, but when their daughter Doïna, 16, turns out to be a new kind of vampire, the fragile balance is shattered. Half-human, half-vampire, Doïna learns to live with her dual nature.
Episodes: *1. Une lycéenne comme les autres [A High School Girl Like Any Other]; 2. Je suis un monstre [I Am A Monster]; 3. Oublie ta vie d'avant [Your Old Life*

Is Gone Now]; 4. Un sang, une loi, une mère [One Blood, One Rule, One Mother]; 5. Tout est possible dans ce monde [Everything is possible in this wsorld]; 6. L'Alpha et l'Oméga [The Alpha and the Omega].

Le Veneur Noir [*The Dark Hunter*] (FR 3, col., Two 85 min. episodes, 29-30 December 1982)
Dir: Paul Planchon; *Wri*: David-André Lang, Paul Planchon, based on the novel *La Baronne Trépassée* [*The Vampire and the Devil's Son*] by Pierre-Alexis Ponson du Terrail.
Cast: Georges Marchal (Le Veneur Noir), François-Eric Gendron (Philippe), Anne Canovas (Lilly), Pierre Banderet (Simiane), Jean Alibert, Antoine Baud, Julien Couty, Maurice Deschamps, Jean-Claude Hirsch, André Lacombe, Serge Pauthe, André Pomarat, Max Ruire, Yves Prunier, Marcel Specht, Lionnel Astier, Isabelle Charraix, René Prost, Robert Chazot, Martine Laisne, Gérard Darrieu, Eddy Roos, Christian Auger.
Story: A young nobleman who is responsible for his wife's death fights a mysterious masked man, the Dark Hunter, allegedly the 900-year-old son of the Devil. He also meets a woman who is an exact double of his dead wife, and who appears to be possessed by her spirit.

Vice Versa (France 2, twenty-six 25 mins. episodes, 13 March 2004-31 December 2005)
Dir: Youcef Hamidi; *Wri*: Loïc Belland.
Cast: Julien Garin (Thomas), Nina-Paloma Polly (Emmanuelle), Jennifer Ducol (Julia), Alix Arbet, Mickaël Gomes Devauchelle, Alexis Campos.
Story: After a strange accident, Thomas, a thirteen-year-old, gains the power to transform into a girl (Emmanuelle) whenever he wants…

Le Village dans les Nuages [*The Village in the Clouds*] (TF1, col, 20 min. episodes,13 September 1982-20 December 1985)
Dir/Wri: Christophe Izard.
Cast: Gérard Camoin, Claude Bordier, Pierre Pirol, Valérie Despuech, Jean-Louis Terrangle, Aline Still, Jean-Pierre Viltange, Patrick Bricard, Yves Brunier, Boris Scheigam.
Story: Children's show featuring the Zabars, two ET families from the distant planet Artas. As they travel through space, their craft suffers a technical failure, and they escape and are forced to stop on the first cloud on their way. There, they discover a strange village perched high above the Earth, inhabited by two old earthlings Oscar and Émilien.

Visions (TF1/RTBF, six 52 mins. episodes, 8-22 May 2022)
Dir: Akim Isker; *Wri*: Jeanne Le Guillou, Bruno Dega.
Cast: Louane (Sarah), Léon Durieux, Soufiane Guerrab (Romain), Jean-Hugues Anglade, Marie-Ange Casta, Robinson Stévenin, Max Boublil, Anne Marivin, Sophie Cattani, Julien Boisselier.
Story: An eleven-year-old girl disappears at her mother's birthday party. Diego, her eight-year-old cousin, then manifests strange visions which alert Romain, the detective in charge of the investigation, as well as his girlfriend Sarah, a psychologist.

Les Visiteurs [*The Visitors*] (TF1, col., six 60 min. episodes, 1980)
Dir: Michel Wyn; *Wri*: Claude Desailly.

Cast: José-Marie Flotats (Jean-Louis Brosec), Barbara Kramer (Renate Mattiesen), Jacques Balutin (Bob), Pierre Piéral, Michèle Bardollet (Colette), François Chaumette (Reka), André Oumansky (Kyrin), Jean-Claude Bouillaud, Jean-René Gossart (Zarko), Pierre Gualdi, Renzo Martini, Feodor Atkine, Amparo Grisales, Patrice Valota, Ronald France.

Story: Arkim and Tolrach, two aliens from a perfect but loveless galactic empire, are reincarnated into the bodies of two comatose Earthlings: Jean-Louis and Renate. Their mission is to find out why six previous "visitors" sent to Earth have vanished without a trace. After a globe-spanning quest, they discover that the visitors like their new lives on Earth better and have decided to remain. Now in love, Arkim and Tolrach (who is pregnant) decide to stay, as well.

Episodes: 1. *Zarko* (3 April 1980); 2. *Alambda* (10 April 1980); 3. *Pirvii* (17 April 1980); 4. *Kyrin* (24 April 1980); 5. *Memno* (1st May 1980); 6. *Reka* (8 May 1980).

Visitors (Warner TV, eight 26 mins. episodes, 10 May 2022).
Dir/Wri: Simon Astier.
Cast: Simon Astier (Marc), Tiphaine Daviot, Vincent Desagnat, Florence Loiret-Caille, Arnaud Joyet.
Story: In the small town of Pointe-Claire, unexpected events occur following the fall of extraterrestrial objects. Richard, on his first day in the police force, takes it upon himself to investigate.

Des Voix dans la Nuit [*Voices In The Night*] (TF1, col., six 60 min. episodes, 1991)
   1. *Succubus* (21 July 1991)

Dir: Patrick Dromgoole; *Wri*: Bob Baker & Dave Martin.
Cast: Barry Foster, Lindsey Baxter, Jeremy Gilley, Aurore Clément.
Story: A young man believes he is being haunted by female ghosts.
Note: Bob Baker and Dave Martin are two British writers who have written many episodes of *Doctor Who*.

2. *La Chambre Secrète* [*The Secret Room*] (9 July 1991)
Dir/Wri: Didier Haudepin, based on a story by Robert Aickman.
Cast: Carol Kane, Jean-François Stévenin, Sabine Haudepin, Eléonor Hirt.
Story: Two children discover a secret room inside a doll house.

3. *Une Main dans l'Ombre* [*A Hand in the Shadow*] (16 July 1991)
Dir/Wri: Peter Duffel.
Cast: Sylvie Granotier, Nicola Pagett, Clive Francis, Helen Cherry.
Story: Two girls have a picnic in a cemetery.

4. *L'Hospice* [*The Retirement Home*] (23 July 1991)
Dir/Wri: Dominique Othenin-Girard, based on a story by Robert Aickman.
Cast: Marthe Keller, Jack Shepherd, Alan Dobie, Gordon Warnecke, Jonathan Cecil.
Story: A driver whose car broke down stays at a strange hotel.

5. *Les Mains d'Orlac* [*The Hands of Orlac*] (30 July 1991)
Dir: Peter Kassovitz; *Wri*: Peter Kassovitz, Patrick Pesnot, based on the story by Maurice Renard.
Cast: Jacques Bonnafé, Laszlo Szabo, Henri Serre, Rebecca Potok, Anne Roussel.
Story: A surgeon grafts a murderer's hands on a pianist.

6. *Les Trains* (6 August 1991)
Dir: György Gat; *Wri*: Unknown.
Cast: Sophie Carle, Nicola Cowper, Robert Koltaï.
Story: Two young woman become lost in the countryside.

Le Voyageur des Siècles [*The Traveler of the Centuries*] (ORTF 1, col., four 60 min. episodes, 1971)
Dir: Jean Dréville; *Wri*: Noël-Noël.
Cast: Robert Vattier, Hervé Jolly, Raymond Baillet, Angelo Bardi, Paul Bisciglia, Anne-Marie Carrière, Roger Carel, Georges de Caunes, Gérard Darrieu, François Darbon, Michel Le Royer, Jean-Marie Proslier, Georgette Anys, Lucien Raimbourg, Léonce Corne, France Delahalle.
Story: An inventor travels back through time to 1884 to meet his great-uncle. Then, together, they travel back to the days of the French Revolution. To save the girl he loves, who is doomed to die on the guillotine, the hero succeeds in preventing the Revolution from taking place, thereby changing the course of history. But the girl nevertheless dies in a balloon accident.
Episodes: 1. *L'Homme au Tricorne* [*The Man With The Three-Cornered Hat*] (7 August 1971); 2. *L'Album de Famille* [*The Family Album*] (14 August 1971); 3. *Le*

Grain de Sable [*The Grain of Sand*] (21 August 1971); 4. *Le Bonnetier de la Rue Tripette* [*The Hosier of Tripette Street*] (28 August 1971).

Chroniques Martiennes

Telefilms

Our definition of telefilms also include a number of short features made for, or first broadcast on, French television, and which attracted a degree of fame by being reviewed in genre magazines. There are, without a doubt, other short features which are not listed here, primarily because information about them is not readily available. Information about running times was not available for all films.

À L'heure Où Le Coq Chantera [*When The Rooster Crows*] (ORTF 2, col., 18 September 1971)
Dir: Jacques Audoir; *Wri*: Jacques Audoir, Jean-Charles Lagneau.
Cast: Geneviève Fontanel, Jean-Pierre Moulin, Françoise Petit, Vernon Dobtcheff.
Story: A ghost story.

L'Adorable Femme des Neiges [*The Adorable Snow-woman*] (col, 90 min, 27 December 2003)
Dir: Jean-Marc Vervoort; *Wri*: Thierry Lassalle, Jeanne Le Guillou, based on the play *Hibernatus* by Jean-Bernard Luc.
Cast: Florence Pernel (Lucie), Pierre Cassignard, Fabienne Mai, Serge Noël, Tsilla Chelton, Pascale Roberts.
Story: The frozen body of Lucie Saint-Pierre, who died in a plane crash in 1919, at the age of twenty-seven, is discovered in a glacier in the Alps, perfectly preserved and alive!

Adrian et Jusemina (RTF, B&W., 20 May 1958)
Dir: René Lucot; *Wri*: Louis Foucher, based on a story by Michel de Ghelderode.
Cast: Robert Fontanet, Huguette Hue, Pierre Giraud, Jenny Clève.
Story: A story about witchcraft.

Ali Baba et les Quarante Voleurs [*Ali Baba and the Forty Thieves*] (TF1, col, 180 min., 2007)
Dir: Pierre Aknine; *Wri*: Michel Delgado, Claude-Michel Rome.
Cast: Gérard Jugnot (Ali Baba), Leïla Bekhti, Saïda Jawad.
Story: Adaptation of the popular *Arabian Nights* tale.

Alice au Pays des Merveilles [*Alice In Wonderland*] (ORTF 2, col., 115 min., 22 December 1970)
Dir: Jean-Christophe Averty; *Wri*: Henri Parisot, based on a story by Lewis Carroll.
Cast: Marie-Véronique Maurin (Alice), Aimée Fontaine, Guy Grosso, Alice Sapritch, Francis Blanche, Hubert Deschamps, Michel Robin, Michel Muller, Pierre Louki, Annette Poivre, Bernard Cara, Michel Modo, Jacques Balutin, Bernard Valdeneige, Daniel Laloux.

Alouqa, ou La Comédie des Morts [*Alouqa, or The Comedy of the Dead*] (TF1, col., 80 min., 13 August 1975)
Dir: Pierre Cavassilas; *Wri*: Francis Lacassin, based on a story by Jean-Louis Bouquet.
Cast: Jean Martin, Max Vialle, Catherine Hubeau, Francis Lax, Roger Pelletier, Pascale Rivault, Karen Blanguenon, Georges Sellier.

Story: A medium hires a troupe of actors to restage a drama that led to an old family curse.

Un Amour de fantôme [*A Lovely Ghost*] (M6, col., 95 min., 3 June 2007)
Dir: Arnaud Sélignac; *Wri*: Catherine Ramberg.
Cast: Virginie Efira (Anna), Bruno Putzulu (Jérémy), Amanda Lear, Dick Rivers.
Story: Anna moves into a haunted house and meets Jeremy, the ghost of a successful disco singer of the 1970s.

L'Archange [*The Archangel*] (1967)
Dir: Olivier Ricard; *Wri*: Roger Blondel, based on his novel.
Cast: Marie-Pierre de Gérando.
Story: An astronaut is selected to go on a dangerous mission.
Note: Roger Blondel wrote numerous science fiction novels under the pseudonym of B.-R. Bruss.

L'Atlantide (ORTF 2, col., 120 min., 24 February 1972)
Dir: Jean Kerchbron; *Wri*: Jean Kerchbron, Armand Lanoux, based on the novel by Pierre Benoît.
Cast: Ludmilla Tcherina (Antinea), Jacques Berthier (Morhange), Denis Manuel (Saint-Avit), Gilles Segal, Marie-Christine Darah, Yves Elliot.
Story: Two French officers, Morhange and Saint-Avit, lost in the Sahara, come across the lost city of Atlantis, ruled by the cruel Queen Antinea.

Au Bois Dormant [*The Sleeping Woods*] (TF1, col., 90 min., 12 February 1975)
Dir/Wri: Pierre Badel, based on the story by Boileau-Narcejac.

Cast: Maureen Kervin, Bernard Alane, René Alone, Jenny Astruc.
Story: A girl succeeds in solving a seemingly supernatural mystery that plagued her boyfriend's ancestor.

Azouk (RTF, B&W., 8 June 1957)
Dir/Wri: Jean Prat, based on a play by Alexandre Rivemale.
Cast: Roger Carel, Lucien Barjon, Jean-Paul Vignon, Henri Virlojeux.
Story: The revenge of African spirits.

Barbara de Lichtenberg (FR 3, col., 11 May 1979)
Dir: Paul Planchon; *Wri*: Paul Sonnendrucker, Paul Planchon.
Cast: Danièle Gueble, Yvette Stahl.
Story: Gothic tale.

La Belle au Bois Dormant [*The Sleeping Beauty*] (ORTF 1, col., 120 min., 22 December 1973)
Dir: Robert Maurice; *Wri*: Romain Weingarten, based on a story by Charles Perrault.
Cast: Isabelle Weingarten (Nuit), Michel de Ré, Marie Dubois, Didier Vallée, Gaby Sylvia, Lucienne Bogaert, Tania Balachova, Marc Eyraud.
Story: In this free adaptation of the classic fairy tale, the Princess (called "Night") must undergo further trials before finding her Prince Charming.

La Belle Endormie [*The Sleeping Beauty*] (TF1, col., 82 min., 3 September 2010)
Dir/Wri: Catherine Breillat based on a story by Charles Perrault.

Cast: Carla Besnaïnou, Julia Artamonov, Kerian Mayan, Peter David Chausse, Luna Charpentier, Rhizlaine El Cohen, Delia Bouglione-Romanès, Diana Rudychenko, Maricha Lopoukhine, Jean-Philippe Tessé, Odile Mallet, Dounia Sichov.
Story: Modern-day adaptation of the classic fairy tale,

La Bête du Gévaudan [*The Beast of Gevaudan*] (ARTE, col., 92 min., 2003)
Dir: Patrick Volson; *Wri*: Brigitte Peskine, Daniel Vigne.
Cast: Sagamore Stévenin, Léa Bosco, Jean-François Stévenin, Guillaume Gallienne, Vincent Winterhalter, Maxime Leroux, Louis-Do de Lencquesaing, Isabelle Leprince.
Story: A somewhat fanciful account of the story of the famous "beast" that terrorized the eponymous French region in the 1760s.

Billénium (ORTF 3, col., 85 min., 10 September 1974)
Dir: Jean de Nesle; *Wri*: Jacques Goimard, based on a story by J. G. Ballard.
Cast: Claude Debord, Albert Simono, Rosita Fernandez, Janine Souchon, Cyril Robichez, Bernard Claudet, Philippe Peltier, Jacques Mussier, Ronny Coutteure.
Story: In an overpopulated world, someone discovers a whole new empty space.
Note: Jacques Goimard is a renowned science fiction critic and editor. This production was intended to be the pilot for an unsold series of science fiction adaptations, entitled *Demain ou Jamais* [*Tomorrow or Never*].

La Bonne Peinture [*The Good Paintings*] (ORTF 2, col., 60 min., 24 November 1967)

Dir: Philippe Agostini; *Wri*: Odette Joyeux based on a story by Marcel Aymé.
Cast: Claude Brasseur, Pierre-Jean Vaillard, René Lefèvre, Jacqueline Coué, Raymond Pelletier, France Rumilly.
Story: A painter's paintings are so realistic that they have the power to appease hunger.

Les Bottes de Sept Lieues [*The Seven League Boots*]
Story: A crotchety old shop-keeper owns the legendary seven-league boots.
Based on a story by Marcel Aymé.

   1. (ORTF 2, col., 90 min., 28 December 1971)
Dir: François Martin; *Wri*: François Martin, François Chevalier.
Cast: Pascal Sellier, France Darry, Jean Bouise, Fernand Berset, Dominique Vincent, Pascal Gillot, Bernard Dumaine, Gilberte Moutier, Eric Baugin, Louise Roblin.

   2. (A2, col., 75 min., 20 December 1990)
Dir: Hervé Baslé; *Wri*: Jean-Claude Grinberg.
Cast: Christine Boisson, Jérémie Semonin, Jacques Dufilho, Pierre-Alexis Hollenbeck, Maxime Boidron, Benoît Robert, Pierre Baslé, Baptiste Vitez, Jean-Claude Bouillaud.

Le Briquet [*The Lighter*] (RTF, B&W., 1954)
Dir: Marcel Bluwal; *Wri*: Marcel Bluwal, René Fallet, based on a story by Hans-Christian Andersen.
Cast: Christiane Minazzoli, Paul Guers, Jean Berger, André Valmy.
Story: Classic fairy tale.

Carmilla, Le Coeur Pétrifié [*Carmilla, The Petrified Heart*] (FR 3, col., 60 min., 10 March 1988)
Dir: Paul Planchon; *Wri*: Paul Planchon, Antonin Robert, based on the story by Sheridan Le Fanu.
Cast: Emmanuelle Meyssignac (Carmilla), Aurelle Doazan, Yvette Stahl, Paulette Schlegel, Roland Kieffer, André Pomarat, Dinah Faust.
Story: Adaptation of Le Fanu's notorious female vampire story.

Ce Soir à Samarcande [*Tonight at Samarkand*] (RTF, B&W., 31 October 1953)
Dir/Wri: Maurice Cazeneuve, based on a play by Jacques Deval.
Cast: Gaby Sylvia, Paul Bernard, Abel Jaquin, Francette Vernillat.
Story: A woman tries to escape from her preordained doom, but in vain.

Cendrillon [*Cinderella*] (RTF, B&W., 24 December 1953)
Dir: Claude Barma; *Wri*: Pierre Dumayet, based on a story by Charles Perrault.
Cast: Christine Carrère, Jean Vinci.
Story: Musical adaptation of the classic fairy tale.

La Chasse au Météore [*The Meteor Hunt*] (ORTF 1, B&W., 90 min., 29 December 1966)
Dir: Roger Iglésis; *Wri*: Jean-Claude Youri, based on the story by Jules Verne.
Cast: Philippe Avron (Zephyrin), Joseph Paster, Bernard Lajarrige, François Maistre, Jacques de Barry, René Clermont, France Delahalle.
Story: Scientists track down a meteor.

Le Château des Carpathes [*The Castle in the Carpathians*] (A2, col., 120 min., 19 December 1976)
Dir: Jean-Christophe Averty; *Wri*: Armand Lanoux, based on the story by Jules Verne.
Cast: Jean-Roger Caussimon (Frik), Jean Martin (Orfanik), Mady Mesplé (Stella), Jacqueline Danno (Fausta), Benoît Allemane (Franz), Guy Grosso, Bernard Valdeneige, Nicole Norden, Yves Arcanel, Jacques Legras, Bernard Cara, Annette Poivre, Sacha Pitoëff, Raymond Meunier.
Story: A lonely nobleman who lost his lover lives in retirement in his castle. A strange inventor uses his devices to preserve the image of the girl and keep strangers away.

Le Château aux Portiques [*The Castle With Porticos*] (ORTF 3, col., 9 October 1973)
Dir: Odette Collet; *Wri*: Charlotte Mercier.
Cast: Maria Meriko, Olivier Deschamps, Natacha Inutine.
Story: A vampire story.

La Chose Qui Ricane [*The Cackling Thing*] (FR 3, col., 11 September 1985)
Dir: Joseph Drimal; *Wri*: Maurice Sarfati, based on a story by Robert-Louis Stevenson.
Cast: Maurice Sarfati, Bernard Tiphaine, Jean Bousquet, Marie Bunel.
Story: Horror story.

Christmas Carol (TF1, col., 90 min., 25 December 1984)

Dir/Wri: Pierre Boutron, based on a story by Charles Dickens.
Cast: Michel Bouquet (Scrooge), Pierre Clémenti, Georges Wilson, Lisette Maslidor, Pierre Olaf, Jean Martin, Manuel Bonnet.
Story: Lavish and well interpreted adaptation of Dickens' classic tale.

Chroniques Martiennes [*The Martian Chronicles*] (ORTF 3, col., 110 min., 13 December 1974)
Dir: Renée Kammerscheit; *Wri*: Louis Pauwels, based on the stories by Ray Bradbury.
Cast: Guy Shelley, Jean-José Fleury, Jean-Claude Amyl, Olivier Sydney, Philippe Murgier, Virginie Billetdoux, Alain Foures.
Story: Television version of a play based on Ray Bradbury's classic collection of short stories. Tim Wilder tells the story of the conquest of Mars as lived by his father.

Le Coeur Cambriolé [*The Stolen Heart*] (A2, col., 90 min., 20 June 1986)
Dir/Wri: Michel Subiela, based on a story by Gaston Leroux.
Cast: Yann Babilée, Katherine Erhardy, Georges Marchal, Arthur Denberg, Roger Carel, Marc François, Olivia Brunaux, Marcello Leone.
Story: A painter uses his psychic powers to steal a young man's bride.

Le Colchique et l'Étoile [*The Colchicum and the Star*] (TF1, col., 26 July 1974)
Dir/Wri: Michel Subiela, based on the novel by Nicole Ciravegna.

Cast: Olivier Norin, Catherine Hubeau, Jean-Pierre Jorris, Gérald Denizot.
Story: In the middle of the 18th century, in the village of Moustiers, a young man dreams of becoming a great painter. He has only one enemy: the village's sorcerer...

Le Coq Noir [*The Black Rooster*] (FR 3, col., 50 min., 3 September 1982)
Dir: Jean-Charles Cabanis; *Wri*: Paul Planchon, Maurice Sarfati, based on the story *"L'Esquisse Mysterieuse"* [*The Mysterious Sketch*] by Erckmann-Chatrian.
Cast: Bernard Freyd, Jean-Pierre Bagot, Germain Muller, Maurice Sarfati, Dinah Faust, Marcel Spegt, Jean-Marie Holterbach, Paul Bru.
Story: A painter accidentally paints a murder scene.

La Couleur de l'Abîme [*The Color From The Abyss*] (TF1, col., 55 min., 5 July 1983)
Dir: Pascal Kané; *Wri*: Gilberto Azevedo, based on a story by H. P. Lovecraft.
Cast: Jean-François Stévenin, Evelyne Dress, Rebecca Pauly, Garrick Maul.
Story: American spelunkers unknowingly awaken a "Colour out of Space" entity, which then attacks a local family.

Le Cyborg, ou Le Voyage Vertical [*The Cyborg, or The Vertical Journey*] (ORTF 2, col., 85 min., 15 September 1970)
Dir: Jacques Pierre; *Wri*: Yves Jamiaque.
Cast: Anne Vernon, Clotilde Joano, Laurence Jyl, Roger Pigault, Marc Michel, Armand Mestral, Gérard Depardieu, Max Vialle.

Story: Seven people from different backgrounds are taken to an underground bunker and told that one of them is a cyborg.

La Dame d'Outre-Nulle Part [*The Lady From Beyond Nowhere*] (Television Romande, B&W, 85 min., 1966)
Dir: Jean-Jacques Lagrange; *Wri*: Jean-Louis Roncoroni, based on a story by Georges Langelaan.
Cast: Marie-Blanche Vergne, Henri Serre, Jean Berger, Serge Nicoloff, Gérard Carrat, Michel Cassagne, Pierre Walker.
Story: Bernard, an engineer in a nuclear power plant, sees young nurse who died during the atomic explosion in Nagasaki, reappear on his TV set, trying to communicate with him...
Note: Georges Langelaan is the author of *The Fly*.

Le Démon Écarlate [*The Scarlet Demon*] (FR 3, col., 60 min., 17 March 1988)
Dir: Joseph Drimal; *Wri*: Maurice Sarfati, based on a story by Sheridan Le Fanu.
Cast: Pierre Vaneck, Pierre Rousseau, Annick Jarry, Tobias Kempf, André Pomarat, Valérie Wolf.
Story: A judge orders the hanging of his mistress' husband, but the dead man returns to exact revenge.

La Dépêche de Nuit [*The Night Wire*] (A2, col., 30 min., 2 April 1984)
Dir: Joseph Lewartowski; *Wri*: Alain Pozzuoli, based on a story by H. F. Arnold.
Cast: Olivier Granier, Ariel Semenoff.
Story: A journalist broadcasts the story of the invasion of a deadly, living fog.

Note: H. F. Arnold's original short story was published in the magazine *Weird Tales* in 1926.

Le Devine-Vent [*The Guess-Wind*] (FR 3, col., 26 Decembre 1980)
Dir/Wri: Régis Forrissier, based on a story by Charles Galtier.
Cast: Paul Crauchet, Anne-Marie Besse, Pierre Boutron.
Story: Provencal folk tale.

Dissimulation: Une Simulation de Philip K. Dick (La Sept, 15 min., 1993)
Dir/Wri: Hervé Nisic.
Cast: Tomacz Bialkowski (Dick).
Story: Surreal made-up video report about Dick's visit to the Metz SF convention.

L'Ensorcelée [*The Spellbound Girl*] (A2, col., 11 April 1981)
Dir: Jean Prat; *Wri*: Jean Prat, Paule de Beaumont, based on the story by Jules Barbey d'Aurevilly.
Cast: Julie Philippe, Jean-Luc Boutté, Elizabeth Kaza, Fernand Berset.
Story: A woman is seemingly possessed by evil.

Entre-Temps [*Between Times*] (A2, col., 29 August 1984)
Dir: José-Maria Berzosa; *Wri*: Carlos Semprun, José-Maria Berzosa.
Cast: Philippe du Janerand, Jean Bouzid, Servane Ducorps, Aïna Walle.
Story: Time travel story.

L'Envolée Belle [*The Beautiful Flight*] (ORTF 2, B&W., 24 December 1969)
Dir: Jean Prat; *Wri*: Alexandre Rivemale.
Cast: Edmond Ardisson, Dominique Rollin, Jean Pignol, Laurence Imbert.
Story: Christmas story.

Et Meurent les Géants [*And The Giants Died*] (FR 3, col., 19 June 1981)
Dir/Wri: Fernand Vincent, based on a story by Louis-François Caude.
Cast: Patrick Raynal, Dominique Dimey, Cyril Robichez, Dominique Sarrazin.
Story: Folk tale.

Esprits de Famille [*Family Ghosts*] (FR 3, col., 19 April 1975)
Wri/Dir: Marc Pavaux, based on a play by Claude Caron.
Cast: Annette Poivre, Raymond Bussières, Brigitte Fossey.
Story: Ghost story.

Les Étonnements d'un Couple Moderne [*The Astonishments of a Modern Couple*] (A2, col., 90 min., 24 December 1986)
Dir: Pierre Boutron; *Wri*: Jean-Claude Carrière.
Cast: Jean Carmet, Delphine Seyrig, Judith Magre, François Perrot, Henri Garcin, Alain Doutey, Anaïs Jeanneret.
Story: A couple discovers that their friends are aliens who have been studying Earth for a quarter of a century, and who are about to return home, deeming the planet doomed.

L'Étrange Château du Docteur Lerne [*The Strange Castle of Dr. Lerne*] (A2, col., 105 min., 28 December 1983)
Dir: Jean-Daniel Verhaeghe; *Wri*: Gérard Brach, based on the novel by Maurice Renard.
Cast: Jacques Dufilho (Lerne), Pierre Clémenti, Dora Doll, Jean-Paul Roussillon, Pierre Etaix, Valérie Jeanneret, Henri Guybet, Claude Villers.
Story: A mad scientist experiments with human grafts.

La Fabrique [*The Factory*] (A2, col., 90 min., 24 December 1979)
Dir/Wri: Pascal Thomas.
Cast: Emilie Gruel, Brigitte Gruel, Renaud Vincent, Armand Gruel, Hervé Bonjean, Frédéric Duru, Sophie Lamoureux, Alexandre Brunner, Emmanuelle Bot, Bernard Menez.
Story: A spoiled little rich girl shares Christmas with a poor little boy from the previous century.

Le Fantôme de mon Ex [*My Ex's Ghost*] (TF1, col., 88 min., 28 May 2007)
Dir: Charlotte Brändström; *Wri*: Florence Philipponnat.
Cast: Bernard Yerlès (Leopold), Florence Pernel (Julia), Carole Richert.
Story: Léopold, a driving school instructor, sees the ghost of Julia, his late ex-wife, who tells him that he has a 6-year-old son.

Le Fantôme de l'Opéra [*The Phantom of the Opera*] (A2, col., 100 min., 28 December 1980)
Dir: Dirk Sanders; *Choreography*: Roland Petit; *Music*: Marcel Landowski; *Art Direction*: Patrick Flynn.

Note: Ballet in 2 acts and 12 scenes based on Gaston Leroux's classic.

Le Fantôme des Canterville [*The Canterville Ghost*] (RTF, B&W., 25 November 1962)
Dir: Marcel Cravenne; *Wri*: Albert Husson, based on a story by Oscar Wilde.
Cast: Jacques Fabbri, Maria Pacôme, Jacques Berlioz, Claude Rich, Pierre Pernet, Claude Nicot.
Story: Claude Rich is a wonderful ghost in this video adaptation of Wilde's famous story about a crude American family's acquisition of a haunted castle.

Le Fantôme du Lac [*The Ghost of the Lake*] (FR3, col., 90 min., 2007)
Dir: Philippe Niang; *Wri*: Patrick Moine, Philippe Niang.
Cast: Bernard Yerlès (Pierre), Linda Hardy, Jean-Louis Foulquier.
Story: After his wife left him for another man, Pierre returns to France with his son. While fishing in a lake, they find a naked young woman and take her to a hospital. The local priest believes she is Jeanne who died in a flood long ago.

Le Fauteuil Hanté [*The Haunted Chair*] (ORTF 1, col., 115 min., 27 June 1970)
Dir/Wri: Pierre Bureau, based on the novel by Gaston Leroux.
Cast: Jacques Grello (Lalouette), Lucien Nat (Loustalot), Jean Mermet (Dédé), Sacha Pitoëff (Eliphas), Renaud Mary (Patard), Noël Roquevert, Olivier Hussenot.

Story: A mad academician uses strange weapons to kill those who have discovered his secret: His son is the real inventor of his designs.

La Femme au Collier de Velours [*The Woman With The Velvet Necklace*] (FR 3, col., 4 September 1986)
Dir: Jean Sagols; *Wri*: Jacques Tephany.
Cast: Pierre Vaneck, Rebecca Pauly, Corinne Dacla, Didier Sauvegrain.
Story: Gothic tale.

La Fenêtre [*The Window*] (ORTF 2, col., 45 min., 2 August 1970)
Dir/Wri: Jacques Pierre, based on the story "*The Spider*" by Hanns Heinz Ewers.
Cast: Michel Lonsdale, Jacqueline Danno, Hélène Dieudonné, Alexandre Rignault.
Story: A spider creature capable of taking the shape of a beautiful young woman lures young men to their deaths.

La Fleur et le Fantôme [*The Flower and the Ghost*] (RTF, B&W., 1953)
Dir: François Chatel; *Wri*: Jacques Floran.
Cast: Isa Miranda, André Valmy, Deryeth Mendel, Christian Fourcade.
Story: A period ghost story.

Des Fleurs pour Algernon [*Flowers for Algernon*] (FR2, col., 95 min., 2006)
Dir: David Delrieux; *Wri*: Anne Giafferi based on the novel by Daniel Keyes.
Cast: Julien Boisselier (Charlie), Hélène de Fougerolles (Alice), Marianne Basler.

Story: After a successful experiment on Algernon, a mouse whose level of intelligence dramatically increases, the scientists decide to experiment on Charlie, a mentally retarded young man.

Frankenstein (ORTF 3, col., 95 min., 7 May 1974)
Dir: Bob Thénault; *Wri*: François Chevallier, based on the novel by Mary Shelley.
Cast: Gérard Berner (Victor), Gérard Boucaron (Frobelius/Monster), Karin Petersen (Elisabeth), Bernard Mesguich (Clerval), Nicolas Silberg, Jean Lepage, Françoise Lugagne, Marc Fayolle.
Story: In this adaptation of Shelley's classic tale, Victor, after having been expelled from the university and repudiated by his family, conducts his experiments on Frobelius, a retarded man. After the latter dies in a mountain accident, Victor brings him back to life.

Le Gentleman des Antipodes [*The Gentleman From The Other Side Of The World*] (A2, col., 90 min., 4 November 1976)
Dir: Boramy Tioulong; *Wri*: Christine Lamorlette, based on the novel by Pierre Véry.
Cast: Gilles Segal (Prosper Lepicq), Armand Mestral, Raymond Gérome, Rosy Varte, Jean Martin, Ginette Garcin, Francis Lax, Jean-Paul Zehnacker, Marc Fayolle, Paul Le Person.
Story: In order to unmask a serial killer, Lepicq infiltrates a club made up of people whose faces resemble animals.

Le Golem (ORTF 2, B&W., 115 min, 18 February 1967)

Dir: Jean Kerchbron; *Wri*: Louis Pauwels, Jean Kerchbron, based on the novel by Gustav Meyrinck.
Cast: André Reybaz (Pernath), Pierre Tabard, Michel Etcheverry, Marika Green, François Vibert, Robert Etcheverry, Magali Noël, Douking, Françoise Winskill, Alfred Baillou, Serge Merlin.
Story: Faithful adaptation of Meyrinck's classic novel.

La Grâce (RTF, B&W., 23 April 1953)
Dir: Jacques-Gérard Cornu; Wri: Jean-Louis Descaves based on a story by Marcel Aymé.
Cast: André de Chauveron, Jean-Pierre Moulinot, Paul Colline, Annie Duguay.
Story: A saintly man is given a halo and must learn to sin to be rid of it.

La Grâce (A2, col., 52 min., 21 April 1979)
Dir/Wri: Pierre Tchernia, based on a story by Marcel Aymé.
Cast: Michel Serrault, Rosy Varte, Roger Carel, Ginette Garcin.
Story: Same as above.

Le Grand Poucet [*Big Thumb*] (A2, col., 25 December 1980)
Dir/Wri: Claude-Henri Lambert, based on a play by Claude-André Puget.
Cast: Christian Marquand, Bruno Devoldère, Carole Coulombe.
Story: Fairy tale.

Gueule d'Atmosphère [*Funny Face*] (FR 3, col., 52 min., 6 June 1980)
Dir: Maurice Château; *Wri*: Jean-Pierre Hubert.

Cast: Bernard Freyd, Hervé Pierre, Claude Bouchery.
Story: Survivors try to flee a pollution-caused plague.
Note: Jean-Pierre Hubert is a noted science fiction writer.

Haute Sécurité [*High Security*] (FR 3, col., 60 min., 17 August 1988)
Dir: Jean-Pierre Bastid; *Wri*: Joël Houssin, Daniel Riche.
Cast: Juliet Berto, Kader Boukhanef, Serge Marquand.
Story: Out of control robocops wreak havoc on a city.
Note: Joël Houssin and Daniel Riche are noted science fiction writers/editors.

L'Herbe Rouge [*The Red Grass*] (A2, col., 90 min., 11 September 1985)
Dir: Pierre Kast, Maurice Dugowson; *Wri*: Pierre Kast, based on the novel by Boris Vian.
Cast: Jean Sorel, Jean-Pierre Léaud, Mijou Kovacs, Yves Robert, Jacques Perrin, Jean-Claude Brialy, Alexandra Stewart, Philippe Clay, Françoise Arnoul.
Story: In a fantastic universe (where grass is red), an engineer builds a machine that will materialise his fears.
Note: Pierre *Kast* died before finishing this film, which was completed by Maurice Dugowson.

Hilda Muramer (ORTF 2, col., 65 min., 12 September 1973)
Dir: Jacques Trébouta; *Wri*: Loys Masson, based on the story *Metzengerstein* by Edgar Allan Poe.
Cast: Loumi Iacobesco (Hilda), Jacques Weber, Paul Crauchet, Dominique Toussaint, Hervé Jolly.
Story: In this free adaptation of Poe's story, the Muramers and the Malirings are two enemy clans. After

Hilda Muramer refuses to save the Malirings from a fatal fire, a horse becomes the instrument of the Malirings' revenge.

L'Histoire Terrible et Douce de la Demoiselle à La Violette [*The Terrible and Kind Story of the Damsel With A Violet*] (FR 3, col., 16 April 1983)
Dir: Jean-Luc Mage; *Wri*: Pierre Dubois.
Cast: Sylvaine Charlet, Hervé Barel, Alain Crampon.
Story: Fairy tale.

L'Homme d'Orlu [*The Man From Orlu*] (ORTF 2, col., 18 May 1971)
Dir/Wri: Jacques Krier.
Cast: Pierre Santini, Jean Lescot, Gérard Darrieu.
Story: An engineer working on a mountain dam meets a man from another dimension.

L'Homme en Rouge [*The Man In Red*] (FR 3, col., 16 January 1981)
Dir: Paul Planchon; *Wri*: David-André Lang, Paul Planchon.
Cast: Christian Baltauss, Yvette Stahl, Henri Muller.
Story: Ghost story.

L'Homme Qui A Perdu Son Ombre [*The Man Who Lost His Shadow*]
Based on the story *The Wonderful Story of Peter Schlemihl* (1814) by Adalbert von Chamisso.
Story: A man sells his shadow to the Devil but comes to regret it.
   1. (RTF, B&W., 60 min., 12 November 1951)
   Dir/Wri: Philippe Agostini, Albert Riera.

Cast: Odette Joyeux, Gérard Oury, Jacques François, Gaston Séverin, Jean Topart, Lucien Blondeau.

2. (ORTF 1, col., 85 min., 16 July 1966)
Dir: Marcel Cravenne; *Wri*: Albert Husson.
Cast: Claude Nicot, Danièle Lebrun, Julien Guiomar, Henri Guisol, Anne Bertin, Catherine Hiegel, Clément Harari.

Le Horla (ORTF 1, col., 80 min., 1966)
Dir/Wri: Jean-Daniel Pollet, based on the story by Guy de Maupassant.
Cast: Laurent Terzieff.
Story: An invisible entity persecutes a man.
Note: Also filmed in 1963 as *Diary of a Madman*, starring Vincent Price.

Hors du Temps [*Out of Time*] (ARTE, col., 90 min., 15 December 2009)
Dir: Jean-Teddy Filippe; *Wri*: Vincent Maillard.
Cast: Natacha Lindinger (Hélène), Bruno Todeschini (Yann), Philippe Duclos, Mathias Mlekuz, Julie Delarme, Alexandre Aubry.
Story: Researchers have succeeded in creating a parallel time loop in the brain of Mab, a guinea pig monkey.

Le Hors-Le-Champ [*Out Of Focus*] (ORTF 3, col., 50 min., 20 February 1973)
Dir: Gérard Guillaume; *Wri*: Michel Suffran.
Cast: Claude Mann, Christiane Laurent, Jean Pignol, Jean Lepage.
Story: A young photographer buys an antique camera which takes him into the past.

La Hotte [*The Basket*] (ORTF 3, col., 23 December 1973)
Dir/Wri: Daniel Georgeot, based on a story by Hervé Bazin.
Cast: Georges Géret, Jean-Jacques Delbo, Anne-Marie Durin.
Story: Christmas story.

Hugues Le Loup [*Hugh The Wolf*]
Based on the novel by Erckmann-Chatrian, a famous writing team who penned numerous fantastic stories revolving around folk tales of their native Alsace) .
Story: Count Nideck and his daughter Odile live in a lonely castle in a countryside plagued by a werewolf.
    1. (TF1, col., 90 min., 29 January 1975)
Dir/Wri: Michel Subiela.
Cast: Patricia Callas, Claude Titre, Jean-Claude Dauphin, Bernard Charnacé, André Valmy.

    2. (FR3, col., 60 min., 19 January 1979)
Dir: Paul Planchon; *Wri*: Paul Planchon, Maurice Sarfati.
Cast: André Pomarat, Margot Lefèvre, Paul Sonnendrucker, Eric de Dadelsen, Marcel Spegt, Christiane Durry, Robert Fuger.

Il n'y a Plus de Héros au Numéro que Vous Avez Demandé [*There's No Hero At The Number You Have Dialed*] (TF1, col., 70 min., 9 December 1980)
Dir/Wri: Pierre Chabartier.
Cast: Serge Reggiani, Hélène Vallier, Léo Campion, Claire Maurier.

Story: A man finds an old telephone which mysteriously connects him with a soldier in the trenches of World War I.

L'Île Bleue [*The Blue Island*] (A2, col., 90 min., 21 May 1983)
Dir: Jean-Claude Giudicelli; *Wri*: Jean-Claude Giudicelli, Michel Jeury.
Cast: Jean-Pierre Kalfon, Aïna Walle, Paul Crauchet, Philippe du Janerand, Féodor Atkine.
Story: In the far future, man has learned to control time and dreams. Everything is white and blue. However, grey rebels have reclaimed the right to dream and die.
Note: Michel Jeury is a major science fiction writer.

Image Interdite [*Forbidden Image*] (A2, col., 90 min., 24 November 1984)
Dir: Jean-Daniel Simon; *Wri*: Claude May, Jean-Daniel Simon.
Cast: Sylvie Fennec, Anne Teyssedre, Jacques Serres, Daniel Langlet, Karol Zubert.
Story: In a future world where images and their transmissions have been forbidden, a young filmmaker discovers a beautiful actress.

Les Indes Noires [*The Black Indies*] (ORTF 1, B&W., 95 min., 25 December 1964)
Dir: Marcel Bluwal; *Wri*: Marcel Moussy based on the novel by Jules Verne.
Cast: Alain Mottet (James), Georges Poujoly (Harry), André Valmy (Simon), Jean-Pierre Moulin (Jack), Paloma Matta (Nell), Geneviève Fontanel, Yvette Étiévant, Christian Barbier, Jean Galland.

Story: Faithful rendition of Verne's classic novel about an underground industrial civilization.

L'Invention de Morel [*Morel's Invention*] (ORTF 2, col., 110 min., 8 December 1967)
Dir: Claude-Jean Bonnardot; *Wri*: Claude-Jean Bonnardot, Michel Andrieu, based on the novel *La Invencion de Morel* by Adolfo Bioy Casares.
Cast: Alain Saury (Luis), Juliette Mills, Didier Conti, Anne Talbot, Anne-Marie Blot, Ursula Kubler, Dominique Vincent, Paula Dehelly, Guy d'Arcangues, Jean Martin.
Story: Luis, a prison escapee, arrives on an island where a sophisticated 3-D projection system endlessly replays scenes featuring the now-deceased guests of the inventor, Morel. Luis falls in love with one of the projections and chooses to die to incorporate himself into the projection.

Le Jardinier [*The Gardener*] (ORTF 3, col., 90 min., 25 December 1973)
Dir: Antoine Léonard; *Wri*: François Possot.
Cast: Pierre Fresnay, Paul Crauchet, Gérard Lorin, Claude Richard, Philippe Laudenbach.
Story: Philosophical tale with fantasy elements.

Le Jardinier Récalcitrant [*The Rebellious Gardener*] (TF1, col., 95 min., 24 February 1983)
Dir: Maurice Failevic; *Wri*: Maurice Failevic, Jean-Claude Carrière.
Cast: Philippe de Cherisey (Martin Blanchet), Jean-Paul Schneider, Maurice Vaudaux, Pierre Londiche, Gabrielle Lazure.

Story: In an antiseptic future where all food is industrially produced *in vitro*, a rebellious gardener uses ancient seeds to again grow vegetables.

Je Tue Il [*I Kill He*] (A2, col., 90 min., 1982)
Dir: Pierre Boutron; *Wri*: Jean-Claude Carrière.
Cast: Nelly Borgeaud, Françoise Dorner, Magali Renoir, Pierre Vaneck.
Story: A novelist sees his world of the imaginary being integrated into his real life. All he has to do is write a few words ans the person for whom they are intended knows of them immediately.

Jour "J" Comme Jouet [*Day "T" For Toy*] (FR 3, col., 13 min., 25 December 1983)
Dir: Jacques Manlay; *Wri*: Michel Jeury.
Cast: Unknown.
Story: Santa Claus overthrows a 1984-like dictatorship.

Kira (Television Romande, 1967)
Dir: Unknown; *Wri*: Serge Leroy, Claude Ligure.
Cast: Unknown.
Story: An alien woman falls in love.

Lancelot du Lac (ORTF 2, col., 135 min., 25 December 1970)
Dir/Wri: Claude Santelli, based on Chrétien de Troyes.
Cast: Gérard Falconetti (Lancelot), Marie-Christine Barrault (Guenevere), Tony Taffin (Arthur), Arlette Tephany, Jean Chevrier, Jean Bouvier, Paul Rieger, Anne Saint-Mor, Jacques Weber, Mariannik Revillon, Jean-Pierre Bernard, Patrick Verde.
Story: The story of the famous Knight of the Round Table, shot on location in Britanny.

La Légende de la Ville d'Ys [*The Legend of the City of Ys*] (FR 3, col., 26 October 1983)
Dir: Renaud Saint-Pierre; *Wri*: Michel Le Bris.
Cast: Pierre Rousseau, Jenny Arasse, Robert Dadles, Jacques Anton.
Story: The legendary city of Ys in Britanny is cursed to be swallowed by the ocean because of the sins of its evil queen, Dahuse.

Le Loup [*The Wolf*] (RTF, B&W., 25 min., 24 December 1958)
Dir/Wri: Jean-Christophe Averty.
Cast: Jacques Fabbri, Jacqueline Bressy, Sylviane Margollé, Paulette Dubost, Jean-Marie Serreau.
Story: A wolf and two little girls play together.

Les Lutteurs Immobiles [*The Motionless Fighters*] (FR 3, col., 60 min., 2 August 1988)
Dir: André Farwagi; *Wri*: Serge Brussolo, based on his novel.
Cast: Bernard-Pierre Donnadieu, Marie Rivière, Fernand Guiot, Jacques Grandjouan, Fernand Kindt, Jean Mourat.
Story: To eliminate waste and protect everyday objects, a future repressive society creates biological links between criminals and a chosen object.
Note: Serge Brussolo is a major science fiction and horror writer.

Mademoiselle B. (A2, col., 90 min., 27 August 1986)
Dir: Bernard Queysanne; *Wri*: Bernard Queysanne, Maurice Pons, based on his novel.

Cast: Claude Avril, Jean-Baptiste Thiérée, André Weber, Marc Fayolle, Dominique Erlanger, Didier Chevalier.
Story: A retired writer in the countryside becomes acquainted with a mysterious girl who is dressed in white and shunned by the local villagers.

Magie Rouge [*Red Magic*] (ORTF 1, col., 23 February 1973)
Dir/Wri: Daniel Georgeot, based on a play by Michel de Ghelderode.
Cast: Jean Le Poulain, Anne Alvaro, Paul Barge, Jean-Roger Caussimon.
Story: Gothic horror tale.

Les Mains de Roxana [*Roxana's Hands*] (France 2, col., 90 min., 20 March 2013)
Dir/Wri: Philippe Setbon based on the novel *The Hands of Orlac* by Maurice Renard.
Cast: Sylvie Testud (Roxana Orlac), Loup-Denis Elion, Micky Sébastian, Coline Leclère, Jean-Marie Winling, Gérard Desarthe, Sylvie Granotier, Anne Canovas, Richard Sammel, Joachim Berger, Anton Yakovlev.
Story: A renowned violinist, Roxana Orlac, has both hands crushed during an accident. She undergoes a transplant of both limbs by an eminent surgeon, whose methods are controversial. The transplant is a complete success. But very quickly, incidents occur in Roxana's environment, including several murders, which lead our heroine and the police to doubt her innocence. Whose grafted hands belonged to? Could these be the hands of a murderess?

Maître Zacharius

Based on the story by Jules Verne.
Story: An old clockmaker dreams of controlling time and invents a robot android.
   1. (ORTF 3, col., 55 min. 26 June 1973)
Dir: Pierre Bureau; *Wri*: Marcel Brion.
Cast: Pierre Vial (Zacharius), Jean-Pierre Sentier, Madeleine Barbulée, Jacques Roussillon, François-Louis Tilly, Jany Gastaldi.

2. (TF1, col., 85 min., 24 March 1984)
Dir: Claude Grinberg; *Wri*: Serge Ganzl, Claude Grinberg.
Cast: Charles Denner (Zacharius), Emmanuelle Béart, Pierre-Louis Rajot.

Malevil (FR3, col., 115 min., 2010)
Dir: Denis Malleval; *Wri*: Jean Rouaud based on the novel by Robert Merle.
Cast: Anémone, Bernard Yerlès, Jean-Pierre Martins, Slony Sow, Émilie de Preissac, Pierre Val, Jean-François Garreaud.
Story: After a nuclear explosion which ravaged the surface of the planet, the inhabitants of the Château of Malevil try to organize themselves.

Marie la Louve [*Marie the Wolf*] (FR 3, col., 95 min., 10 December 1991)
Dir: Daniel Wronecki; *Wri*: Daniel Wronecki, Rodolphe-Maurice Arlaud, based on a story by Claude Seignolle.
Cast: Aurélie Gilbert, Frédéric Pellegeay, Pierre Debauche, Dora Doll, Etienne Bierry, Sylvie Herbert, Jean-Paul Roussillon, Marie Pillet.

Story: A young girl tries, unsuccessfully, to reject the powers she inherited, which enable her to cure wolf bites and lead wolves.

Mars: Mission Accomplie [*Mars: Mission Accomplished*] (ORTF, B&W, 77 min., 1967)
Dir: Edmond Tyborowsky; *Wri*: Edmond Tyborowsky, Henri Viard based on his novel *L'Enfer est dans le ciel* [*Hell in the Sky*].
Cast: Sady Rebbot, Alain Saury, Didier Chereau, Georges Claisse, Christian Barbier, Pierre Gatineau.
Story: A rivalry develops between American and Soviet spacemen en route to Mars.

Le Matin des Jokers [*The Morning of the Jokers*] (FR 3, col., 60 min., 18 November 1988)
Dir: Robert Mugnerot; Wri: Pierre Pelot.
Cast: Greg Germain, Blanche Ravalec, Patrick Messe, Claire de Beaumont.
Story: A doctor has created cloned twins of his wife (murdered by her clone) and politicians.
Note: Pierre Pelot is a major science fiction writer.

Melmoth Réconcilié [*Melmoth Reconciled*] (RTF, B&W., 15 May 1964)
Dir: Georges Lacombe; *Wri*: Pierre Latour, based on the novel by Honoré de Balzac.
Cast: Robert Porte, François Maistre, Régine Blaess, Anne-Marie Coffinet.
Story: The eternal wanderer finally finds peace.

Merlin (TF1, col., 180 min., 27-28 October 2012)
Dir: Stéphane Kappes; *Wri*: Michel Delgado, Karine de Demo.

Cast: Gérard Jugnot (Merlin), Joséphine de Meaux (Viviane), Marilou Berry (Morgane), Arthur Molinier, Michel Vuillermoz, Fred Epaud, Cristiana Capotondi, Jean-Baptiste Maunier, Fanie Zanini.
Story: At 50, Merlin would like nothing more than to retire to the woods and live in peace…
Episodes: 1. *L'Enchanteur désenchanté [The Disenchanted Enchanter]*; 2. *Le Secret de Brocéliande [The Secret of Broceliande]*.

La Métamorphose [*The Metamorphosis*] (FR 3, B&W., 50 min., 5 June 1983)
Dir: Jean-Daniel Verhaeghe; *Wri*: Jean-Daniel Verhaeghe, Roger Vrigny, based on the novel by Franz Kafka.
Cast: Madeleine Robinson, Julien Guiomar, Anne Caudry, Pierre Etaix.
Story: Faithful adaptation of Kafka's classic allegorical novel in which a man wakes up to find himself transformed into a giant insect.

Le Millième Cierge [*The Thousandth Candle*] (Television Suisse Romande, col., 80 min., 27 November 1969)
Dir/Wri: Raymond Barrat, based on a story by Claude Seignolle.
Cast: Raoul Guillet, Pierre Ruegg, Jacques Richard (The Devil), Serge Nicoloff, Caroline Cartier:
Story: Folk legend.

Le Miroir Opaque [*The Opaque Mirror*] (TF1, col., 90 min., 25 July 1985)
Dir: Alain Boudet; *Wri*: Christian Watton, Alain Boudet.
Cast: Aïna Walle, Yves Beneyton, Georges Marchal, Roland Monod.

Story: A young woman's dreams lead her to solve a murder.

La Mission, ou L'Aube du Rat [*The Mission, or The Dawn of the Rat*] (FR 3, col., 1986)
Dir: Michel Guillet; *Wri*: Pierre Pelot.
Cast: Unknown.
Story: A post-apocalyptic saga.

Le Modèle [*The Model*] (ORTF 2, col., 90 min., 5 July 1969)
Dir/Wri: Jacques Pierre.
Cast: Robert Manuel, Maike Jansen, Gabriel Jabbour, Jacques Duby, Jacqueline Danno.
Story: A young woman helps a writer with writer's block.

Mon Faust [*My Faust*] (ORTF 2, col., 1st December 1970)
Dir/Wri: Daniel Georgeot, Pierre Franck, based on a play by Paul Valéry.
Cast: Pierre Fresnay, Pierre Dux, Danièle Delorme.
Story: Variation of the *Faust* story.

La Montre du Doyen [*The Dean's Watch*] (FR 3, col., 3 January 1988)
Dir: Joseph Drimal; *Wri*: Maurice Sarfati, based on a story by Erckmann-Chatrian.
Cast: André Pomarat, Yves Aubert, Claude Lergenmuller, Marcel Grandidier.
Story: A tale of rural witchcraft.

La Mort Amoureuse [*Death In Love*] (TF1, col., 85 min., 16 November 1977)

Dir: Jacques Ertaud; *Wri*: René Fallet.
Cast: Marcel Dalio (God), Françoise Lugagne (Death), Guy Marchand, Myriam Boyer, Michel Creton, Pierre Saintons, Françoise Dupré.
Story: Death's human lover cheats on her, causing her to become jealous.

Le Nain [*The Dwarf*] (RTF, B&W., 19 March 1961)
Dir: Pierre Badel; *Wri*: Jean Cathelin, based on a story by Marcel Aymé.
Cast: Roland Lacoste, Jean Houbé, Paul Frankeur, Jacques Gripel, Evelyne Lacroix, Fernande Albany, Dominique Davray, Arthur Allan.
Story: After thirty-five years, a circus dwarf begins to grow taller.

Le Navire Étoile [*The Starship*] (RTF, B&W., 11 December 1962)
Dir: Alain Boudet; *Wri*: Michel Subiela, based on the novel *The Space Born* (1956) by E. C. Tubb.
Cast: Dirk Sanders, Geneviève Casile, Pierre Massimi, François Maistre, René Arrieu, Roger Blin, André Charpak, Yves Brainville.
Story: A revolution takes place in a generation starship ruled by a computer. It is eventually revealed that the ship is nearing its destination, and the revolt was all part of a plan to restore a sense of initiative in the crew.

Nemo (ORTF 1, col., 95 min., 21 March 1970)
Dir: Jean Bacque, based on a play by Alexandre Rivemale inspired by the character created by Jules Verne.

Cast: Michel Le Royer (Nemo), Lucien Barjon (Arronax), Agnès Desroches, Bernard Cara, Jean Franval, Gilberte Rivet, Pierre Mirat, Fernand Guiot.
Story: Captain Nemo decides to retire and leaves the *Nautilus*.

La Nonne Sanglante, ou Roberta la Flétrie [*The Bloody Nun, or Roberta the Branded*] (FR 3, col., 10 May 1981)
Dir: Bernard Maigrot; *Wri*: Maurice Sarfati, based on a novel by Albert Bourgeois.
Cast: Maria Laborit, Edith Perret, Nathalie Roussel.
Story: Gothic melodrama.

La Nuit des Fantômes [*Night of the Ghosts*] (FR 3, col., 75 min., 18 December 1990)
Dir: Jean-Daniel Verhaeghe; *Wri*: Gérard Brach.
Cast: Frédéric Deban, Marie Bunel, Jean-Pierre Bisson, Clément Harari, Laurent Paris, Baptiste Roussillon, Pauline Delfau.
Story: A modern-day teenager (Deban) falls in love with the ghost of a noblewoman from the Crusades (Bunel).

La Nuit Se Lève [*Night Is Rising*] (ORTF 2, col., 20 October 1970)
Dir: Roland Bernard; *Wri*: Jean-Claude Brisville.
Cast: Pascale Audret, Régine Blaess, Paul Bergé, André Julien.
Story: A contemporary vampire story set in the mountain region of the Gévaudan.

Objets Trop Identifiés [*Too Identified Flying Objects*] (TF1, col., 6 August 1984)
Dir: Alain Dhouailly; *Wri*: Victor Haïm.

Cast: Dominique Arden, Hubert Deschamps, Maurice Chevit.
Story: UFO story.

On A Feulé Chez M. Sloop [*Something Growled at Mr. Sloop's*] (A2, col., 22 November 1981)
Dir/Wri: Claude Ventura, based on a play by Bernard Mazéas.
Cast: Rosine Favey, Bernard Mazéas.
Story: Gothic story.

L'Oreille Absolue [*The Absolute Ear*] (ORTF 2, col., 24 August 1972)
Dir: Philippe Condroyer; *Wri*: François-Régis Bastide.
Cast: Michel Subor, Hannah Peschar, Jacques Seiler, Guy Tréjean.
Story: Satirical science fiction.

L'Orgue Fantastique [*The Fantastic Organ*] (ORTF 1, col., 73 min., 24 December 1968)
Dir: Jacques Trébouta; *Wri*: Frédéric Ardant, Claude Santelli based on the story *M. Ré Dièze et Mlle. Mi Bémol* by Jules Verne.
Cast: Xavier Depraz (Takelbarth), Fernand Ledoux (Hartman), Sabine Haudepin (Christel), Philippe Normand, François Valorbe, Marcel Cuvelier, Jacques Rispal, Francis Lax, François Vibert.
Story: After an old organist's death, a demon comes to a village and uses its children to create a fantastic new organ.

Les Palmiers du Métropolitain [*The Palm Trees of the Metro*] (A2, col., 3 August 1978)
Dir/Wri: Jean-Claude Youri.

Cast: Linda Thorson, Maurice Biraud, Pierre Tornade, Françoise Taillandier.
Story: Comedy with light fantasy overtones.

Panique ! [*Panic*] (TF1, col., 120 min., 2009)
Dir: Benoît d'Aubert; *Wri*: Emmanuelle Sardou, Vincent Solignac.
Cast: Richard Anconina (François), Alessandra Martines, Clara Ponsot, Pierre Derenne, Charlie Dupont, Jean-Baptiste Puech.
Story: No one wants to hear François' warnings about the bees attack...

Le Passe-muraille [*The Walker Through The Walls*] (ARTE, col, 95 min., December 2016)
Dir/Wri: Dante Desarthe, d'après la nouvelle de Marcel Aymé.
Cast: Denis Podalydès (Dutilleul), Marie Dompnier, Scali Delpeyrat, Claude Perron, Maryvonne Schiltz, Roger Jendly.
Story: M. Dutilleul discovers he has the power to walk through walls.

La Peau de Chagrin [*The Sorrow's Skin*]
Based on the novel by Honoré de Balzac.
Story: A young man receives the gift of a strange talisman which grants his wishes but shortens his life in exchange.

1. (A2, col., 150 min., 29 December 1980)
Dir: Michel Favart; *Wri*: Armand Lanoux,.
Cast: Marc Delsaert, Catriona McCall, Anne Faudry, Richard Fontana, Alain Cuny, Alexandre Rignault, Jean-Marie Galey, Raymond Jourdan, Robert Favart.

2. (TF1, col., 98 min., 24 April 2010)
Dir: Alain Berliner; *Wri*: Alexandra Deman, Alain Berliner.
Cast: Thomas Coumans, Annabelle Hettmann, Julien Honoré, Mylène Jampanoï.

Petit Claus et Grand Claus [*Little Claus and Big Claus*] (ORTF 2, B&W., 70 min., 25 December 1964)
Dir: Pierre Prévert; *Wri*: Pierre Prévert, Jacques Prévert, based on the story by Hans Christian Andersen.
Cast: Elisabeth Wiener, Maurice Baquet, Roger Blin, Jean-Jacques Steen, Madeleine Damiens, Laure Paillette, Hubert Deschamps, Roger Pigault (Narrator).
Story: Big Claus has four horses, while Little Claus has only one. After Big Claus kills his rival's horse, Little Claus plots revenge.

Le Petit Manège [*The Little Merry-Go-Round*] (FR 3, col., 30 November 1984)
Dir/Wri: Daniel Tragarz, based on a story by Gilbert Rozes and Michel Rouzière.
Cast: Jean Franval, Vanessa Zaoui, Yolande Gilot, Mimie Mathy.
Story: Children's fantasy.

Photo-Souvenir [*Souvenir Shots*] (ORTF 3, col., 35 min., 10 May 1978)
Dir: Edmond Séchan; *Wri*: Edmond Séchan, Jean-Claude Carrière.
Cast: Jean-Claude Carrière, Vania Vilers, Bernard Lecoq, Danièle Aymé, Ginette Mathieu, Jean-Paul Venel.
Story: A mysterious camera shows a surgeon pictures of the future.

La Planète des Cons [*The Planet of Idiots*] (Canal+, col. 98 min., 19 June 2013)
Dir: Gilles Galud, Charlie Dupont; *Wri*: Julien Simonet, Philippe Plunian, based on a concept by Laurent Foulon.
Cast: Thomas Séraphine, Stéphanie Crayencour, Claire Pataut, Arnaud Ducret, Issa Doumbia, Pierre Boulanger, Frédéric van den Driessche.
Story: A man named Boris vows to make idiots disappear. This is granted and some idiots are teleported to another planet. Accidentally, Boris is also teleported to that planet.

Pleine Lune [*Full Moon*] (FR 3, col., 45 min., 1982)
Dir/Wri: Jean-Pierre Richard.
Cast: Laurent Mallet, Thérèse Liotard.
Story: A tale of love among vampires.

Président Faust (ORTF 1, col., 105 min., 12 January 1974)
Dir: Jean Kerchbron; *Wri*: Jean Kerchbron, Louis Pauwels.
Cast: François Chaumette (Faust), François Simon, France Dougnac, Elina Labourdette, Maurice Chevit, André Oumansky, Jacques Mauclair, Jean-Luc Boutté, Laurence Ragon.
Story: In this modern variation of the classic tale, Faust is a powerful captain of industry who eventually falls in love with the daughter of a trade union leader.

Le Prince Porcher [*The Pig-Keeping Prince*] (RTF, B&W., 20 April 1962)

Dir: Monique Chapelle; *Wri*: Michèle Angot, based on "*The Pig-Keeper and the Princess*" by Hans-Christian Andersen.
Cast: Marie Dubois, Jacques Grello, Madeleine Barbulée, Anne Zamire.
Story: A classic fairy tale.

Le Puits et le Pendule [*The Pit and the Pendulum*] (ORTF 1, B&W., 45 min., 9 January 1964)
Dir/Wri: Alexandre Astruc, based on the story by Edgar Allan Poe.
Cast: Maurice Ronet.
Story: Brilliant adaptation of Poe's story. The prisoner escapes by getting rats to chew his bonds.

Que Voyez-Vous, Miss Ellis? [*What Do You See, Miss Ellis?*] (FR 3, col., 35 min., 24 August 1975)
Dir: Claude Mourthé; *Wri*: Anny Mourthé, based on a story by Roderick Wilkinson.
Cast: Edith Scob, Roger Blin, Jean-Paul Cisife, Edgar Duvivier.
Story: A young girl and her companion are pulled inside a painting.

Le Recyclage de Georges B. [*The Recycling of Georges B.*] (TV Romande, 1967)
Dir: Unknown; *Wri*: Pierre-Henri Zoller.
Cast: Unknown.
Story: The hero tries to escape from a world where everything is literally kept under wraps.

La Redevance du Fantôme [*The Ghost's Rent*] (ORTF 1, B&W., 100 min., 17 April 1965)

Dir: Robert Enrico; *Wri*: Jean Gruault, based on a story by Henry James.
Cast: Stéphane Fey, François Vibert, Marie Laforêt, Reine Courtois, Michel Lonsdale, Philippe Sautrec.
Story: A classic ghost story.

Le Réquisitionnaire [*The Commanding Officer*] (ORTF 1, B&W., 14 May 1968)
Dir: Georges Lacombe; *Wri*: Didier Goulard, Maurice Fabre, based on a story by Honoré de Balzac.
Cast: Alice Sapritch, Jacques Dacqmine, Sylvie Vaneck, Paul Barge.
Story: Ghost story.

Rhésus B (1967)
Dir: Unknown; *Wri*: Gébé (Georges Blondeau).
Cast: Unknown.
Story: In 2067, any type of work is prohibited.

Roc, ou La Malédiction [*Roc, or The Curse*] (FR 3, col., 90 min., 6 February 1973)
Dir: Daniel Wronecki; *Wri*: Daniel Wronecki, Claude Seignolle, based on his short story "*Le Diable en Sabots*" [*The Devil In Clogs*].
Cast: Claude Titre (Roc), Laurence Imbert, François Darbon, Françoise Le Bail, Raymond Meunier, Aline Bertrand, Paul Bisciglia, Thérèse Clay, André Dumas, Arlette Ménard, Jean Nehr.
Story: Roc, a newcomer, seemingly gifted with mysterious powers, takes over the trade of a smith who hanged himself.

Les Roses de Manara [*The Roses of Manara*] (TF1, Col., 24 March 1976)

Dir: Jean Kerchbron; *Wri*: Louis Pauwels, Jean Kerchbron.
Cast: Jean-Claude Drouot, Jean-Roger Caussimon, Jean Rupert, Denise Roland, Aniouta Florent.
Story: Jean, a modern cynical journalist, meets a strange pilgrim in a convent in Seville who tells him about the adventures of Miguel de Mnatra, a sort of repentant Don Juan of the 17th century who ends his life in the orders and rests in the crypt of the convent.

Rubis [*Ruby*] (A2, col., 95 min., August 1984)
Dir: Daniel Moosmann; *Wri*: Jean Bany, based on the short story "*To See the Invisible Man*" by Robert Silverberg.
Cast: Pierre Vaneck, Claude Mathieu, Georges Chatelain, Stéphane Bouy.
Story: In the 22nd century, Avignon is ruled by an authoritarian pope. A music teacher who publicly claimed not to like Wagner is condemned to a year of "social invisibility", evidenced by a ruby-like gem implanted on his forehead.
Note: Robert Silverberg's story originally appeared in *Worlds of Tomorrow* in 1963. It was adapted again in *The New Twilight Zone* on CBS on 31 January 1986, directed by Noel Black, written by Steven Barnes, starring Cotter Smith.

Une Seconde d'Éternité [*A Second of Eternity*] (TF1, col., 70 min., 13 July 1977)
Dir: Gérard Chouchan; *Wri*: Jean Ferry, based on a story by Daphne du Maurier.
Cast: Loleh Bellon, Catherine Lafond, Pascale Berger, Renée Duchâteau, Anne Denieul.

Story: A woman is suddenly thrown into a nightmarish reality.

Le Secret de Monsieur L. [*The Secret of Mister L.*] (A2, col., 22 August 1983)
Dir/Wri: Pierre Zucca.
Cast: Pierre Arditi, Michel Bouquet, Irina Brook.
Story: Satirical tale with fantasy elements.

Le Secret de Rembourg [*The Secret of Rembourg*] (ORTF 2, col., 21 December 1974)
Dir: Jeannette Hubert; *Wri*: Georges Sonnier, based on a tale by E.T.A. Hoffmann.
Cast: Christian Rist, François Perrot, René Bernan, Jenny Arasse.
Story: Ghost story.

Le Secret de Wilhelm Storitz [*The Secret of Wilhelm Storitz*] (ORTF 1, Col., 110 min., 28 October 1967)
Dir: Eric Le Hung; *Wri*: Claude Santelli based on the novel by Jules Verne.
Cast: Jean-Claude Drouot (Storitz), Bernard Verley, Pascale Audret, Monique Mélinand, Robert Vattier, Pierre Leproux, Michel Vitold.
Story: This story, about a scientist who has discovered the secret of invisibility, also incorporates elements from another Verne novel, *Le Château des Carpathes* [*The Castle in the Carpathians*].

Sherlock Holmes en Amérique [*Sherlock Holmes in America*] (RTF, B&W., 24 December 1957)
Dir/Wri: Françoise Dumayet.
Cast: Ronald Howard (Holmes), Jean Paqui, Joël Flateau, Georges Janney, Maurice Sarfati.

Story: Sherlock Holmes pastiche.

Si j'étais vous [*If I Were You*] (ORTF 2, col., 22 October 1971)
Dir: Ange Casta; *Wri*: Ange Casta, Robert de Saint-Jean, based on the novel by Julien Green.
Cast: Dominique Maurin, Grégoire Aslan, Jacques Debary, Gérard Darrieu, Henri Virlojeux, Patrick Dewaere, Jean-Paul Moulin.
Story: An old man (Aslan) gives a young, disillusioned man (Maurin) the power to mentally switch bodies and live other people's lives.

Le Spectre de Tappington [*Tappington's Ghost*] (ORTF 2, B&W., 9 April 1965)
Dir: Paul Renty; *Wri*: Christiane Dupont, based on a story by Richard Harris Barham.
Cast: Pierre Tornade, Cécile Arnold, Jean-Louis Le Goff, Odette Piquet.
Story: A period ghost story.

Strangers dans la Nuit [*Strangers In The Night*] (FR 3, col., 8 October 1991)
Dir: Sylvain Madigan; *Wri*: Gérard Krawczyk, Marcel Gotlib.
Cast: Karin Viard, Philippe Ulchan, Patrick Braoudé.
Story: Satirical tale.
Note: Marcel Gotlib is a renowned French cartoonist.

La Surprenante Invention du Prof. Delalune [*The Surprising Invention of Prof. Delalune*] (1964)
Dir: Marcel Cravenne; *Wri*: Albert Husson.

Cast: Christian Alers, Marie Daëms, Barbara Sommers, Roger Carel, Maurice Porterat, Denise Péron, Renée Gardes.
Story: Science fiction comedy for children included in the program *Theâtre de la Jeunesse* [*Youth's Theater*].

Sylvie et le Fantôme [*Sylvie and the Ghost*] (RTF, B&W., 24 July 1954)
Dir/Wri: Stellio Lorenzi, based on a play by Alfred Adam.
Cast: Marianne Lecène (Sylvie), Alfred Adam, Suzanne Dentès, Charles Deschamps, Jean Ozenne, Madeleine Barbulée, Solange Certain, Albert Rémy.
Story: Sylvie falls in love with a gallant ghost. During a party for her sixteenth birthday, she discovers real love.

Temps Mort [*Dead Time*] (Television Romande, B&W, 65 min., 1969)
Dir: Jean-Jacques Lagrange; *Wri*: Jean-Louis Roncoroni, based on a story by Georges Langelaan.
Cast: Jacques Riberolles, Bernard Rousselet, Erika Dentzler.
Story: Two aviators serve as guinea pigs for scientists seeking to slow down their biological functions for long-duration space travel. But instead of slowing down, the two airmen live an hour what a normal man lives in a day.

Le Testament du Dr. Cordelier [*The Testament of Dr. Cordelier*, trans. as *The Doctor's Horrible Experiment*, aka *Experiment in Evil*] (RTF, B&W., 100 min., 16 November 1961)
Dir/Wri: Jean Renoir, based on the novel by Robert-Louis Stevenson.

Cast: Jean-Louis Barrault (Dr. Cordelier/Opale), Teddy Bills, Michel Vitold, Jean Topart, Micheline Gary, Gaston Modot.
Story: French transposition of Stevenson's *Dr. Jekyll and Mr. Hyde*.
Note: This film was originally made in 1959 and screened that year at the Venice Film Festival. However, its release was delayed because of a conflict between film and television distributors.

Tête d'Horloge [*Clock Head*] (ORTF 2, col., 100 min., 11 April 1970)
Dir: Jean-Paul Sassy; *Wri*: Jean Pradeau, based on his novel.
Cast: Pierre Fresnay (Clock Head), Claude Cerval, Sophie Grimaldi, Bruno Balp, Denise Benoit.
Story: One day, all of the world's clocks mysteriously stop, except for the watch of an old professor nicknamed "Clock Head" because of his punctuality.

Thanatos Palace Hôtel
Story: People wishing to die but afraid to commit suicide come to a hotel where they will be killed painlessly.
Based on the short story by André Maurois, a famous writer and essayist.

1. (FR3, col., 60 min., 8 May 1973)
Dir: Pierre Cavassilas; *Wri*: Maurice Toesca
Cast: Max Vialle, Barbara Lass, Jacques Monod, Roger Pelletier.

2. (FR3, col., 14 November 1979)
Dir: James Thor; *Wri*: Maurice Toesca, James Thor.
Cast: Jean-Pierre Bacri, Aïna Walle, Igor Tyczka, Gérard Hérold.

Le Tour d'Écrou [*The Turn of the Screw*] (ORTF 2, col., 100 min., 25 December 1974)
Dir: Raymond Rouleau; *Wri*: Paule de Beaumont, Jean Kerchbron, based on the novel by Henry James.
Cast: Suzanne Flon, Andrée Tainsy, Laure Jeanson, Stéphane Guiraud, Robert Hossein, Marie-Christine Barrault, Robert Rimbaud,.
Story: Psychoanalytical version of Henry James' classic story in which two children are haunted by the ghosts of an evil gardener and his lover.

Tout Spliques étaient les Borogoves [*Mimsy Were The Borogoves*] (ORTF 2, col., 85 min., 6 September 1970)
Dir: Daniel Lecompte; *Wri*: François-Régis Bastide, Daniel Lecompte, Marcel Schneider, based on the eponymous short story by Lewis Padgett, a.k.a. Henry Kuttner & Catherine L. Moore.
Cast: Eric Damain, Laurence Debia, Malka Ribowska, William Sabatier, Madeleine Ozeray, Jean-Roger Caussimon, Pierre Didier, Muse Dalbray, Max Desrau.
Story: Two children find educational toys from another dimension which eventually teach them to travel there.

Le Travail du Furet [*The Weasel's Work*] (FR 2, col., 100 min., 31 January 1994)
Dir: Bruno Gantillon; *Wri*: Gérard Carré, Alain Minier, based on the novel by Jean-Pierre Andrevon.
Cast: Fabrice Eberhard, Marine Delterme, Richard Sammut, Charlie Nelson, Mircea Abulescu, Dan Condurache, Roman Saint-Ourens, Carmen Ionescu, Valentin Uritescu, Luana Stoica.
Story: In an overpopulated near-future, people are randomly selected to die, and are then killed by a cadre of

executioners dubbed "Weasels." One of the Weasels (Eberhard) falls in love with his intended victim (Delterme) and refuses to kill her, then goes on discover that the system is rigged.
Note: Jean-Pierre Andrevon is a famous science fiction writer.

Vacances au Purgatoire [*Holidays in Purgatory*] (FR 3, col., 90 min., 26 December 1992)
Dir: Marc Simenon; *Wri*: Valentine Albin.
Cast: Marie-Anne Chazel, Michel Pilorge, Louba Guertchikof, Mylène Demongeot, Thierry de Peretti, Michel Peyrelon.
Story: After her death, a call-girl is sent back to Earth in the body of a harried housewife.

La Vénus d'Ille [*The Venus of Ille*]
Story: A bridegroom mistakenly places his wedding ring on the finger of the statue of a pagan goddess, and thus seals his doom.
Based on a story by Prosper Mérimée.

    1. (RTF, B&W., 13 December 1957)
Dir: Pierre Badel; *Wri*: Jean-Claude Youri.
Cast: Jacques Castelot, François Vibert, F. Albani, André Oumansky, Alain Bouvette, Michèle Nadal, Pierre Leproux.

    2. (FR3, col., 4 July 1980)
Dir/Wri: Jean-Jacques Bernard, Robert Réa.
Cast: François Marthouret, Jean-Pierre Bacri, Yves Favier, Raymonde Aubray.

Vie et Mort d'Untel [*Life and Death of Anyone*] (FR 3, col., 55 min., 11 April 1980)

Dir: Fernand Vincent; *Wri*: Pierre Dupriez, Serge Martel.
Cast: Jean-Paul Zehnacker, Alain Doutey, Maud Rayer.
Story: A man finds a book which tells the story of his life.

La Voix Venue d'Ailleurs [*The Voice From Beyond*] (ORTF 3, col., 50 min., 20 March 1973)
Dir: Odette Collet; *Wri*: Pierre Dupriez, Serge Martel.
Cast: Elia Clermont, Paul Guers, Michel Fortin.
Story: A mysterious female voice on the telephone causes the disappearance of a writer.

Le Vol d'Icare [*The Flight of Icarus*] (A2, col., 100 min., 22 November 1980)
Dir/Wri: Daniel Ceccaldi, based on a novel by Raymond Quéneau.
Cast: Michel Galabru, Caroline Cellier, Henri Garcin, Evelyne Buyle, Roger Carel, Pierre Malet.
Story: A writer hires a detective to locate the hero of his latest novel who has, literally, left the author's manuscript.

Le Voyageur Imprudent [*The Careless Traveler*] (A2, col., 90 min., 2 January 1982)
Dir/Wri: Pierre Tchernia; based on the novel by René Barjavel.
Cast: Thierry Lhermitte, Anne Caudry, Jean-Marc Thibault, Lily Fayol, Jean Bouise.
Story: A time traveler returns to the past and mistakenly kills his grandfather, thus creating a time paradox.

Les Voyageurs de l'Espace [*The Space Travelers*] (ORTF 1, B&W., 22 July 1966)

Dir: Edmond Tybo; *Wri*: Maurice Toesca, based on his play.
Cast: Jacques Duby, Didier Cherreau, Sady Rebot, Bérangère Vattier.
Story: On another planet, Greek spacemen discover the ancient Greek Gods exiled from Earth 2000 years ago.

Léo Campion
La Brigade des Maléfices

Helmut Berger
Fantômas

RADIO

Overview

The golden age of French Radio took place in the 1950s and the early 1960s, when up to fifteen million listeners remained glued to their sets for a variety of programs including music, comedy, game shows and serials.

If most serials were soaps like the hugely popular *La Famille Duraton* (Radio-Luxembourg, 1937-66!), a few relied on the traditional forms of pulp literature for their inspiration: fearless heroes fighting mysterious villains bent on world domination. Some played it straight (*L'Homme à la Voiture Rouge* [*The Man With The Red Car*]); others with a hearty dose of humor, like the classic *Signé Furax* [*Signed: Furax*]; one, *Ça Va Bouillir* [*It's Gonna Boil*], even managed to have it both ways, featuring Zappy Max, a real radio personality playing himself as the hero of incredible adventures.

From 1968 on, television took over the place that had been occupied by radio in the family bosom. Radio was relegated to sports, news and music, until the 1980s when so-called "free" radio and FM radio exploded on the air waves.

Zappy Max

Serials

L'Apocalypse Est Pour Demain (Les Aventures de Robin Cruzo) [*The Apocalypse Is For Tomorrow*] (France-Inter, 65 eps., April 1978)
Wri/Voices: Jean Yanne.
Story: A "salubrious and ecological" comedy serial in which movie star/comedian Jean Yanne tells the adventures of Robin Cruzo in a world invaded by pollution and cars.

L'Arme Invisible [*The Invisible Weapon*] (France-Culture, 10 eps., February 1989)
Dir: Evelyne Frémy; *Wri*: Serge Martel based on the novel by Paul Féval.
Story: The actions of Magistrate Remy d'Arx threatens the Black Coats.
Note: Adaptation of the keystone novel in the prodigious crime saga.

Astérix (France-Inter, 1966-68)
Voices: Roger Carel (Astérix), Jacques Morel (Obélix), Bernard Lavalette.
Story: Based on the famous graphic novels by Albert Uderzo and René Goscinny the radio adaptations expanded the original stories and added new characters and new layers of plot.

Une Aventure de Ferdinand Straub [*An Adventure of Ferdinand Straub.*]
   1. Docteur Radar à Paris [*Doctor Radar in Paris*] (France-Culture, 5 eps., July 1989)
   2. Docteur Radar en Italie [*Doctor Radar in Italy*] (France-Culture, 5 eps., July 1989)
   3. *Le Retour du Docteur Radar* [*The Return of Doctor Radar*] (France-Culture, 10 eps., February 1991)
Dir: Jean-Jacques Vierne; *Wri*: Noël Simsolo.
Story: Ferdinand Straub, a former French aviation ace turned detective, investigates a series of extraordinary murders and discovers that the person responsible for these crimes is Doctor Radar, a mysterious and dangerous individual who has become a master in the art of disguise.

Les Aventures de Peter Gay [*The Adventures of Peter Gay*] (Europe 1, 1963-64)
Wri: Jacques Antoine.
Voices: Pierre Gay.
Story: Peter Gay was an aerospace engineer who became involved in adventures blending cutting edge scientific discoveries and spy thrillers. He took part in telepathic experiments between the Pentagon and a nuclear submarine cruising under the Pole; he thwarted a terrorist assassination attempt against UN Secretary Dag Hammarskjöld, etc.

Les Aventures de Tchitchklov (France-Culture, 17 eps., December 1978)
Dir: Bronislaw Horowicz; *Wri*: Sylvie Marville, based on the novel *Dead Souls* by Nikolai Gogol.
Story: The travels and strange adventures of Pavel Ivanovich Chichikov

Balaoo (France-Culture, 10 eps., February 1989)
Dir: Claude Roland-Manuel; *Wri*: Philippe Derrez based on the novel by Gaston Leroux.
Story: The tale of a murderous man-ape.

La Baronne Trépassée [*The Dead Baroness* aka *The Vampire and the Devil's Son*] (France-Culture, 10 eps., March 1988)
Dir: Evelyne Frémy; *Wri*: Serge Martel based on the novel by Pierre-Alexis Ponson du Terrail.
Story: Baron de Nossac returns from a daring military mission in Eastern Europe when, crossing the forests of Bohemia, he is captured by the legendary Black Huntsman, a 900-year-old wraith who is none other than the Devil's son. Held prisoner at the Hunstman's enchanted castle, the Baron is then seduced by a female vampire who resembles his dead wife.

Blake & Mortimer (ORTF/France II, 1960-63)
Dir: Jacques Langeais, Nicole Strauss.
Voices: Jacques Morel (Mortimer), Roger Carel, Jean Rochefort, Jean-Pierre Marielle.
Story: Adaptations of two of the popular graphic novels: *SOS Météores* [*SOS Meteors*] and *Le Piège Diabolique* [*The Time Trap*] by Edgar-Pierre Jacobs.

Bons Baisers de Partout [*From Everywhere With Love*] (France-Inter, 1966-68)
Wri/Voices: Pierre Dac, Louis Rognoni.
Story: This madcap *James Bond* satire tells the adventures of Nicolas Leroidec, anvil salesman and French intelligence ace. All the characters sport punnish names: Hubert de Guerlasse, l'Adjudant Tifrisse, etc. Some of

the stories involve SF elements, as when two agents are sent a year back in time.

Le Carnaval du Choléra [*The Carnival of Cholera*] (France-Culture, 22 eps. September 1983)
Dir: Jean-Pierre Colas; *Wri*: Pierre Bodin, based on *Champavert, contes immoraux* by Petrus Borel.
Story: Horror story.

La Cinquième Planète [*The Fifth Planet*] (France-Culture, 17 eps., August 1981)
Dir: Jean-Jacques Vierne; *Wri*: Emile Noël, Chantal Richemont based on the novel by Fred & Geoffrey Hoyle.
Story: Another star is due to pass close to the sun, close enough for conventional spacecraft to reach it. The first planets observed are four gas giants, but then an inner Fifth Planet is found. Signs of chlorophyll are detected, suggesting that it supports life. Rival Soviet and US expeditions are launched to visit it.

Christina (France-Culture, 109 eps., January 1980)
Dir: Jean-Pierre Colas; *Wri*: Miron Niculescu based on the novel by Mircea Eliade.
Story: A story of vampires in a world plagued by blasphemy; to exorcise her, a young man kills a vampire twice by piercing her heart.

Les Contes du Whisky [*Tales From Whisky*] (two episodes included in the anthology serries *Samedi Noir*) (France-Culture, March 2016).
Dir/Wri: Étienne Valles based on stories by Jean Ray.
Story: Horror stories.

Le Cousin de Lavarede [*Lavarede's Cousin*] (France-Culture, 10 eps., juillet 1990)
Dir: Claude Roland-Manuel; *Wri*: Philippe Derrez based on the novel by Paul d'Ivoi.
Story: Vernian tale featuring the heroes of *Around the World on Five Sous*.

De la Terre à la Lune [*From the Earth to the Moon*] (France-Culture, 2 eps., January 2014)
Dir: Michel Sidoroff; *Wri*: Hervé Prudon based on the novel by Jules Verne.
Story: Faithful adaptation of the classic sf story.

Doyle, Sir Arthur Conan (France-Culture, 1981)
Story: A series of adaptations of Sir Arthur Conan Doyle's stories dealing with reincarnation, the occult, parapsychology, and ancient curses.

1. *La Main Brune* [*The Brown Hand*] (19 September 1981)
Dir: Anne Lemaître; *Wri*: Edith Loria.

2. *La Hachette d'Argent* [*The Silver Axe*] (28 September 1981)
Dir: Claude Roland-Manuel; *Wri*: M. Loran, Edith Loria.

3. *La Grande Experience de Keinplatz* [*The Great Keinplatz Experiment*] (5 October 1981)
Dir: Guy Delaunay; *Wri*: M. Loran.

4. *Le Lot No. 249* (12 October 1981)
Dir: Arlette Dave; *Wri*: M. Loran, Edith Loria.

5. *L'Anneau de Toth* [*The Ring of Toth*] (26 October 1981)
Dir: Georges Peyrou; *Wri*: Edith Loria.

Dracula (France-Culture, 12 eps., January 1982)
Dir: Jean-Pierre Colas; *Wri*: Jacques Bransolle, based on the novel by Bram Stoker.
Story: Faithful adaption of the horror classic.

Les Elixirs du Diable [*The Devil's Elixirs*] (France-Culture, 10 eps., September 1990)
Dir: Anne Lemaître; *Wri*: Pascal Amel, Dominique Mehadji based on the story by E.T.A. Hoffmann.
Story: Gothic fantasy tale.

L'Ensorcelée [*The Spellbound*] (France-Culture, 5 eps., February 1994)
Dir: Jacques Taroni; *Wri*: Geneviève Bray based on the story by Jules Barbey d'Aurevilly.
Story: Gothic fantasy tale.

L'Eve future [*Future Eve*] (France-Culture, 10 eps., May 1990)
Dir/Wri: Jean-Jacques Vierne based on the story by Philippe-Auguste Villiers de l'Isle Adam.
Story: Classic tale about a female android.

Le Fauteuil hanté [*The Haunted Armchair*] (France-Culture, 5 eps., août 1990)
Dir: Claude Roland-Manuel; *Wri*: Charlotte Messer based on the novel by Gaston Leroux.
Story: Extravagant murders at the French Academy.

Frankenstein (France-Culture, 5 eps., February 1989)

Dir: Anne Lemaître; *Wri*: Alain Pozzuoli, Jean-Frédéric Vernier, Joe Ceurworst based on the novel by Mary Shelley.
Story: Faithful adaption of the horror classic.

Le Golem (France-Culture, 10 eps., December 1988)
Dir: Arlette Dave; *Wri*: Jean-Pierre Spilmont, Denise Meunier based on the novel by Gustav Meyrinck.
Story: Adaptation of the classic story.

Gormenghast (France-Culture, 3 eps. January 1980)
Dir: Georges Peyrou; *Wri*: Gilberte Lambrichs, Patrick Reumaux based on the novel by Mervyn Peake.
Story: Adapotation of the fantasy novel about the inhabitants of Castle Gormenghast, a sprawling, decaying castle.

Le Grand Décret [*The Edict*] (France-Culture, 20 eps., September 1982)
Dir: Jean-Jacques Vierne; *Wri*: Emile Noël, Jacques Ovion, Chantal Plancon based on the novel by Max Ehrlich.
Story: A future when the uncontrolled growth of the human population has pushed the world to the brink of total disaster.

Han d'Islande [*Hans of Iceland*] (France-Culture, 24 eps., août 1983)
Dir: Jean-Pierre Colas; *Wri*: Dominique Wahiche based on the novel by Victor Hugo.
Story: Fantasy adventure story set in 17th-Century Norway, back when it was part of Denmark.

Histoires insolites et contes cruels [*Strange Tales & Cruel Stories*] (France-Culture, 5 eps. April 1984).
Dir: Anne Lemaître; *Wri*: Jean Steen, based on stories by Philippe-Auguste Villiers de l'Isle-Adam.

Joseph Balsamo (France-Culture, 20 eps., janvier 1997)
Dir: Georges Peyrou; *Wri*: Annie Mercier based on the novel by Alexandre Dumas.
Story: Adaptation of the classic novel about the masonic conspiracy aiming to overthrow the French Monarchy.

Le Joyau aux Sept étoiles [*The Jewel of Seven Stars*] (France-Culture, 10 eps., March 1991)
Dir: Christine Bernard-Sugy; *Wri*: Alain Pozzuoli, Jacques Parsons based on the novel by Bram Stoker.
Story: A young man pulled into an archaeologist's plot to revive Queen Tera, an ancient Egyptian mummy.

L'Homme à la Voiture Rouge [*The Man With The Red Car*] (Radio-Luxembourg, 1962-64)
Dir: Jean Maurel; *Wri*: Yves Jamiaque.
Story: Reporter Stéphane Berrier and his red car, Ruby (which seems gifted with some kind of intelligence, as it appears to warn or rescue him from tight spots) fights a worldwide conspiracy led by the "*Grand Patron*" [*Big Boss*], from a secret base under a volcano in Sicily to one protected by a deadly force field in the Amazon Delta.

L'homme qui rit [*The Man Who Laughs*] (France-Culture, 20 eps., October 2001)
Dir: Claude Guerre; *Wri*: Claude Dufresne based on the novel by Victor Hugo.

Story: Adaptation of the classic gothic novel about the plights of a disfigured man.

Le Nommé Jeudi [*The Man Who Was Thursday*] (France-Culture, 10 eps., September 1981)
Dir: Claude Roland-Manuel; *Wri*: Roger Pillaudin, Jean Florence, based on the novel by G. K. Chesterton.
Story: Adaptation of the classic metaphysical thriller.

Littérature Populaire & Fantastique aux 18ème & 19ème Siècle [*Fantastic & Popular Literature of the 18th & 19th Century*] (France-Culture, 1976-1980)
Wri/Host: Maurice Sarfati.
Story: Adaptations of popular gothic fantasy stories.

Le Juif Errant [*The Wandering Jew*] (January-March 1976)
Dir: Bronislaw Horowicz based on a story by Eugène Sue.

Caftan Rouge le Sorcier [*Red Caftan the Wizard*] (18 August 1980)
Dir: Bronislav Horowicz based on a story by Nikolai Gogol.

Les Chiennes Blanches [*The White Dogs*] (19 August 1980)
Dir: Evelyne Frémy based on a story by James Hogg.

Poing de Fer [*Iron Fist*] (20 August 1980)
Dir: Anne Lemaître based on a story by Walter Scott.

Le Château d'Otranto [*The Castle of Otranto*] (21 August 1980)

Dir: Bronislav Horowicz based on a story by Horace Walpole.

Wolfstein et Mégalena (23 August 1980)
Dir: Georges Peyrou based on a story by Percy Bysshe Shelley.

Le Maître du Silence [*The Master of Silence*] (France-Culture, 10 eps., January 1998)
Dir: Jean Couturier *Wri*: Philippe Bardy, based on characters created by Arthur Conan Doyle.
Story: Sherlock Holmes pastiche.

Manuscrit trouvé à Saragosse [*The Manuscript Found in Saragossa*] (France-Culture, 6 eps., March 1985)
Dir: Jacques Taroni; *Wri*: Paule Chavasse based on the novel by Jan Potocki.
Story: Intertwining stories set in whole or in part in Spain with a large and colorful cast of Romani, thieves, inquisitors, a cabbalist, etc.

Le Mystérieux Dr. Cornelius [*The Mysterious Dr. Cornelius*] (France-Culture, 35 eps., 1978)
Dir: Alain Barroux; *Wri*: Edith Loria, based on the novels by Gustave Le Rouge.
Cast: Jean Topart (Fritz), Michel Bouquet (Cornelius), Denis Manuel (Harry Dorgan), Guy Tréjean (G. de Maubreuil), Jean Wiener (Bondonnat), Pierre Vaneck (Burydan), Catherine Hubeau (Isidora), Naïa Simon (Andrée), Catherine Laborde (Frédérique).
Story: Radio adaptation of the famous pulp serial novel about a mad plastic surgeon and the heroes who band together to defeat him.

Nostradamus (France-Culture, 30 eps., October 1977)
Dir: Evelyne Frémy; *Wri*: Serge Martel, Pierre Dupriez, based on the novel by Michel Zevaco.
Story: Marie, daughter of Baron Croixmart, the great witch hunter in the time of François I, consults a seer who predicts the death of her father. She warns him and the latter has the "witch" burned at the stake. The crowd, rebel and massacre the Baron and his men. Renaud, the seer's son, swears revenge on Marie, but falls in love with her...

Nous autres [*We*] (France-Culture, 10 eps., January 1991)
Dir: Michel Sidoroff; *Wri*: Irina Vavilova, Gérard Conio based on the novel by Yevgeny Zamyatin.
Story: A world of harmony and conformity within a united totalitarian state.

Panix (France Inter, 1973-76)
Wri/Voices: Claude Villers, Patrice Blanc-Francard.
Story: The comedic adventures of French super-hero Panix, who protects his girl-friend Mireille Pamieux from the evil schemes of villainous Elvis Sansfin.

Passeport pour l'Inconnu [*Passport For The Unknown*] (Radio-Genève, 1957)
Dir: Roland Sassi; *Wri*: Pierre Versins.
Story: Adaptations of classic novels and short stories by Asimov, Van Vogt, Heinlein, etc. Original radio plays include:
   Procyon Simple Course [*Procyon Simple Run*] by Robert Pibouleau (18 February 1959)

Le Robot Mal-Aimé [*The Ill-Loved Robot*] by Laurent Lourson (18 March 1959)

A-t-il fait sauter la Maison ? [*Has He Blown Up The House?*] by Roland Sassi?(7 May 1965)

Hier le Jour, Hier la Nuit [*Yesterday The Day, Yesterday The Night*] by Martine Thomé (16 June 1966)

Peter Pan (France-Culture, 5 eps., November 2004)
Dir/Wri: Marguerite Gateau based on the story by James Barrie.
Story: Adaptation of the classic children's tale.

Pierre de lune [*The Moonstone*] (France-Culture, 20 eps., May 2006)
Dir: Myron Meerson; *Wri*: Pierre Senges based on the novel by Wilkie Collins.
Story: Adaptation of the classic gothic novel.

Plate-Forme 70 (RTF, 1946)
Dir: Bernard Gandrey-Réty; *Wri/Voice*: Jean Nocher.
Story: Prof. Hélium (Nocher) warns the listeners that Earth is in imminent danger of being destroyed by a freak atomic explosion.
Note: This *War of the Worlds*-like broadcast was taken seriously by many listeners and generated 28,000 letters. It was novelized by Nocher in 1946.

Princesses d'ivoire et princes de nacre [*Ivory Princesses and Mother of pearl Princes*] (France-Culture, 6 eps., October 1993)

Dir: Christine Bernard-Sugy; *Wri*: Alain Pozzuoli based on the stories from *Princesses d'ivoire et d'ivresse* of Jean Lorrain.
Story: Drawing his inspiration through the ages with characters like Illys, Mandosiane, Oriane, or Mélusine, Lorrain immerses us in his marvelous and fantastic universe.

Le Prisonnier de la Planète Mars [*The Prisoner of Planet Mars*] (France-Culture, 1978)
Dir/Wri: Marguerite Cassan, based on the novel by Gustave Le Rouge.
Story: Radio adaptation of the famous pulp serial novel about the war against Martian vampires.

Maurice Renard (France-Culture, January 1981)
Dir: Evelyne Frémy, Claude Roland-Manuel; *Wri*: , based on the stories by Maurice Renard.
Story: A series of adaptations of science fiction short-stories by this great author.

1. *La Berlue de Mme d'Estrailles* [*Mrs. D'Estrailles' Vision*] (9 November)

2. *L'Homme qui Voulait Être Invisible* [*The Man Who Wanted To Be Invisible*] (16 November)

3. *L'Homme Truqué* [*The Doctored Man*] (20 November)

4. *L'Homme au Corps Subtil* [*The Man With a Subtle Body*] (23 November)

5. *Le Brouillard du 26 Octobre* [*The Mist of October 26th.*] (30 November)

6. *L'Affaire du Miroir* [*The Mirror Affair*] (7 December)

7. *L'Image au Fond des Yeux* [*The Image at the Bottom of the Eyes*] (14 December)

Rocambole (RTF, 1941)
Based on the famous character created by popular writer Pierre-Alexis Ponson du Terrail.

Rouletabille: Le Mystère de la Chambre Jaune [*The Mystery of the Yellow Room*] (France-Culture, 24 eps., December 1982)
Dir: Jean-Jacques Vierne; *Wri*: Philippe Derrez based on the novel by Gaston Leroux.
Story: Classic locked room mystery.

La Science-Fiction (France-Culture, 1980-81)
Dir: Henri Soubeyran; *Wri*: Catherine Bourdet.
Note: A series of adaptations of classic science fiction novels by major American writers.

1. *The Dreaming Jewels* (Theodore Sturgeon) (26 July 1980)

2. *The Man in the High Castle* (Philip K. Dick) (2 August 1980)

3. *Les Vampires de l'Alfama* (Pierre Kast) (19 August 1980)

4. *Le Correcteur* (Isaac Asimov) (21 August 1980)

5. *The Lovers* (Philip José Farmer) (25 July 1981)

6. *A Door Into Summer* (Robert A. Heinlein) (1st August 1981)

Sherlock Holmes contre Fu-Manchu [*Sherlock Holmes vs Fu-Manchu*] (France-Culture, 10 eps., August 1997
Dir: Christine Bernard-Sugy; *Wri*: Denis Boissier based on characters created by Arthur Conan Doyle and Sax Rohmer.
Story: Sherlock Holmes pastiche.

Sherlock Holmes: L'Affaire Frankenstein [*Sherlock Holmes: The Frankenstein Affair*] (France-Culture, 15 eps., May 1999
Dir: Christine Bernard-Sugy; *Wri*: Denis Boissier based on characters created by Arthur Conan Doyle and Mary Shelley.
Story: Sherlock Holmes pastiche.

Signé Furax
1. *Malheurs aux Barbus* [*Woe To The Bearded Ones*] (RTF, 1951-1952)
Wri: Pierre Dac, Francis Blanche; *Dir*: Cédric Aussir.
2. *Signé Furax* [*Signed: Furax*] (Europe 1, 1956-1960)
Wri: Pierre Dac, Francis Blanche; *Dir*: Pierre-Arnaud de Chassy-Poulay.
Voices: Pierre Dac (Black), Francis Blanche (White), Jean-Marie Amato (Furax, Asti), Jeanne Dorival (Malvina), Maurice Biraud (Socrate, Maurice Champot), Edith Fontaine (Carole, Mademoiselle Fiotte), Claude Dasset (Klakmuf), Louis Blanche (Hardy-Petit), Roger Pierre, Jean-Marc Thibault, Raymond Devos, Pauline Carton, Jean Poiret, Laurence Riesner, François Chevrais.

Story: *Signé Furax* began modestly on 15 October 1951 at 1:10 p.m. on French channel RTF as a short-lived radio serial of ten-minute instalments entitled *Malheurs aux Barbus* [*Woe To The Bearded Ones*]. Written by renowned humorists Pierre Dac and Francis Blanche (who also starred in it), it narrated the fight of two private investigators. Black and White. against the megalomaniacal villain, Edmond Furax, a cross between Arsène Lupin and Fantômas. In this madcap serial, Furax kidnapped 642 Bearded Men, took over an island in the Hebrides, then traveled through space to Antares, and through time back to the days of Louis XIV.

Four years later, in 1956, Furax returned in a new radio serial entitled *Signé Furax* [*Signed: Furax*], this time on the Europe 1 channel. *Signé Furax* lasted four years, totalling over 1200 episodes, and became a national media event. This time, Furax and his girlfriend, the beautiful Malvina, came out of retirement to fight on the side of good and thwart the nefarious schemes of the evil sect of the Babus (no "r"), led by the diabolical Klakmuf. Furax's allies included a colorful gallery of characters, such as Police Commissioner Socrate, his old enemies and now friends private investigators Black and White, former hitman Asti Spumante, genial scientist Hardy-Petit, his daughter Carole and son-in-law Théo Courant, gang leader Maurice Champot, aka La Grammaire, and even the president of the far-off planet Asterix, Clodomir.

The first serial, entitled *Le Boudin Sacré* [*The Sacred Sausage*] (1956-57), began with an attempt by the Babus to frame Furax in a plot involving the dehydratation of Paris' best-known monuments to better transport them to their own, middle-eastern state, Filikistan. Furax, however, outwitted the Babus and gained control of the sect through the stealing of their sacred sausage, but his secret identity—that of France's Chief of Police Fouveaux—was exposed. The story ended with a temporarily insane Furax traveling back in time to the Crimean War in a ultimtely aborted effort to rewrite history.

The next serial, entitled *La Lumière qui Éteint* [*The Light That Dims*] (1957-58), began with an investigation into a new plot by the Babus to take over the world, using a strange, blue light which saps people's wills discovered by Babu scientist Gregory Mouchmouch. The story then moved to the discovery of the Babus' secret base on the atoll Anatole, which, as it turns out, is also a space-faring vehicle. Anatole took our heroes to the far-off planet Asterix, where they met friendly aliens led by President Clodomir. Upon their return to Earth, Furax thwarted a last Babu plan to release an army of giant spiders.

The third saga, entitled *Le Gruyère Qui Tue* [*The Swiss Cheese That Kills*] (1958-59), saw Furax and his friends team up again to save Earth from an invasion of body-snatching alien parasites, the Gsbrr, who literally inhabit swiss cheese. Anyone who ate contaminated cheese eventually woke up with a Gsbrr inside his head. The Gsbrr used the Babus to try to enslave Earth, but with the help of President Clodomir, and of some parmesan cheese, Furax and his friends eventually defeated the space parasites.

There was a fourth radio series entitled *Le Fils de Furax* [*The Son of Furax*] (1959-60).

Finally, five shorter Furax adventures were recorded and sold as 45 rpm records in the early 1960s, but they are generally considered to be outside the main continuity:

- *Menace sur Tancarville* [*Threat Over Tancarville*]

- *La navrante comédie des proverbes* [*The Sorry Comedy of Proverbs*]
- *Trafic de larmes* [*Tear Traffic*]
- *L'Enlèvement du Père Noël* [*The Kidnapping of Santa Claus*]
- *Alerte aux homards* [*Alert: Lobsters*]

CDs: All of the Furax stories (except *Son of Furax*) are now available in CD audio collections.

Novelizations: The first radio serial, *Malheur aux Barbus*, presumably adapted by Dac & Blanche themselves from their own radio scripts, was published in four novels by Martel in 1952-53:

1. *Malheur aux Barbus* [*Woe To The Bearded Ones*] (Martel, 1952)
2. Confession de Furax [*Furax's Confession*] (Martel, 1952)
3. Mangez de la Salade [*Eat Salad*] (Martel, 1952)
4. Les Barbus de l'Espace [*The Bearded Ones In Space*] (Martel, 1953)

A second series of novelizations, this time penned by writer Henri Marc, adapted the *Signé Furax* radio scripts, and were published by Jean-Claude Lattès in the 1970s. First, Lattès published four standard-size paperbacks,

1. *Le Boudin Sacré* [*The Sacred Sausage*] (JCL, 1970)
2. *Malheur aux Babus* [*Woe To The Babus*] (JCL, 1970)
3. *Crimée... Châtiment* [*Crimea... Punishment*] (JCL, 1971)
4. *La Lumière qui Éteint* [*The Light That Dims*] (JCL, 1971)

then three larger-size trade paperbacks:

1. *Signé Furax* (collects 1-3 above) (JCL, 1971)

2. *Furax et les Autres* [*Furax & Others*] (collects 4, plus the unpublished 5. *L'Atoll Anatole* [*The Atoll Anatole*] and 6. *M... comme* [*M as in...*] which were not released as separate paperbacks) (JCL, 1973)

3. *Le Gruyère qui Tue* [*The Swiss Cheese That Kills*] (JCL, 1976)

Comic Strip: *Furax*' success also led to a comic-strip adaptation by Roger Mallat & Paul Gordeaux, drawn by artist Henry Blanc. It was serialized as 1174 daily strips in the newspaper *France-Soir* in 1957-60, roughly broken down into 4 stories:

1. *Le Boudin Sacré* [*The Sacred Sausage*] (strips 1-255)

2. *La Lumière qui éteint* [*The Light That Dims*] (strips 256-571)

3. *Le gruyère qui tue* [*The Swiss Cheese That Kills*] (strips 572-920)

4. *Le fils de Furax* [*The Son of Furax*] (strips 921-1174)

Two collections of the strip were reprinted by Pressibus in 1991 and 1992.

Motion Picture: Finally, in 1980, the first *Signé Furax* story, *Le Boudin Sacré* [*The Sacred Sausage*], was adapted by Marc Simenon into a live action feature film. (See Section 1.)

Le Théâtre de l'Étrange [*Theater of the Strange*] (France-Inter, 1963-74). (The episode guide below is incomplete as a large number of plays are not listed in the official records at the French Institut National de l'Audiovisuel.)

Akatan Bloc NC 22. *Dir*: Unknown. *Wri*: René Brant (1964).

La Musique d'Erich Zann [*The Music of Erich Zann*]. *Dir/Wri*: Claude Mourthé, based on the story by H. P. Lovecraft (1965).

Juin 2003 à travers les airs [*June 2003: Way In The Middle Of The Air*]. *Dir*: Jeanne Rollin Weisz, based on the story by Ray Bradbury (1965).

Les Hordes de la nuit [*The Night Hordes*]. Dir: Georges Gravier; *Wri*: René Brant (1965).

Le Ruum [*The Ruum*]. *Dir/Wri*: Philippe Guinard, based on the story by Arthur Porges (1965).

L'Exception [*The Exception*]. *Dir*: Claude Dupont; *Wri*: Claude Aveline (1965).

L'Hôte de Bessarion [*The Guest from Bessarion*]. *Dir*: Gilbert Caseneuve; *Wri*: Gérard Klein (1965).

Le Vieil Armand [*Old Armand*]. *Dir/Wri*: Bernard Saxel based on the story by George Langelaan (1965).

Les Rats [*The Rats*]. *Dir*: Albert Riera; *Wri*: Nino Frank based on the story by Dino Buzzati (1965).

Dracula (2 episodes). *Dir*: Jean Chouquet; *Wri*: Dominique Mauclair, Jean Patrick based on the novel by Bram Stoker; *Voices*: Daniel Gélin, Jean Rochefort (1965).

La Crapaude [*The She-Toad*]. *Dir*: Jacques Adrien Blondeau; *Wri*: Robert Arnaut (1965).

Ce Mur infranchissable [*That Impassable Wall*]. *Dir/Wri*: Emile Noël (1965).

La Sentinelle [*The Sentinel*]. *Dir/Wri*: Bernard Latour based on the story by Nathalie Henneberg (1965).

Eratos. *Dir*: Unknown. *Wri*: Pierre Feuga (1965).

Beleybuse ou L'Etoile morte [*Beleybuse or The Dead Star*]. *Dir*: Georges Gravier; *Wri*: Geneviève Ballac (1965).

La Route au Clair de Lune [*The Moonlit Road*]. *Dir/Wri*: Albert Riera based on the story by Ambrose Bierce (1965).

Bénédiction en gris [*Dark Benediction*]. *Dir/Wri*: Jeanne Rollin Weisz based on the story by Walter M. Miller (1965).

Epha que j'aimais [*Epha Whom I Loved*]. *Dir*: Bernard Latour; *Wri*: Frédéric Christian (1965).

Le Désert à deux faces / Fahel [*The Desert With Two Faces / Fahel*] (2 stories). *Dir*: Claude Roland-Manuel; *Wri*: Marguerite Cassan (1965).

L'Étrange Amitié de Charles-Louis de Lignières [*The Strange Friendship of Charles-Louis de Lignières*]. *Dir*: Jean-Wilfrid Garrett; *Wri*: Alain Franck (1965).

Le Vieil Homme et l'Espace [*The Old Man and Space*]. *Dir*: Arlette Dave; *Wri*: Gérard Klein (1965).

Ils avaient la peau brune et les yeux dorés [Dark They Were and Golden-Eyed]. *Dir/Wri*: Jeanne Rollin Weisz based on the story by Ray Bradbury (1965).

Reviens, veux-tu ? [Will You Come Back?]. *Dir*: Philippe Guinard; *Wri*: Michael Maltravers (1965)

La Chanson de Nika [Nika's Song]. Dir/Wri: Bernard Saxel based on the story by George Langelaan (1965).

On frappe pourtant à la porte [Yet They Knocked at the Door]. *Dir*: Albert Riera; *Wri*: Nino Frank based on the story by Dino Buzzati (1965).

Programmation corrigée [Correct Program]. *Dir/Wri*: Bernard Latour based on the story by Nathalie Henneberg (1965)

Frère Hans, Mon Frère Hans [Brother Hans, My Brother Hans]. *Dir*: Gilbert Caseneuve. *Wri*: Jacqueline H. Osterrath (1965).
Note: Jacqueline H. Osterrath was the editor of *Lunatique*, one of the earliest French science fiction fanzines and the translator of the German *Perry Rhodan* book series.

L'Apprentie Sorcière [The Sorceress's Apprentice]. *Dir*: Guy Delaunay; *Wri*: Milorad Pavic based on *Journal d'un inconnu* by Jean Cocteau. (1965)

Les Mains d'Anicette [*The Hands of Anicette*]. *Dir*: Guy Delaunay; *Story* by René Barjavel read by Didier Conti (1965).

Ligeia la Revenue [*Ligeia the Revenant*]. *Dir*: Arlette Dave; *Wri*: Loys Masson based on the story by Edgar Allan Poe (1965).

Dessus et Dessous [*Above and Below*]. *Dir*: Henri Soubeyran; *Wri*: Nino Frank based on the story by Alexandre Arnoux (1965).

Voyage Inaugural [*First Journey*]. *Dir*: Philippe Guinard; *Wri*: Bernard Soulet (1965).

Ecoute le temps [*Listen to Time*]. Dir: Olivier d'Horrer; *Wri*: Richard Puydorat (1965).

La Dot [*The Dowry*]. *Dir*: Claude Mourthé; *Wri*: Georges Govy (1965).

Anna Laub. *Dir*: Bronislaw Horowicz; *Wri*: Jakov Lind, Roger Richard (1965).

Une Nuit Interminable [*An Endless Night*]. *Dir*: Eléonore Cramer; *Wri*: Marguerite Cassan based on the story by Pierre Boulle (1965)

Ni fleurs, ni étoiles [*Neither Flowers, Nor Stars*]. *Dir*: Jeanne Rollin Weisz; *Wri*: Nino Frank (1965).

L'Ambassadeur de Xonoï [*The Ambassador from Xonoï*]. *Dir*: Bernard Latour; *Wri*: Frédéric Christian (1966)

Note: A computer-generated voice played the part of an alien.

Pernicia. *Dir*: Philippe Guinard; *Wri*: Pierre Dupriez (1966).

La Tour Grise [*The Grey Tower*]. *Dir*: Bernard Latour; *Wri*: Michel Suffran (1966).

Le Miroir [*The Mirror*]. *Dir*: Claude Roland-Manuel; *Wri*: Véra Feyder (1966).

Le Paradis Oublié [*The Forgotten Paradise*]. *Dir*: Olivier d'Horrer; *Wri*: Alain Franck (1966).

La Dernière Traversée [*The Last Crossing*].
Dir: Gilbert Caseneuve; *Wri*: René Brant based on the story by George Langelaan (1966).

Bonne nuit, Sophia [*Good Night, Sophia*]. *Dir/Wri*: Claude Mourthé based on the story by Lino Aldani (1966).

Les Chiens de Cébolène [*The Dogs of Cebolene*]. *Dir*: Jean-Wilfrid Garrett; *Wri*: Gérard Klein (1966).

Ce Que Me Raconta Jacob [*What Jacob Told Me*]. *Dir/Wri*: René Jentet, based on a story by Claude Seignolle. *Voices*: Gérard Darrieu, Léon Spiegelman.

A l'auberge de Manjoala [*At the Manjoala Inn*]. *Dir*: Alain Barroux; *Wri*: Hubert Juin based on the story by Ion Luca Caragiale (1966).

Le Monde que j'avais quitté [*The World That I Left*]. *Dir*: Jean-Wilfrid Garrett; *Wri*: Robert Arnaut based on the story by Anatoly Dneprov (1966).

Cabine 10 [*Cabin 10*]. *Dir*: Bernard Saxel; *Wri*: Roger Richard based on the story by Ermanno Macario (1966).

Humanité Provisoire [*Conditionally Human*]. *Dir/Wri*: Jeanne Rollin Weisz based on the story by Walter M. Miller (1966).

Si la vie ne meurt [*If Life Survives*]. *Dir*: Claude Mourthé; *Wri*: Véra Feyder (1966).

Un Bruit de Guêpes [*The Sound of Wasps*](2 episodes). *Dir*: Jean Chouquet; *Wri*: Louis Rognoni based on the novel by Jean Paulhac (1966).

Le Dernier Métro [*The Last Metro*]. *Dir*: Bernard Latour; *Wri*: Frédéric Christian (1966).

Dans la Gueule du Lion [*In the Jaws of the Lion* aka *Night Has A Thousand Eyes*]. *Dir*: Jacques Adrien Blondeau; *Wri*: Serge Douay based on the novel by Cornell Woolrich (1966).
Note: The same novel was already filmed in 1948 by John Farrow starring Edward G. Robinson. The book was originally published under the *nom-de-plume* of "George Hopley".

Les Polypes Musiciens [*The Musical Polyps*]. *Dir*: Guy Delaunay; *Wri*: Antoinette Riva based on the story by Sandro Sandrelli (1966).

Monsieur Chtoss. *Dir*: Bernard Latour; *Wri*: Georges Govy (1966).

Désillusions interplanétaires, ou Mars en Carême [*Cosmic Desillusion*]. *Dir*: Unknown; *Wri*: Irving Le Roy (1966).

Récession. *Dir*: Henri Soubeyran; *Wri*: Emile Noël based on the story by George Langelaan (1966).

Le Labyrinthe [*The Labyrinth*]. *Dir*: Philippe Guinard; *Wri*: Denise Miège Simansky (1966).

Harry. *Dir*: Gilbert Caseneuve; *Wri*: Serge Douay based on the story by Rosemary Timperley (1966).

Le Bal de Miss Tessa Benton [*Miss Tessa Benton's Ball*]. *Dir*: Alain Barroux; *Wri*: Pierre Dupriez (1966).

Plaque Sensible [*Sensitive Plate*]. *Dir*: Claude Roland-Manuel; *Wri*: Marguerite Cassan (1966).

Le Mal des Mots [*The Evil of Words*]. *Dir*: Jeanne Rollin Weisz; *Wri*: Stella Malard (1966).

Les Fantasmes d'Otrante [*The Phantoms of Otranto*] (3 episodes). *Dir*: Jean Doat; *Wri*: Loys Masson based on *The Castle of Otranto* by Horace Walpole (1966).

Le Portrait. *Dir*: Philippe Guinard; *Wri*: Denise Miege Simansky based on the story by Nikolai Gogol (1966).

Le Personnage [*The Character*]. *Dir*: Alain Barroux; *Wri*: Andrée Chedid (1966).

La Ruelle Ténébreuse [*The Dark Alley*]. *Dir*: Arlette Dave; *Wri*: Jacqueline Clancier based on the story by Jean Ray (1966).

Génocide [*Now let us sleep*]. *Dir*: Unknown. *Wri*: Serge Douay based on the story by Avram Davidson (1966).

Si vous vous perdez à Elfaciano [*If you get lost in Elfaciano*]. *Dir*: Claude Roland-Manuel; *Wri*: Véra Feyder (1966).

Le Bruit du Moulin [*The Sound of the Mill*]. *Dir/Wri*: José Pivin based on the story by Marcel Béalu (1966).

Le Tableau au dessus du lit [*The Painting Above the Bed*]. *Dir*: Bronislaw Horowicz; *Wri*: Dominique Vincent (1966).

La Main de l'autre [*The Other's Hand*]. *Dir*: Bernard Latour; *Wri*: René Brant based on the story by George Langelaan (1966).

Chant de Noël [*A Christmas Carol*]. *Dir*: Bronislaw Horowicz; *Wri*: Jeanne Rollin Weisz based on the story by Charles Dickens (1966).

Les Prétendants [*The Pretenders*]. *Dir*: Jean-Wilfrid Garrett; *Wri*: Louis Rognoni based on the story by Pierre Joffroy (1967).

Traduit du Martien [*Translated from the Martian*]. *Dir*: Bernard Saxel; *Wri*: Francis Didelot (1967).

Des Sons et des Couleurs [*Sounds and Colors*]. *Dir*: Claude Mourthé; *Wri*: Nino Frank (1967).

Les Mines [*The Mines*]. *Dir*: Jean-Pierre Colas; *Wri*: Pierre Roudy (1967).

Et pourtant elle tourne [*And Yet It Moves*]. *Dir*: Bernard Latour; *Wri*: Philippe Derrez, Serge Petrof (1967)

Les Hommes Sandouiches [*The Sandwich Men*]. *Dir*: Olivier d'Horrer; *Wri*: Jean Féron (1967).

Delphine. *Dir*: Alain Barroux; *Wri*: Hubert Juin based on the story by Claude Seignolle *Voices*: Michel Bouquet, Fernand Ledoux (1967).

Coup de foudre [*Thunderstruck*]. *Dir*: Claude Roland-Manuel; *Wri*: Marguerite Cassan (1967).

Amanda et les Colibris [*Amanda and the Hummingbirds*]. *Dir*: Evelyne Frémy; *Wri*: Pierre Dupriez (1967).

La Photo. *Dir*: Marcel Sicard; *Wri*: Frédéric Christian (1967).

D'un Autre Monde [*From Anorther World*]. *Dir*: Arlette Dave; *Wri*: Marcelle Hagen (1967)

Les Saules [*The Willows*]. *Dir*: Guy Delaunay; *Wri*: Monique Rousselet based on the story by Algernon Blackwood (1967).

Un Saint au Néon [A Neon Saint]. *Dir/Wri*: Jeanne Rollin Weisz based on the story by Jean Louis Curtis (1967).

Dans le Tableau [*In The Picture*]. *Dir*: Alain Barroux; *Wri*: Catherine Chraibi based on the story by Roderick Wilkinson (1967).

Une Alice au Hasard [*An Alice At Random*]. *Dir*: Jean-Pierre Colas; *Wri*: Gébé (1967).

Le Détective [aka *Pressure*]. *Dir*: Michel Duplessis; *Wri*: Catherine Birckel based on the story by Roderick Wilkinson (1967)

L'Implacable Soleil [Merciless Sun]. *Dir*: Claude Mourthé; *Wri*: René Brant (1967).

L'Énigme d'Erstein [*The Erstein Enigma*]. *Dir*: Bernard Latour; *Wri*: Serge Robillard (1967).

Le Cinquième au Bridge [*The Fifth at the Bridge Table*]. *Dir*: Bronislaw Horowicz; *Wri*: Georges Lisowski based on the story *Der Fünfte zum Bridge* by Michal Tonecki (1967).

Le Dernier Gerfaut [*The Last Falcon*]. *Dir*: Arlette Dave; *Wri*: Jean *Serres* (1967),

Duo Nombreux [*Numerous Duos*]. *Dir*: Guy Delaunay; *Wri*: Nino Frank (1967).

La Planète Myra [*Planet Myra*]. *Dir*: José Pivin; *Wri*: Gébé (1967).

L'Hypnotiseur [*The Bohemian*]. *Dir*: Georges Gravier; *Wri*: Jean-François Hauduroy based on the story by Fitz James O'Brien (1967).

Défense de... [*Forbidden To...*]. *Dir*: Georges Peyrou; *Wri*: Francis Didelot (1967).

Je Reviendrai [*I Shall Return*]. *Dir*: Arlette Dave; *Wri*: Marcelle Hagen (1967).

Vol 270 [*Flight 270*]. *Dir*: Guy Delaunay; *Wri*: Thalie de Molenes (1967).

Le Saint énigmatique [*The Enigmatic Saint*]. *Dir*: Olivier d'Horrer *Wri*: Marguerite Cassan based on the story by Pierre Boulle (1967).

La Démangeaison [*The Itch*]. *Dir*: Jean-Pierre Colas; *Wri*: Alain Spiraux (1967).

Transfusion. *Dir*: Claude Roland-Manuel; *Wri*: Véra Feyder (1967).

La Machine à désintégrer [*The Disintegration Machine*]. *Dir*: Bernard Saxel; *Wri*: Jacques-Bernard

Brunius based on the story by Arthur Conan Doyle (1967).

La Métempsycose [*The Metempsychosis*] (2 episodes). *Dir*: Philippe Guinard; *Wri*: Roger Richard based on a story by Robert Macnish translated by Gérard de Nerval (1967).

Le Dernier Pape [*The Last Pope*]. *Dir*: Evelyne Frémy; *Wri*: Geneviève Gennari (1967).

L'Anacardier [*On Anacardium*]. *Dir*: Arlette Dave; *Wri*: Marianne Monestier based on the story by Gloria Alcorta (1967),

Une Pierre dans leur Jardin [*A Stone in their Garden* aka *The Golden Bugs*]. *Dir*: Philippe Guinard; *Wri*: Patrice Galbeau based on the story by Clifford D. Simak (1968).

Biennale An 6000 [*Biennal Year 6000*]. *Dir*: Guy Delaunay; *Wri*: Antoinette Riva based on the story by Guido Raiola (1968).

Le Solitaire [*The Lonesome Man*]. *Dir*: Bronislaw Horowicz; *Wri*: Jean Francis based on the story by Franz Hellens (1968).

Onze légère [*Light Eleven*]. *Dir*: Alain Barroux; *Wri*: Gébé (1968).

Marée basse [*Low Tide*]. *Dir/Wri*: Jeanne Rollin Weisz based on the story by Jacques Sternberg (1968).

Les Feux de Kahlrousein [*The Fires of Kahlrousein*] (4 episodes). *Dir*: Jean-Pierre Colas; *Wri*: Loys Masson based on the novel *The Mysteries of Udolpho* by Ann Radcliffe (1968).

Le Chupador. *Dir/Wri*: Jeanne Rollin Weisz, based on a story by Claude Seignolle. *Voices*: Michel Vitold, François Maistre, France Descaux.

Le Lion a peur / L'Ange gardien [*The Lion Is Scared / The Guardian Angel*]. *Dir*: Bernard Latour; *Wri*: story #1 by Charles Hamilton; story #2 by Marcel Béalu read by Michel Bouquet (1968).

Les Orgues du Vent [*The Organs of the Wind*]. *Dir*: Unknown; *Wri*: Louis Thirion (1968).

Le Galoup. *Dir/Wri*: Jeanne Rollin Weisz, based on a story by Claude Seignolle (1968).

Le Petit Homme de San Francisco [*The Little Man of San Francisco*]. *Dir*: Unknown; *Wri*: Louis Thirion (1968).

Le Millième Cierge [*The Thousandth Candle*]. *Dir/Wri*: René Jentet, based on a story by Claude Seignolle. *Voices*: Gérard Darrieu, Jean-Roger Caussimon, Catherine Sellers.

Appartement 6000 ou Le Gardien [*Apartment 6000, or The Watchman*]. *Dir*: Unknown; *Wri*: Louis Thirion (1969).

Eudes, l'Enfant venu d'Ailleurs [*Eudes, The Child From Beyond*]. *Dir*: Unknown; *Wri*: Louis Thirion (1970).

Marc Gillipendie. Dir: Jeanne Rollin Weisz; Wri: Charles Gilbert (1970).

Le Matagot. *Dir/Wri*: Jeanne Rollin Weisz based on a story by Claude Seignolle (1970).

Rosalba. *Dir*: Evelyne Frémy; *Wri*: Monique Ruyssen based on the story by Jules Barbey d'Aurevilly (1972).

Tintin (Europe 1, 1964)
Voices: Jacques Hilling (Haddock), Jacques Dufilho (Tournesol).
Story: Adaptations of the graphic novels.

Les Tréteaux de la Nuit [*The Night Stage*] (France-Inter, 1979-80)
Hosts: Patrice Galbeau, Jean-Jacques Vierne.
Dirs: Bronislav Horowicz, Claude Roland-Manuel, Bernard Saxel, Georges Godebert, Anne Lemaître, Olivier d'Horrer, Jeanne Rollin Weisz, Jacques Taroni, Henri Soubeyran, Arlette Dave, Jean-Wilfrid Garrett, etc.
Story: A series of weekly 50-minute original plays featuring fantasy, horror or science fiction elements. Stories for the 1979 and 1980 seasons are listed below:

La Tête [*The Head*] by Jacques Mauclair (13 January 1979).

Le Dernier des Rabasteins [*The Last of the Rabasteins*] by Philippe Derrez (20 January 1979).

Le Reportage [*The Reporting*] by Marie-Blanche Dumet (27 January 1979).

Oh! Quelle Famille [*What A Family!*] by Jean Brach (3 February 1979).

Djamilia by Marie O. (10 February 1979).

La Très Humide Histoire de Fusain Canson et de sa Goelette [*The Very Humid Story of Fusain Canson and of His Schooner*] by Colette Piat (17 February 1979).

La Caverne de la Nuit [*The Cavern of Night*] by Philippe Brunet-Schneider (24 February 1989).

Le Vent Kuona [*The Wind Kuona*] by Jacques Floran (3 March 1979).

Un Poisson dans la Ville [*A Fish in the City*] by Jean-François Menard (10 March 1979).

La Marque [*The Mark*] by Maurice-Étienne Dantan (17 March 1979).

Une Funeste Expérience [*A Sinister Experiment*] by Dominique Cir (24 March 1979).

Une Nuit de Solstice [*Solstice Night*] by Katherine Robineau (31 March 1979).

Les Cerceaux Domestiques [*The Domestic Hoops*] by Odile Marcel (7 April 1979).

M comme Mithra [*M As In Mithra*] by Catherine d'Etchea (14 April 1979).

L'Homme en Noir [*The Man In Black*] by Frédéric Christian (21 April 1979).

Une Singuliere Journée [*A Singular Day*] by Louis Rognoni (28 April 1979).

L'Étrange Partie d'Échecs de Douglas McLloy [*The Strange Chess Game of Douglas McLloy*] by Catherine Tolstoï (5 May 1979).

Alex et Odilon by Jean Emmanuel (12 May 1979).

La Bombe Glacée [*The Ice Cream Surprise*] by Michèle Tourneur (19 May 1979).

Du Cyanure dans la Rivière [*Cyanide In The River*] by Henri Mitton (26 May 1979).

C'est Mon Papa qui a Gagné la Bataille [*My Daddy Won The Battle*] by Jean-Jacques Steen (9 June 1979).

La Leçon de Chine [*China Lesson*] by Francis Roure (16 June 1979).

L'Homme aux Yeux Gris [*The Man With Grey Eyes*] by Jean-Jacques Varoujean (23 June 1979).

Un Testament Provençal [*A Provencal Testament*] by Pierre Magnan (30 June 1979).

Opération Osiris by Jacques Idier (7 July 1979).

La Marée Était en Noir [*The Tide Wore Black*] by Jean-Claude Danaud (14 July 1979).

L'Hôtel du Progrès by Jean Brach (28 July 1979).

Saint Petersbourg by Patrick Besson (4 August 1979).

Mademoiselle Else by Arthur Schitzer (11 August 1979).

La Grande Entourloupe [*The Great Trick*] by Roald Dahl (18 August 1989).

Bouche Cousue [*Closed Mouth*] by Charles Goupil (25 August 1979).

Le Fantôme Inconnu [*The Unknown Ghost*] by Daniel Zerki (1st September 1979).

Un Château de Sable [*A Sand Castle*] by Jacques Bens (15 September 1979).

Paradise Bar by Gilbert Simourre (22 September 1979).

Clamuche, ou La Vertu Récompensée [*Clamuche, or Rewarded Virtue*] (29 September 1979).

Comme à la Fin d'une Danse [*As At The End of a Dance*] by Marie-Bénédicte Charon (6 October 1979).

La Mort Caméléon [*Chameleon Death*] by Martin Lewis (13 October 1979).

Requiem pour un Inconnu [*Requiem For An Unknown Man*] by Gérard Houlet (20 October 1979).

Place Clichy by Jean-Jacques Varoujean (27 October 1979).

Un Poète m'a dit [*A Poet Told Me*] by Marc Audouard (3 November 1979).

La Fille de Lady Edwina [*Lady Edwina's Daughter*] by Gabriel Douchkine (17 November 1979).

Le Trou [*The Hole*] by Daniel Goldenberg (1st December 1979).

Rendez-vous à Sainte Adresse by Patrick Liegebel (8 December 1979).

Numéro Huit, Au Bout de l'Impasse [*No.8 At The End of the Dead End*] by Michèle Tourneur (15 December 1979).

La Visitation by Henri Weitzmann (22 December 1979).

Mort d'un Vampire Trop Honnête [*Death Of A Too Honest Vampire*] by Bernard Da Costa (29 December 1979).

Bonjour Philippine by Fred Kassak (12 January 1980).

Dossier CX by Louis Rognoni (26 January 1980).

L'Entrée de Service [*The Service Entrance*] by Guy Haurey (9 February 1980).

Hasard ou Vengeance [*Chance Or Revenge*] by Ida Savignac (16 February 1980).

Du Muguet en Hiver [*Lilies in the Winter*] by Claude Dufresne (23 February 1980).

Trains Espace Tour by Bernard Mazeas (8 March 1980).

Quai 17 [*Platform 17*] by Pascal Hamel (29 March 1980).

L'Adjudant by Patrick Besson (12 April 1980).

Allo! C'est toi? C'est moi [*Hello? Is it you? It's me*] by Philippe Clay (26 April 1980).

Le Mal d'Aurore [*Dawn's Disease*] by Catherine Tolstoï (17 May 1980).

Le Jeune Garçon au Bord de la Rivière [*The Young Man By The River*] by Guy Haurey (14 June 1980).

Les Voyageurs de Nulle Part [*The Travelers From Nowhere*] by Luc Sylvair (21 June 1980).

Les Gens du Dessus [*The People From Above*] by Gilles Laurent et Marie Borrel (5 July 1980).

Angelina et son Armoire [*Angelina And Her Dresser*] by Daniel Goldenberg (2 August 1980).

Le Juke-box Jouait du Wagner [*The Juke-Box Played Wagner*] by Jean-Claude Danaud (9 August 1980).

Le Tueur de Temps [*The Time Killer*] by Alain Spiraux (27 Septembre 1980).

Le Fantôme de la Maoulinière [*The Ghost of The Maouliniere*] by Henri Weitzmann (8 November 1980).

Attention: Une Sorciere peut en cacher une autre [*Watch Out: One Witch Can Hide Another*] by Katherine Robineau (6 December 1980).

La Planète du Temps [*Time's Planet*] by Louis Rognoni (20 December 1980).

Trois Hommes à la Recherche d'une Comète [*Three Men In Search Of A Comet*] (France-Culture, 20 eps., 4-29 August 1980)
Wri: Lazare Kobrynski.
Story: To avoid nuclear war, the super-powers are duped into sending missiles toward a threatening comet. But the missiles destroy the Moon instead.

Les Tyrans Sont Parmi Nous [*The Tyrants Are Among Us*] (RTF, 1953)
Wri: Jacques Antoine.
Story: A mysterious, international organization, Point Zero, has found the secret of making gold (artificial gold is, however, slightly radioactive) and prepares to use it to conquer the world.

Le Vagabond des Etoiles [*The Star Rover*] (France-Culture, 23 eps., February 1978)
Dir: Georges Peyrou; *Wri*: Maurice Chevit based on the novel by Jack London.
Story: A novel of mysrticism and reincarnation.

Voyages Au Bout De La Science [*Voyage To The Ends Of Science*] (Radio-Lausanne, 1952)
Wri: Stephen Spriel.
Story: This thirteen-episode magazine series also broadcast a number of original radio plays written by Spriel (the co-founder of the science fiction imprint *Le Rayon Fantastique*) and Georges-Michel Bovay (except where otherwise mentioned):

   1. *Ils Sont Parmi Nous* [*They Walk Among Us*]

   2. *Les Sur-Animaux* [*The Over-Animals*]

   3. *Un Maître du Monde* [*A Master of the World*]

   4. *Les Passagers de l'Avenir* [*The Passengers From The Future*]

   5. *Fort-de-France Appelle Mont-Pelé* (written by René-Maurice Picard)

6. *Menace sur la Terre* [*Menace Over Earth*]

7. *La Reine de la Jungle* [*The Queen of the Jungle*]

8. *Le Jour où la Terre s'arrêta* [*The Day The Earth Stood Still*] (radio adaptation of the classic film)

9. *Le Congrès de '39* [*The Congress of '39*] (written by René-Maurice Picard)

10. *Quand le Soleil Reviendra* [*When The Sun Returns*]

11-12. *Le Nouveau Déluge* [*The New Flood*] (based on the novel by Noelle Roger)

13. *Les Révoltés de l'an 3000* [*Revolt In The Year 3000*]

XT-1 (Radio-Luxembourg, 1957)
Dir/Host: Georges H. Gallet, Jacques Tourneur.
Note: Short-lived magazine series created by the co-founder of the science fiction imprint *Le Rayon Fantastique*. Jacques Tourneur was the son of Maurice Tourneur.

Zappy Max
1. *Vas-y Zappy* [*Go For It, Zappy*] (Radio-Luxembourg, 1952-57)
2. *Ça Va Bouillir* [*It's Gonna Boil!*] (Radio-Luxembourg, 1957-63)
3. *C'est Parti Mon Zappy* [*Zappy Max Is Go!*] (Radio-Luxembourg, 1963-66)

Wri: Saint-Julien (Hugo de Hahn).
Voices: Zappy Max (Himself), Gérard Sire (Kurt von Straffenberg), Roger Carel, Jacques Balutin, Jean Daurant, André Le Gall.
Story: Radio personality Zappy Max (real name: Max Doucet) plays himself as an investigative reporter who thwarts the evil, world-conquering schemes of the obese mad scientist Kurt von Straffenberg, a.k.a. *Le Tonneau* [*The Barrel*], and the secret criminal society known as *Les Treize* [*The Thirteen*].
Note: This is one of the longest serials on French radio, totaling over 3300 episodes. The name change was due to a change of sponsors in 1963, from Unilever to Procter & Gamble. A comic-strip adaptation entitled *Ça Va Bouillir* drawn by Maurice Tillieux was published in 1959 in *Pilote*.

Radio Plays

Over the years, France-Inter and France-Culture, a cultural channel, have broadcast numerous radio plays featuring fantastic elements; some were original stories, others adaptations of literary classics. A comprehensive listing of such plays is virtually impossible to assemble, as records of these are incomplete and no study has been published. We have listed here a selection of some of the more interesting plays.

L'Arc-en-Ciel, ou Naissance d'un Mutant [*The Rainbow, or Birth of a Mutant*] (France-Culture, 1966)
Dir/Wri: René-Jean Chauffard.
Story: Post-cataclysmic tale.

L'Attentat en Direct [*Terrorism On Live TV*] (France-Culture, 1969)
Dir/Wri: Claude Ollier.
Story: Political fiction.

L'Autre Monde [*The Other World*] (France-Culture, 1980)
Dir/Wri: Bronislav Horowicz, based on the stories by Hercule-Savinien Cyrano de Bergerac.
Story: Radio dramatization of the famous utopia.

Les Aventures Génétiques [*The Genetic Adventures*] (France-Inter, 1981)
Dir: Olivier d'Horrer; *Wri*: Jean Loisy.

Story: Two geneticists produce a superbaby.

Le Bal des Affamés [*The Ball of the Starving*] (France-Inter, 1981)
Dir: Jacques Taroni; *Wri*: Alain Page.
Story: A writer's fictional characters assume lives of their own.

La Brume Ne Se Lèvera Plus [*The Mist No Longer Rises*] (Radio-Montpellier, 1966)
Dir/Wri: Maurice Bardoulat, based on a story by Claude Seignolle.
Voices: Madeleine Attal.
Story: Ghost story.

Coeur de Chien [*Heart of a Dog*] (France-Culture, 1981)
Dir: Claude Roland-Manuel; *Wri*: Geneviève Bray, based on the novel by Mikhail Bulgakov.
Story: A satire of Soviet society based on a popular Russian genre novel.

Les Cris du Coeur [*The Screams of the Heart*] (France-Inter, 1981)
Dir: Pierre Billard; *Wri*: Robert Nahmias.
Story: Is personality transferred after a heart transplant?

Le Diable Amoureux [*The Devil In Love*] (France-Culture, 1980)
Dir: Jeanne Rollin Weisz; *Wri*: Henri Weitzmann, based on the novel by Jacques Cazotte.
Story: A nobleman summons a demon.

Le Diable en Sabots [*The Devil In Clogs*] (Radio-Montpellier, 1964)
Dir/Wri: Maurice Bardoulat, based on a story by Claude Seignolle.
Voices: Madeleine Attal.

Electrodome 2006 (France-Culture, 1979)
Dir: Bernard Saxel; *Wri*: Verell Pennington Ferguson.
Story: Rollerball inside a giant electronic billiard.

Etat Civil [*Civil State*] (France-Culture, 1968)
Dir: Unknown; *Wri*: Pierre Gripari.
Story: Social satire.

Le Fantastique Inceste [*The Fantastic Incest*] (France-Culture, 1967)
Dir: Unknown; *Wri*: Pierre Le Quellec.
Story: Time travel story.

Les Fleurs de Systèle [*The Flowers of Systele*] (France-Culture, 1981)
Dir: Eléonore Cramer; *Wri*: Myrielle Marc.
Story: Women of the future revolt by refusing to bear female babies.

Grand-Guignol
Dir: Georges Godebert; *Wri*: Gabriel Germinet (*Marémoto* written in collaboration with Pierre Cusy).
Story: Two radio plays written for the Grand-Guignol Theater and broadcast by the BBC: *Great-Guignol* (1923) and *Marémoto* (1924).

Inutile de s'inquiéter [*No Need To Worry*] (France-Inter, 1981)

Dir: Anne Lemaître; *Wri*: Serge Ganzl.
Story: Two aliens study mankind through the eyes of dogs.

La Lune Comme Un Point Sur Un I [*The Moon As A Dot On The I*] (France-Inter, 1981)
Dir: Henri Soubeyran; *Wri*: Michèle Tourneur.
Story: Ghost story.

Marie la Louve [*Mary The Wolf*]
Version No. 1: Radio-Toulouse, 1965; Version No. 2: Radio-Limoges, 1968
Dir/Wri: Maurice Bardoulat, based on a story by Claude Seignolle.
Voices: Madeleine Attal.

Le Martien [*The Martian*] (Radio-Luxembourg, 1954)
Dir: Unknown; *Wri*: Georges Chaulet.
Story: Fake Martian.

Le Mystère de la Mary-Céleste [*The Mystery of the Mary-Celeste*] (France-Culture, 1981)
Dir: Jean-Wilfrid Garrett; *Wri*: Philippe Clay.
Story: A shipwreck survivor tells the truth.

Noë, ou L'Épopée d'un Survivant [*Noah, or A Survivor's Odyssey*] (France-Culture, 1979)
Dir: René Jentet; *Wri*: Lazare Kobrynski.
Story: A post-cataclysmic tale.

Nouvelles Scènes de la Vie Future [*New Scenes Of A Future Life*] (France-Culture, 1981)
Dir: Georges Godebert; *Wri*: Dominique Kergall.
Story: People are programmed to die at age 75.

On A Sonné! [*Someone Rang!*] (France-Culture, 1981)
Dir: Jean-Jacques Vierne; *Wri*: Serge Martel.
Story: Several dreamers dream the same dream.

Où Est Donc La Nuit ? [*Where Is The Night?*] (France-Culture, 1980)
Dir: Anne Lemaître; *Wri*: Marian Georges Valentini.
Story: A post-cataclysmic tale.

Le Péril Vert [*The Green Peril*] (France-Culture, 1980)
Dir: Jeanne Rollin Weisz; *Wri*: Serge Martel, Pierre Dupriez.
Story: Deprived of oxygen, plants find a way to steal it from humans.

La Peste Blanche [*The White Plague*] (France-Culture, 1980)
Dir/Wri: Jean-Wilfrid Garrett.
Story: The world ends in bacteriological war.

Le Premier Matin [*The First Morning*] (France-Culture, 1981)
Dir/Wri: Jean Couturier based on a story by Jan Potocki.

Quelques Instants de la Vie de mon Concierge [*Some Instants In The Life Of My Concierge*] (France-Inter, 1981)
Dir: Georges Godebert; *Wri*: Michèle Angot.
Story: Dracula as a Parisian concierge.

Rendez-Vous avec le Démon [*Rendezvous With The Devil*] (RTF, 9 December 1958)
Wri: Jean-Louis Bouquet.

Une Soirée Comme Les Autres [*An Evening Like Any Other*] (France-Culture, 1972)
Dir: Unknown; *Wri*: Jacques Sternberg.
Story: Social satire.

Sous un Ciel Couleur d'Aubergine [*Under An Aubergine-Colored Sky*] (France-Culture, 1967)
Dir: Unknown; *Wri*: Roger Blondel.
Story: Alien encounter.
Note: Roger Blondel wrote numerous science fiction novels under the pseudonym B.-R. Bruss.

Le Tabernacle [*The Tabernacle*] (France-Culture, 1968)
Dir: Unknown; *Wri*: André Quéderosse.
Story: Post-cataclysmic story.

Tête à Tête [*Head To Head*] (France-Culture, 1981)
Dir: Jean-Jacques Vierne; *Wri*: Maurice Toesca.
Story: After having his limbs amputed, a British Naval officer survives as an immortal head.

Le Trio, ou Le Triomphe de la Mécanique [*Triangle, or The Triumph Of Machines*] (France-Inter, 1981)
Dir: Georges Gravier; *Wri*: Daniel Goldenberg.
Story: Robots in love.

Les Trois Cases Blanches [*The Three White Squares*] (France-Culture, 1980)
Dir: Jean-Pierre Colas; *Wri*: Alain Didier.
Story: Three people are mysteriously omitted from a telephone directory.

3, Rue Bréa [*3, Brea Street*] (France-Culture, 1981)

Dir: Jean-Jacques Vierne; *Wri*: Bernard Mazeas.
Story: In a strange city, everyone is named Berthier, lives at the same address and works at the same job.

Les Yaquils (France-Culture, 1967)
Dir: Unknown; *Wri*: Emmanuel Robles.
Story: Social satire.

FRANCIS BLANCHE & PIERRE DAC
LE GRUYERE QUI TUE

roman

JClattès

Index

A.D.G., 48
Abdelmalek, Bellamine, 61
Abiteboul, Michaël, 110
Ablanalp, Armand, 103
Abulescu, Mircea, 185
Achache, Mona, 107
Ackermann, Kathrin, 19, 20
Adam, Alfred, 183
Adda, Fabien, 110
Adkins, Scott, 98
Agacinski, Sophie, 20
Agogué, Raphaëlle, 101
Agostini, Philippe, 146, 160
Aickman, Robert, 137
Aknine, Pierre, 107, 142
Alane, Bernard, 50, 84, 144
Alari, Nadine, 18, 112
Alba, Christian, 124
Albani, F., 186
Albany, Fernande, 172
Albert, Didier, 102
Albin, Valentine, 186
Albray, Muse d', 116
Alcorta, Gloria, 223
Alcover, Catherine, 50
Aldani, Lino, 216
Alers, Christian, 183

Alexandrakis, Claire, 71, 72
Alexandre, Michel, 97
Alexandre, Michèle, 77
Alfonsi, Philippe, 117
Alibert, Jean, 134
Allain, Marcel, 12, 63, 64
Allan, Arthur, 40, 172
Allemane, Benoît, 148
Allières, Annick, 35
Alma, Gil, 108
Alone, René, 36, 144
Alric, Catherine, 24
Alric, Jacques, 129
Alvarez, Isaac, 37
Alvaro, Anne, 167
Alyx, Karen, 120
Amamra, Mounir, 133
Amamra, Oulaya, 133
Amat, Christine, 118
Amato, Jean-Marie, 207
Amédée, 127
Amel, Pascal, 198
Amidou, Souad, 79
Amoussou, Ralph, 99
Amyl, Jean-Claude, 149
Amyl, Max, 31
Anconina, Richard, 175
Andersen, Hans Christian, 146, 176, 178
Andrae, Manfred, 53
André, Robert, 18

Andreani, Jean-Pierre, 45
Andrevon, Jean-Pierre, 56, 185, 186
Andrews, Natasha, 99
Andrieu, Michel, 164
Andrieux, Roger, 54
Anémone, 69, 168
Anfousse, Lisette, 107
Anglade, Jean-Hugues, 135
Angot, Michèle, 178, 239
Anscutter, Julien, 108
Antoine, Jacques, 194, 232
Anton, Jacques, 166
Anys, Georgette, 138
Arasse, Jenny, 33, 106, 166, 181
Arbessier, Louis, 19
Arbet, Alix, 134
Arcanel, Yves, 148
Arcangues, Guy d', 164
Ardant, Fanny, 76, 102
Ardant, Frédéric, 174
Arden, Dominique, 174
Ardisson, Edmond, 153
Arditi, Pierre, 181
Arenal, Jacqueline, 27
Ariel, Hariette, 17
Arlaud, J. M., 40, 41, 44
Arlaud, Rodolphe-Maurice, 168
Armand, Jacques, 19, 36, 78, 104
Armand, Pierre, 115
Armontel, Roland, 43, 78, 109

Arnal, Philippe, 117
Arnaud, Claude Main, 123
Arnaud, Françoise, 52
Arnaud, Jean-Yves, 51
Arnaut, Robert, 212, 217
Arnold, Cécile, 182
Arnold, H. F., 151, 152
Arnoul, Françoise, 35, 159
Arnoux, Alexandre, 215
Arnulf, Christophe, 71
Arrieu, René, 80, 172
Artamonov, Julia, 145
Artarit, Régine, 40, 41, 42, 43
Arthapignet, Émilie, 70
Asimov, Isaac, 206
Aslan, Grégoire, 182
Assié, Victor, 15
Assumçao, Patrick d', 80
Astier, Alexandre, 71, 84, 85, 89, 90
Astier, Lionnel, 69, 70, 84, 89, 134
Astier, Simon, 70, 71, 72, 73, 84, 101, 136
Astruc, Alexandre, 23, 76, 178
Astruc, Jenny, 144
Atkine, Féodor, 60, 79, 136, 163
Atlas, Georges, 32, 34
Attal, Henri, 77
Attal, Madeleine, 236, 237, 238
Attal, Yvan, 15
Aubert, Benoît d', 175
Aubert, Clément, 99

Aubert, Georges, 133
Aubert, Yves, 171
Aubray, Raymonde, 186
Aubry, Alexandre, 161
Auclair, Maurice, 118
Auclair, Michel, 57
Audhuy, Christine, 131
Audibert, Mireille, 48
Audier, Marc, 126
Audoir, Jacques, 141
Audouard, Marc, 229
Audret, Pascale, 173, 181
Auger, Christian, 134
Auger, Michel, 33
August, Amadeus, 111
Aussir, Cédric, 207
Avanac, Jacques, 26, 27, 28
Aveline, Claude, 212
Averty, Jean-Christophe, 49, 142, 148, 166
Avril, Claude, 167
Avron, Philippe, 147
Ayadi, Naidra, 108
Aymard, Brigitte, 64, 66
Aymé, Danièle, 176
Aymé, Marcel, 11, 33, 34, 52, 146, 158, 172, 175
Azabal, Lubna, 104, 128
Azemar, Frédéric, 82
Azevedo, Gilberto, 150
Azoulay, Anne, 15
Ba, Pennda, 51
Babel, Armand, 82
Babilée, Yann, 28, 149
Bach, Simone, 29
Bachelier, Louvia, 51

Bachschmidt, Fritz, 25
Bacque, Jean, 172
Bacri, Jean-Pierre, 184, 186
Badel, Anne, 107
Badel, Pierre, 73, 74, 80, 130, 131, 143, 172, 186
Badie, Laurence, 101, 115
Baetens, Veerle, 30
Bagot, Jean-Pierre, 150
Baillet, Raymond, 138
Bailleul, Maxime, 82
Baillot, Quentin, 73
Baillou, Alfred, 158
Bailly, Raymond, 39, 40
Bairam, Clément, 131
Bajraktaraj, Arben, 99
Baker, Bob, 137
Balachova, Tania, 114, 144
Balard, Jean-Claude, 44
Balasuriya, Laura, 73
Baldi, Marcello, 19
Balembois, Jean-Marie, 124
Ballac, Geneviève, 213
Ballard, J. G., 145
Balme, Karyn, 45
Balp, Bruno, 184
Baltauss, Christian, 160
Balutin, Jacques, 18, 136, 142, 234
Balzac, Honoré de, 169, 175, 179
Bancou, Pascal, 64
Banderet, Pierre, 134
Baptiste, Muriel, 132

Baquet, Maurice, 176
Barbé, Marc, 114
Barbey d'Aurevilly, Jules, 152, 198, 225
Barbey, Mathieu, 78
Barbier, Christian, 117, 125, 163, 169
Barbier, Gilette, 70
Barbier, Stéphane, 65, 66
Barbulée, Madeleine, 168, 178, 183
Bardem, Juan Antonio, 81
Bardem, Rafaël, 81
Bardi, Angelo, 138
Bardollet, Michèle, 136
Bardoulat, Maurice, 236, 237, 238
Bardy, Philippe, 202
Barel, Hervé, 160
Barell, Renée, 70
Barge, Paul, 167, 179
Barham, Richard Harris, 182
Barino, Vittorio, 24, 27
Barjac, Sophie, 24
Barjavel, René, 68, 187, 215
Barjon, Lucien, 144, 173
Barlier, Alexia, 58
Barma, Claude, 12, 16, 36, 147
Barnes, Steven, 180
Barney, Jean, 132
Barone, Carina, 111
Baroude, Patrick, 118
Barraco, Adriano, 19
Barrat, Raymond, 170

Barrault, Jean-Louis, 184
Barrault, Marie-Christine, 165, 185
Barré, Robert, 41
Barrie, James, 204
Barrio, Sebastian, 104
Barroux, Alain, 202, 216, 218, 219, 220, 221, 223
Barry, Jacques de, 147
Barsacq, Yves, 43
Barthélémy, Olivier, 58
Bas, Philippe, 68
Basedow, Rainer, 59
Baslé, Hervé, 146
Baslé, Pierre, 146
Basler, Marianne, 156
Bassis, Antarès, 128
Bastid, Jean-Pierre, 159
Bastide, François-Régis, 174, 185
Bastien, Fanny, 60
Bats, Guillaume, 73
Battaglia, Rik, 81
Bauchau, Patrick, 102
Baud, Antoine, 134
Baugin, Eric, 146
Baxter, Lindsey, 137
Baye, Nathalie, 104
Bazin, Hervé, 162
Béalu, Marcel, 219, 224
Béart, Emmanuelle, 168
Beauchamps, Edmond, 117
Beaumont, Claire de, 169
Beaumont, Paule de, 50, 116, 152, 185
Beaune, Caroline, 120

Beaune, Michel, 112
Becker, Hugo, 107
Becker, Rolf & Alexandra, 19, 20, 22, 23
Beckmann, Franck, 73
Begovic, Ena, 26
Behat, Gilles, 53
Béjart, Maurice, 125, 126, 127, 128
Bekhti, Leïla, 142
Bel, Frédérique, 98, 120
Belhousse, Yacine, 55
Belko., Aurélie, 107
Belland, Loïc, 134
Belle, David, 98
Bellon, Loleh, 131, 180
Belvedere, Vittoria, 28
Ben Gharbia, Khalil, 114
Benchetrit, Samuel, 114
Benedek, Patrick, 121
Beneyton, Yves, 81, 170
Bennett, Elsa, 51
Benoît, Daniel, 123
Benoit, Denis, 184
Benoit, Denise, 129
Benoît, Nadine, 48
Benoît, Pierre, 143
Bens, Jacques, 228
Bento, Serge, 34
Bénureau, Didier, 70
Béranger, Anne, 96, 115
Berard, Jack, 43
Bérard, Jacques, 124
Berenson, Marisa, 102
Berg, Julius, 107
Bergé, Francine, 112
Bergé, Paul, 173
Berger, Éric, 82
Berger, Helmut, 63
Berger, Jean, 50, 146, 151
Berger, Joachim, 167
Berger, Pascale, 132, 180
Bergeron, Maxime, 108
Bergeron, Mireille, 124
Bergier, Jacques, 30, 31, 32
Berliner, Alain, 176
Berling, Charles, 82, 128
Berlioz, Jacques, 155
Berlot, Georges, 22
Berman, Marc, 119
Bernan, René, 181
Bernard , Paul, 147
Bernard, Dominique, 116
Bernard, Jean-Jacques, 186
Bernard, Jean-Pierre, 70, 165
Bernard, Jean-Toussaint, 99
Bernard, Jérémy, 61
Bernard, Ludovic, 29
Bernard, Roland, 173
Bernardi, Mario, 19
Bernard-Sugy, Christine, 200, 205, 207
Bernède, Arthur, 12, 36
Berner, Gérard, 132, 157
Bernhard, Edmond, 125
Bernheim-Dennery, Arauna, 128
Bernicat, Jean-Marie, 76
Berno, Nicolas, 73

Berry, Dennis, 96
Berry, Etienne, 117
Berry, Marilou, 170
Berry, Serge, 23
Berset, Fernand, 146, 152
Berteau, Alain, 74
Berthe, Frédéric, 51
Berthier, Jacques, 33, 143
Berthier, Michel, 133
Bertholier, Christine, 105
Bertin, Anne, 161
Bertin, Françoise, 52
Bertin, Jérôme, 59
Bertin, Roland, 56
Berto, Juliet, 77, 159
Bertrand, Aline, 179
Bertrand, Martine, 127
Berzosa, José-Maria, 152
Besnaïnou, Carla, 145
Besnard, Jacques, 24
Besse, Anne-Marie, 152
Besson, Patrick, 24, 228, 230
Bessou, Marc, 124
Beuf, Géo, 31
Bia, Ambroise, 81
Bialkowski, Tomacz, 152
Bierce, Ambrose, 213
Bierry, Etienne, 117, 168
Bilis, Teddy, 18, 133
Billard, Pierre, 236
Billetdoux, Virginie, 149
Billon, Pierre, 28
Bills, Teddy, 184
Binard, Arnaud, 58, 102
Bion, Joël, 132
Bioy Casares, Adolfo, 164

Biraud, Maurice, 23, 175, 207
Birckel, Catherine, 221
Bisciglia, Paul, 112, 121, 138, 179
Bisson, Dorian, 72
Bisson, Jean-Pierre, 173
Bista, Henryk, 26
Bitton, Gérard, 65, 67, 68
Black, Noel, 180
Blackwood, Algernon, 221
Blaess, Régine, 169, 173
Blaise, Jean, 61
Blaise, Paul, 97
Blanc, Henry, 211
Blanc-Francard, Patrice, 203
Blanchard, Aude, 71
Blanche, Francis, 142, 207, 208, 210
Blanche, Louis, 207
Blanco, Maria, 25, 103
Blanguenon, Karen, 142
Blin, Roger, 172, 176, 178
Blondeau, Jacques, 212
Blondeau, Jacques Adrien, 217
Blondeau, Lucien, 161
Blondel, Roger, 143, 240
Blot, Anne-Marie, 164
Bluwal, Marcel, 146, 163
Bodin, Pierre, 196
Bodin, Samuel, 97
Boëglin, Bruino, 85
Bogaert, Lucienne, 144
Böhm, Christine, 22

Boidron, Emmanuelle, 109
Boidron, Maxime, 146
Boileau-Narcejac, 143
Boisrond, Michel, 24, 25
Boisselier, Julien, 51, 135, 156
Boissery, Jean, 83
Boisset, Yves, 113
Boissier, Denis, 207
Boissol, Claude, 30, 31, 32, 33
Boisson, Christine, 146
Boivin, Ginette, 121
Bollery, Jean, 105
Bolo, Pierre, 48
Bona, Julie de, 97
Bonitzer, Agathe, 107
Bonjean, Hervé, 154
Bonnafé, Jacques, 138
Bonnardot, Claude-Jean, 164
Bonnet, Manuel, 149
Bonnín, Hermann, 26
Bordier, Claude, 135
Borel, Petrus, 196
Borgeaud, Nelly, 165
Borrel, Marie, 231
Bosco, Léa, 145
Bossair, Georges, 125
Bossis, Héléna, 36
Bot, Emmanuelle, 154
Boublil, Max, 135
Boucaron, Gérard, 157
Bouchard, Louise Anne, 123
Bouchard, Yvon, 17, 122

Bouchery, Claude, 159
Bouclet, Philippe, 111
Boudet, Alain, 83, 130, 131, 132, 170, 172
Boudet, Jacques, 24
Boudjera, Mohamed, 25
Bouglione-Romanès, Delia, 145
Bouillaud, Jean-Claude, 79, 136, 146
Bouillette, Christian, 57
Bouillon, Bruno, 60
Bouise, Jean, 103, 106, 146, 187
Boujenah, Lucie, 97
Boukhanef, Kader, 159
Boulanger, Armande, 110
Boulanger, Pierre, 118, 177
Boulet, Denise, 124
Boulle, Pierre, 215, 222
Bouquet, Jean-Louis, 142, 239
Bouquet, Michel, 149, 181, 202, 220, 224
Bourbon, Maurice, 105, 129
Bourdet, Catherine, 206
Bourgeois, Albert, 173
Bourgine, Elisabeth, 57
Bourgoin, Sylvie, 131
Bourguine, Elisabeth, 74
Boury, Agnès, 70
Bousquet, Jean, 148
Boutron, Pierre, 149, 152, 153, 165

Boutté, Jean-Luc, 152, 177
Bouveron, Christian, 65, 66
Bouvette, Alain, 186
Bouvier, Jean, 165
Bouy, Stéphane, 102, 104, 180
Bouzid, Jean, 152
Bovay, Georges-Michel, 232
Bovloc, René, 23
Bowen, Christopher, 111
Boyer, Marie-France, 112
Boyer, Myriam, 172
Bozzuffi, Marcel, 56
Brabo, Michèle, 16
Brac, Virginie, 101
Brach, Gérard, 154, 173
Brach, Jean, 226, 228
Bracho, Diana, 75
Bradbury, Ray, 149, 212, 214
Brainville, Yves, 172
Brändström, Charlotte, 154
Brandt, Carlo, 85
Bransolle, Jacques, 198
Brant, René, 211, 212, 216, 219, 221
Braoudé, Patrick, 182
Brasseur, Claude, 45, 146
Brasseur, Pierre, 45, 113
Bray, Geneviève, 132, 198, 236
Bréal, Sylvie, 61
Breillat, Catherine, 144
Breillat, Marie-Hélène, 77, 78
Brel, Jacques, 125, 126, 127
Brel, Stéphane, 101
Bremans, Gilbert, 127
Bresch, Manon, 101
Bressy, Jacqueline, 166
Bret, Roxane, 61
Breteuil, Martine de, 78
Breton, Marie-Claude, 43, 52
Brialy, Jean-Claude, 23, 159
Briat, Guillaume, 85
Briault, François, 73
Bricard, Patrick, 135
Brière, Florence, 109
Brigaud, Philippe, 33
Brion, Françoise, 79
Brion, Marcel, 168
Brione, Benoist, 106
Briquet, Sacha, 23
Brisebois, Eric, 37, 123
Brisville, Jean-Claude, 173
Broche, Olivier, 108
Brook, Irina, 181
Brook, Kelly, 98
Brouer, Jerry, 31
Bru, Paul, 150
Brulé, Claude, 18, 20, 21, 22
Brunaux, Olivia, 149
Brunet-Schneider, Philippe, 226
Bruni, Roberto, 78

Brunier, Yves, 135
Brunius, Jacques-Bernard, 223
Brunner, Alexandre, 154
Bruno, Fabrice, 101
Bruno, Jean, 118
Brunot, Jean-Pierre, 70
Bruss, B.-R., 143, 240
Brussolo, Serge, 166
Bruzat, Michel, 121
Bucci, Flavio, 119
Buchegger, Christine, 20
Buhr, Gérard, 23
Bujeau, Christian, 70, 84
Bulgakov, Mikhail, 236
Bunel, Marie, 60, 148, 173
Buñuel, Juan Luis, 57, 63, 75, 78
Buñuel, Luis, 75
Bureau, Pierre, 168
Bureau, Yves, 50
Burgel, Patrick, 111
Burnand, Jacqueline, 118
Bussières, Raymond, 50, 106, 153
Butler, Yvan, 53
Buyle, Evelyne, 187
Buzzati, Dino, 212, 214
Cabanis, Jean-Charles, 150
Cadena, Jordi, 26
Caillaud, Gérard, 53
Cailley, Thomas, 15, 128
Caillois, Roger, 61
Calatayud, Jacky, 36, 42
Callas, Patricia, 162
Caltagirone, José, 107
Calve, Jean, 129
Calvé, Jean-François, 70
Calvet, Roberto, 58
Calvi, Gérard, 120
Cambo, Paul, 36
Cammermans, Paul, 19
Camoin, Cora, 16
Camoin, Gérard, 135
Campanacci, Alexandra, 51
Campillo, Robin, 110
Campion, Cris, 69
Campion, Léo, 44, 101, 162
Campos, Alexis, 134
Candé, Jacques de, 66
Canolle, Jean, 17
Canovas, Anne, 68, 69, 134, 167
Cantien, Grégory, 65, 66
Cantin, Roger, 122, 123
Canuyt, Sacha, 80
Cap, Jean-Louis, 105
Capelluto, Laurent, 100
Capillery, Franck, 26
Capotondi, Cristiana, 170
Capponi, Pier Paolo, 28
Caprioli, Vittorio, 75, 76
Cara, Bernard, 142, 148, 173
Cara, Raffaela, 19
Caragiale, Ion Luca, 216
Cardinski, Juliette, 133
Carel, Roger, 17, 34, 35, 52, 120, 138, 144, 149, 158, 183, 187, 193, 195, 234

Carette, Bruno, 105
Carle, Sophie, 37, 138
Carlisi, Olympia, 84
Carmet, Jean, 60, 119, 153
Carmona, Christophe, 51
Carney, Matt, 102
Caroit, Philippe, 53
Caron, Claude, 153
Caron, Mine, 124
Caron, Richard, 28
Carrat, Gérard, 151
Carré, Gérard, 185
Carrer, Emilio, 43
Carrère, Anne, 43
Carrère, Christine, 147
Carrère, Emmanuel, 110
Carrié, Céline, 65
Carrière, Anne-Marie, 138
Carrière, Bruno, 122, 123
Carrière, Jean-Claude, 60, 153, 164, 165, 176
Carrière, Mathieu, 69, 76, 83
Carrière, Nicole, 60
Carroll, Lewis, 142
Cartier, Caroline, 170
Carton, Pauline, 207
Carvajal-Alegria, Esteban, 80
Caseneuve, Gilbert, 212, 214, 216, 218
Casey, Marie-Pierre, 69
Casile, Geneviève, 172
Casini, Stefania, 57
Cassagne, Michel, 118, 151
Cassan, Marguerite, 48, 52, 205, 213, 215, 218, 220, 222
Cassignard, Pierre, 141
Cassot, Marc, 132
Casta, Ange, 182
Casta, Marie-Ange, 135
Castelnau, Véronique, 61
Castelot, Jacques, 186
Cathelin, Jean, 172
Cattand, Gabriel, 60
Cattani, Sophie, 104, 135
Caude, Louis-François, 153
Caudry, Anne, 170, 187
Caunant, Charles, 121
Caunes, Antoine de, 84
Caunes, Georges de, 138
Caussimon, Céline, 67
Caussimon, Jean-Roger, 49, 116, 117, 148, 167, 180, 185, 224
Cavalli, Marina Giulia, 28
Cavalli, Valeria, 59, 85, 109
Cavassilas, Pierre, 142, 184
Cavayé, Fred, 104
Cayatte, André, 68
Cazenave, Anne, 80
Cazeneuve, Maurice, 147
Cazotte, Jacques, 236
Ceccaldi, Daniel, 120, 187
Cecil, Jonathan, 137
Cellier, Caroline, 77, 114, 187
Cerisola, Thomas, 69

Certain, Solange, 183
Cerval, Claude, 41, 184
Ceurworst, Joe, 199
Ceyleron, Bernard, 112
Chabartier, Pierre, 162
Chabat, Alain, 105
Chabrol, Claude, 63, 64, 75, 76, 77, 83, 118
Chalonge, Christian de, 77
Chamarat, Georges, 129
Chambon, Jacques, 84
Chambon, Luc, 85
Chamisso, Adalbert von, 160
Champel, Marcel, 48, 129, 132
Champion, Jean, 113
Champreux, Jacques, 12, 50, 78, 81
Chanteux, Sylvie, 30, 59, 107, 133
Chapelle, Monique, 178
Chaplin, Geraldine, 30
Chaplin, Josephine, 75, 78
Chapuis, Alain, 85
Charby, Jacques, 123
Charlan, Bernard, 42
Charlet, Sylvaine, 160
Charnacé, Bernard, 48, 162
Charnay, Jean-Claude, 123
Charon, Jacques, 115
Charon, Marie-Bénédicte, 229
Charpak, André, 172
Charpentier, Luna, 145

Charraix, Isabelle, 134
Charras, Charles, 76
Charreyron, Antoine, 121
Charrier, Anne, 54
Chasseriaud, Zacharie, 54
Chassy-Poulay, Pierre-Arnaud de, 207
Château, Maurice, 158
Chatel, François, 103, 156
Chatelain, Georges, 180
Chauffard, René-Jean, 235
Chaulet, Georges, 64, 238
Chaumeau, André, 123
Chaumette, François, 31, 36, 136, 177
Chausse, Peter David, 145
Chauveron, André de, 158
Chauveron, Philippe de, 119
Chavasse, Paule, 202
Chazel, Marie-Anne, 186
Chazot, Robert, 134
Chedid, Andrée, 219
Chelton, Tsilla, 16, 141
Chenail, Roland, 33, 47
Chereau, Didier, 169
Chérino, Lénie, 110
Cherisey, Philippe de, 164
Cherreau, Didier, 188
Cherry, Helen, 137
Chesnais, Patrick, 57, 69, 85
Chesterton, G. K., 116, 201
Chevalier, Didier, 167
Chevalier, François, 25, 146

Chevallier, Alain, 17
Chevallier, François, 157
Chevallier, Martine, 82
Chevalme, Cédric, 59
Chevit, Maurice, 34, 174, 177, 232
Chevrais, François, 207
Chevrier, Jean, 165
Chiche, Gabriel, 107
Chiche, Louis, 107
Chiche, William, 107
Chilton, Gisèle, 16
Chodat, François, 36
Cholet, Antoine, 72
Chomel, Thomas, 108
Chouchan, Gérard, 180
Chouquet, Jean, 212, 217
Chraibi, Catherine, 221
Chrétien de Troyes, 165
Christian, Eva, 30
Christian, Frédéric, 213, 215, 217, 220, 227
Christianssens, Serge, 123
Christine, Théo, 58
Cinque, Gabriel, 50
Cir, Dominique, 226
Ciravegna, Nicole, 149
Ciriez, Catherine, 103
Cisife, Jean-Paul, 178
Cissé, Anne, 133
Civil, François, 46
Clair, Eléa, 58
Claisse, Georges, 75, 113, 169
Clancier, Jacqueline, 219
Claude, Francis, 83
Claudet, Bernard, 145

Clay, Philippe, 45, 159, 230, 238
Clay, Thérèse, 179
Clech, Yvonne, 49
Clément, Aurore, 137
Clément, Charles, 71
Clément, Suzanne, 133
Clémenti, Pierre, 76, 149, 154
Clermont, René, 112, 147, 187
Clève, Jenny, 142
Cocteau, Jean, 214
Coffinet, Anne-Marie, 169
Cohen, Ami, 99
Cohen, Hélène, 98
Cohen, Jonathan, 71, 73
Cohen, Michaël, 96
Dyrek, Fran, 50
Colant, Jean-Louis, 20
Colas, Jean-Pierre, 196, 198, 199, 220, 221, 222, 224, 240
Colin, Erik, 49
Collet, Odette, 148, 187
Collet, Pierre, 78
Colline, Paul, 158
Collins, Conny, 20
Collins, Wilkie, 204
Collombert, Laurent, 59
Colmant, Jean-Louis, 127
Colpi, Henri, 81
Condamines, Laura, 74
Condo, Anna, 24
Condroyer, Mariette, 27
Condroyer, Philippe, 24, 27, 174

Condurache, Dan, 185
Conio, Gérard, 203
Consigny, Anne, 110
Constantine, Eddie, 57, 119
Conte, Louise, 83, 129
Conti, Didier, 164, 215
Corbusier, Nelly, 128
Cordier, Antony, 108
Cordier, Arnaud, 58
Corne, Léonce, 84, 138
Cornet, Dominique, 124
Cornil, Christelle, 61
Cornu, Jacques-Gérard, 158
Corod, Michel, 118
Coroner, Gilles, 38, 39, 40, 41
Corot, Jacqueline, 112
Corraface, Georges, 59
Corsales, Antoine, 124
Cortazar, Julio, 76
Coryn, William, 74
Costa, Artur, 26
Coste, Jean, 103
Côté, Stéphan, 122
Cottençon, Fanny, 102
Couchard, Jean-Luc, 71
Coué, Jacqueline, 146
Coulombe, Carole, 158
Coumans, Thomas, 176
Courchesne, Marie-Andrée, 123
Courtemanche, Michel, 71
Courtois, Reine, 179
Courtois-Brieux, Jean, 69
Cousseau, Thomas, 84
Coussoneau, Philippe, 80
Coutterand, Leslie, 58
Coutteure, Ronny, 145
Couturier, Jean, 202, 239
Couty, Julien, 134
Couzinié, Jonathan, 80
Covillault, Jérémie, 51
Cowper, Nicola, 138
Cramer, Eléonore, 215, 237
Cramoisan, Guillaume, 58, 62, 109
Crampon, Alain, 160
Crampon, Julien, 97
Crauchet, Paul, 36, 129, 152, 159, 163, 164
Cravenne, Marcel, 182
Cravenne, Maurice, 12, 81, 109, 155, 161
Crayencour, Stéphanie, 177
Crelli, Anne, 41
Crémadès, Michel, 65, 66, 67
Crémieux, Henri, 78
Creton, Michel, 33, 172
Creusvaux, Marion, 85
Crochemore, Jean-Yves, 124
Crocitti, Vincenzo, 28
Crouzet, Roger, 49, 129, 133
Cruz, Carlos, 27
Cuche, Nicolas, 54
Cuny, Alain, 175
Cuq, Katia, 59
Curet, Raoul, 34, 70, 112

Curtis, Jean-Louis, 221
Curzi, Pierre, 122
Cuse, Carlton, 111
Cusy, Pierre, 237
Cuvelier, Marcel, 132, 174
Cvejic, Branko, 26
Cyr, Isabelle, 122
Cyrano de Bergerac, Hercule-Savinien, 235
D'Amour, Marie-Pierre A., 124
Da Costa, Bernard, 230
Dabry, Bernard, 113
Dac, Pierre, 195, 207, 208, 210
Dacla, Corinne, 156
Dacqmine, Jacques, 23, 76, 102, 179
Dacquin, Michel, 44
Dadelsen, Eric de, 162
Dadles, Robert, 166
Daëms, Marie, 183
Dahl, Roald, 228
Dahmen, Andrea, 23
Dalban, Robert, 32
Dalbray, Muse, 48, 185
Dalio, Marcel, 50, 172
Dalou, François, 70
Damain, Eric, 185
Damecour, Pierre-Antoine, 58
Damian, Elyette, 23
Damien, Gilbert, 97, 133
Damiens, Madeleine, 35, 130, 176

Danaud, Jean-Claude, 228, 231
Dancourt, Julia, 70
Dang Tran, Quoc, 82, 97, 104, 108
Daninos, Rugger de, 27
Danno, Jacqueline, 35, 148, 156, 171
Danot, Serge, 120, 121
Dansereau, Sophie, 124
Dantan, Maurice-Étienne, 226
Darah, Marie-Christine, 143
Darbon, François, 138, 179
Dard, Hippolyte, 51
Dargent, Clémence, 108
Darier, Gérard, 70
Darlan, Eva, 119
Darras, Jean-Pierre, 77, 120
Darrieu, Gérard, 134, 138, 160, 182, 216, 224
Darry, France, 146
Dary, René, 36, 50
Dasset, Claude, 207
Daubin, Jean-Jacques, 16
Daude, Gilles, 105
Dauphin, Jean-Claude, 162
Daurant, Jean, 234
Dave, Arlette, 197, 199, 213, 215, 219, 221, 222, 223, 225
David, Mario, 63
Davidson, Avram, 219

Daviot, Tiphaine, 97, 136
Davis, Robin, 59
Davray, Dominique, 172
De Ahna, Kerstin, 41
De Baerdemaeker, Hilde, 114
De Meyst, Émile-Georges, 127
De Prekel, Antoine, 102
De Santis, Louis, 33
Deban, Frédéric, 173
Debary, Jacques, 29, 131, 182
Debauche, Pierre, 168
Debeurme, Henri, 99
Debia, Laurence, 185
Deblin, Jean-Marie, 126
Deblock, François, 30
Debord, Claude, 145
Decaux, Alain, 129
Decourt, Jean-Pierre, 18, 97, 112
Deffin, Soizic, 69
Dega, Bruno, 135
Degliame, Claude, 21
Degrave, Jean, 112
Dehelly, Paula, 164
Dehors, Olivier, 58
Dekock, Alain, 112
Del, Eric, 123
Deladonchamps, Pierre, 128
Delafosse, Éric, 55
Delahalle, France, 138, 147
Delair, Suzy, 124
Delaître, Didier, 62

Delannoy, Philippe, 24, 25, 26, 27, 28
Delarme, Julie, 161
Delaroche, Christine, 36, 115
Delarue, Marie, 117
Delasoie, Gilbert, 124
Delaunay, Guy, 197, 214, 215, 217, 221, 222, 223
Delbat, Germaine, 83, 109
Delbo, Jean-Jacques, 162
Delbourg, Véronique, 63, 78
Delfau, Pauline, 173
Delfosse, Raoul, 44, 50
Delgado, Michel, 142, 169
Delire, Jean, 125, 126, 127
Delorme, Danièle, 171
Delpeyrat, Scali, 175
Delrieux, David, 109, 156
Delsaert, Marc, 175
Delterme, Marine, 185, 186
Deman, Alexandra, 176
Demarch, Aimé, 113
Demarty, Joël, 69
Demas, Georges, 44
Demay, Henri, 16
Demo, Karine de, 169
Demolon, Pascal, 72
Demongeot, Mylène, 186
Denberg, Arthur, 149
Denie, Danièle, 125, 127
Denieul, Anne, 180
Denis, Jacques, 53
Denizot, Gérard, 131, 133, 150

Denner, Charles, 168
Dentès, Suzanne, 183
Dentzler, Erika, 183
Deny, Pierre, 69
Denys, Claude, 39, 42, 43
Depardieu, Gérard, 150
Depraz, Xavier, 174
Derenne, Pierre, 175
Deret, Jean-Claude, 16
Dermo, Pierre, 128
Deroisy, Lucien, 126
Derrez, Philippe, 195, 197, 206, 220, 225
Desagnat, Jean-Pierre, 20, 21, 22, 23
Desagnat, Vincent, 136
Desailly, Claude, 59, 78, 135
Desailly, Marcel, 78
Desarnauts, Virginie, 59
Desarthe, Dante, 175
Desarthe, Gérard, 74, 103, 167
Descamps, Patrick, 121
Descaux, France, 224
Descaves, Jean-Louis, 158
Deschamps, Charles, 183
Deschamps, Hubert, 23, 32, 112, 142, 174, 176
Deschamps, Maurice, 134
Deschamps, Olivier, 148
Descraques, François, 55
Desjardins, Guillaume, 61
Desmare, RFoger, 50
Despaux, Julien, 114
Despuech, Valérie, 135
Desrau, Max, 32, 185

Desroches, Agnès, 173
Dessailly, Nicole, 33
Destailles, Pierre, 74
Desvallées, André, 130, 132
Detcheva, Malina, 102
Deval, Jacques, 147
Devime, Raymond, 36
Devoldère, Bruno, 158
Devos, Raymond, 207
Dewaere, Lola, 58
Dewaere, Patrick, 182
Dewolf, Patrick, 97
Dhénault, Alain, 117
Dhéran, Bernard, 20
Dhouailly, Alain, 173
Diamant, Elise, 108
Dick, Philip K., 152, 206
Dickens, Charles, 116, 149, 219
Didelot, Francis, 220, 222
Didier, Alain, 240
Didier, Pierre, 185
Diefenthal, Frédéric, 54
Dietl, Jurad, 119
Dietrich, Wolf, 20, 22
Dieudonné, Hélène, 130, 156
Diffring, Anton, 102
Dillane, Richard, 80
Dillys, Manon, 62
Dimey, Dominique, 153
Dion, Paul, 122
Diop, Aïssatou, 29, 121
Disiz, 71
Divorne, Gilbert, 118
Dneprov, Anatoly, 217

Doat, Jean, 218
Doazan, Aurelle, 111, 147
Dobie, Alan, 137
Dobtcheff, Vernon, 141
Doelnitz, Max, 76
Dol, Juliette, 114
Doll, Dora, 154, 168
Dolmaire, Quentin, 108
Dombasle, Arielle, 75
Dompnier, Marie, 58, 175
Dona, Tamara, 27
Donnadieu, Bernard-Pierre, 69, 166
Donnadieu, Ingrid, 51
Donzelli, Valérie, 104
Doris, Pierre, 35
Dorival, Jeanne, 207
Dorner, Françoise, 129, 165
Dorysse, Françoise, 124
Douaire, Martin, 108
Douay, Serge, 217, 218, 219
Douchka, 132
Douchkine, Gabriel, 229
Douglas, Pierre, 63
Dougnac, France, 49, 177
Douieb, Laurent, 48
Doumbia, Issa, 177
Doumerg, Jo, 121
Doutey, Alain, 117, 153, 187
Doutey, Mélanie, 114
Doyle, Arthur Conan, 197, 202, 207, 223
Dress, Evelyne, 22, 150
Dréville, Jean, 12, 138

Drevon, Josée, 70, 84
Drimal, Joseph, 148, 151, 171
Dromgoole, Patrick, 137
Drouot, Jean-Claude, 75, 115, 180, 181
Du Bois, Victoire, 97
Dubart, Marvin, 101
Dubernet, Isabeklle, 66
Dubois, Jean-Pol, 53
Dubois, Marie, 144, 178
Dubois, Pierre, 160
Dubost, Paulette, 115, 166
Duby, Jacques, 106, 171, 188
Duc, Christian, 121
Duc, Hélène, 63, 131
Ducados, Coco, 75
Ducharme, Camille, 47
Duchâteau, Renée, 180
Duchaussoy, Michel, 60, 77, 97, 115
Duchez, Serge, 130
Duclos, Philippe, 74, 161
Ducol, Jennifer, 134
Ducommun, Fabien, 107
Ducorps, Servane, 152
Ducrest, Philippe, 61
Ducret, Arnaud, 177
Dufer, Laetitia, 125
Duffel, Peter, 137
Dufilho, Jacques, 63, 146, 154, 225
Dufour, Thierry, 49
Dufresne, Claude, 200, 230
Duggan, Tom, 116

Dugowson, Maurice, 159
Duguay, Annie, 158
Duléry, Antoine, 27, 62
Dumaine, Bernard, 146
Dumas, Alexandre, 84, 200
Dumas, André, 179
Dumayet, Françoise, 181
Dumayet, Jean-Luc, 16
Dumayet, Pierre, 16, 147
Dumet, Marie-Blanche, 226
Dumur, Pierre, 123
Dunoyer, François, 23, 26, 49, 79, 109
Dupas, Benjamin, 133
Duperey, Anny, 45
Duplessis, Michel, 221
Dupont, Charlie, 175, 177
Dupont, Christiane, 182
Dupont, Claude, 212
Dupont, Manoël, 107
Dupont, Pascale, 122
Dupré, Françoise, 172
Dupriez, Pierre, 187, 203, 216, 218, 220, 239
Durand-Zouky, Nicolas, 59
Durieux, Léon, 135
Durin, Anne-Marie, 162
Duroy, Marie, 58
Durry, Christiane, 162
Duru, Frédéric, 59, 154
Dusaugey, Satya, 104
Duthion, Zoé, 54
Dutoit, Roger, 20
Duval, Jacques-Henry, 16

Duvall, Shelley, 56
Duvivier, Edgar, 178
Dux, Pierre, 53, 81, 171
Dynam, Jacques, 36, 112
Dyrek, François, 129
Eber, Victoria, 108
Eberhard, Fabrice, 185, 186
Écoffey, Jean-Philippe, 102
Efira, Virginie, 143
Ehrlich, Max, 199
Eïdo, Lilly, 71
Eine, Simon, 79
El Cohen, Rhizlaine, 145
El Maghraby, Essam, 29
El Mechri. Mabrouk, 104
El Zein, Judith, 82
Eliade, Mircea, 196
Elion, Loup-Denis, 98, 167
Elkabetz, Ronit, 128
Elliot, Yves, 143
Elso, Pascal, 69
Emilfork, Daniel, 48
Emmanuel, Jean, 227
Enard, Jean-Pierre, 124
Englander, Lucas, 99
Enrico, Robert, 179
Epaud, Fred, 170
Epiere, Germaine, 118
Epstein, Yan, 111
Erckmann-Chatrian, 150, 162, 171
Erhardy, Katherine, 38, 67, 68, 149
Erlanger, Dominique, 167

Ernotte, André, 128
Ertaud, Jacques, 172
Esposito, Gianni, 116, 127
Estange, Frank, 129
Etaix, Pierre, 154, 170
Etchea, Catherine d', 227
Etcheverry, Michel, 80, 81, 158
Etcheverry, Robert, 158
Etienne, Claude, 127
Étiévant, Yvette, 163
Evrard, Claude, 42
Ewers, Hanns Heiz, 156
Eynard, Marie, 108
Eyraud, Marc, 144
Fabbri, Jacques, 155, 166
Fabre, Maurice, 179
Facco, Fabienne, 59
Facon, Francis, 122
Fadel, Yvan, 126
Fague, Etienne, 70, 84
Failevic, Maurice, 164
Falavigna, Louis, 112
Falcon, André, 129
Falconetti, Gérard, 165
Falk, Suzy, 126
Fallet, René, 146, 172
Fansten, Jacques, 60
Fansten, Jérôme, 104
Farenc-Deramond, Julie, 55
Farmer, Philip José, 206
Farner, Ellen, 41
Farré, Jean-Paul, 37
Farrow, John, 217
Farrugia, Dominique, 105
Farwagi, André, 166

Faucher, Sophie, 124
Faudry, Anne, 175
Faure, André, 118
Faure, Brigitte, 104
Faurie, Jacques, 119
Faust, Dinah, 147, 150
Favard, Robert, 38
Favart, Michel, 60, 175
Favart, Robert, 175
Favey, Rosine, 174
Favier, Yves, 186
Fayol, Lily, 187
Fayolle, Marc, 157, 167
Fegyvères, Ivan, 114
Felsner, Ursule, 39
Fennec, Sylvie, 45, 163
Ferguson, Verell Pennington, 237
Ferjac, Anouk, 79, 131
Fernagut, Etienne, 118
Fernandez, Miguel, 69
Fernandez, Rosita, 145
Féron, Jean, 220
Ferréol, Andréa, 34
Ferrière, Jacques, 79
Ferrière, Martine, 131
Ferrus, Caroline, 84
Ferry, Jean, 180
Festraëts, Marion, 100
Feuga, Pierre, 213
Féval, Paul, 70, 97, 193
Fey, Stéphane, 179
Feyder, Véra, 216, 217, 219, 222
Fierry, Patrick, 60
Fila, Corentin, 101
Filippe, Jean-Teddy, 161

Filliozat, Jean-Denis, 60
Fink, Julia, 65
Finkielkraut, Thomas, 107
Fisher, Terrence, 58
Fisichella, Enzo, 78
Flaadt, Tony, 19
Flamand, Didier, 24
Flanigan, Joe, 98
Flateau, Joël, 181
Fleurot, Audrey, 61, 62, 69, 84
Fleury, Jean-José, 149
Flon, Suzanne, 185
Floran, Jacques, 156, 226
Florence, Jean, 201
Florent, Aniouta, 82, 83, 180
Flotats, José-Marie, 136
Flynn, Patrick, 154
Foïs, Marina, 46
Folliot, Yolande, 24, 109
Fombelle, Laetitia de, 110
Fontaine, Aimée, 142
Fontaine, Anne, 103
Fontaine, Bruno, 84
Fontaine, Edith, 207
Fontana, Richard, 104, 175
Fontanel, Geneviève, 60, 141, 163
Fontanel, Jacques, 70
Fontanet, Robert, 142
Fontanille, Pascal, 109
Fontenay, Vladimir de, 133
Forestier, Éric, 107
Forquet, Philippe, 102
Forrissier, Régis, 152
Forster, Nadine, 126
Fortin, Michel, 187
Fossey, Brigitte, 153
Foster, Barry, 137
Fouché, André, 42
Fouché, Audrey, 107
Foucher, Louis, 142
Fougerolles, Hélène de, 156
Foulon, Laurent, 177
Foulquier, Jean-Louis, 54, 155
Fourcade, Christian, 156
Foure, Sébastien, 97
Foures, Alain, 149
Fournier, Brice, 84
Fournier, Jean-Vincent, 97
Fox, Olivier, 104, 107
Frachon, James L., 120
Fraioli, Justine, 64
France, Ronald, 136
Francis, Clive, 137
Francis, Jean, 223
Franck, Alain, 213, 216
Franck, Pierre, 171
François, Claude, 115
François, Jacques, 44, 103, 161
François, Marc, 149
Françoise, Alain, 124
Franju, Georges, 12, 78
Frank, Nino, 212, 214, 215, 220, 222
Frankeur, Jean-Paul, 76
Frankeur, Paul, 172
Franklin, Eric, 23

Franquet, Sabine, 64
Franval, Jean, 39, 61, 173, 176
Frapier, François, 71
Frédérick, André, 120
Frémy, Evelyne, 193, 195, 201, 203, 205, 220, 223, 225
Fresnay, Pierre, 164, 171, 184
Freyd, Bernard, 79, 150, 159
Freyer, Biggi, 40
Friedman, Serge, 26
Froebe, Gert, 77, 78
Fröhlich, Josef, 19
Frohlich, Marieli, 64
Froidebise, Lucien, 125
Fromental, Jean-Luc, 79
Frydland, Maurice, 12, 103
Fuchs, Gaby, 111
Fuger, Robert, 162
Führer, Éric, 66
Gabin, Mata, 68
Gabion, Nicolas, 84
Gabrielli, Laetitia, 25
Gadebois, Grégory, 110
Gagnon, Hubert, 107
Gai, Claude, 122
Galabru, Michel, 187
Galbeau, Patrice, 223, 225
Galey, Jean-Marie, 175
Galipeau, Jacques, 119
Galland, Jacques, 75
Galland, Jean, 163
Gallet, Georges H., 233

Gallienne, Guillaume, 145
Galtier, Charles, 152
Galud, Gilles, 177
Gamond, Raoul, 57
Gandrey-Réty, Bernard, 204
Gantillon, Bruno, 59, 185
Ganzl, Serge, 168, 238
Garcia, Frédéric, 101
Garcia, Nicole, 108
Garcin, Ginette, 34, 157, 158, 187
Garcin, Henri, 153
Gardes, Renée, 130, 183
Garin, Julien, 134
Garland, Michel, 31
Garnier, Edith, 130
Garnier, Michel, 31
Garreaud, Jean-François, 37, 75, 168
Garrel, Maurice, 83, 129
Garrello, Stafania Orsola, 28
Garrett, Jean-Wilfrid, 213, 216, 217, 220, 225, 238, 239
Garrivier, Victor, 63, 74
Garry, Didier, 123
Gary, Micheline, 184
Gary, Nadia, 126, 127
Gascon, Gabriel, 28
Gascon, Jean, 17
Gastaldi, Jany, 168
Gat, György, 138
Gateau, Marguerite, 204
Gatineau, Pierre, 169
Gatterburg, Gail, 119

Gaudron, Didier, 59
Gaum, Ludwig, 109
Gaurin, Manon, 97
Gauthier, Vincent, 75
Gautier, Jean-Yves, 29
Gautier, Maurice, 36
Gautier, Théophile, 74
Gauvin, Réjean, 122
Gauvin, Robert, 122
Gay, Pierre, 194
Gayet, Julie, 97
Gazzolo, Nando, 24
Gébé, 179, 221, 222, 223
Gégauff, Paul, 57, 75, 77
Gélin, Daniel, 18, 212
Gélin, Hugo, 29
Gélin, Xavier, 117, 119
Gelinas, Gratien, 33
Geller, Pierre, 53
Genay, Julien, 47
Gence, Denise, 76
Gendron, François-Eric, 103, 134
Gennari, Geneviève, 223
Gens, Xavier, 101
Gensac, Claude, 109
Georgeot, Daniel, 162, 167, 171
Georgi, Marc de, 32, 130
Gérando, Marie-Pierre de, 143
Gerbaud, Guy, 132
Géret, Georges, 33, 103, 162
Gerken, Erik, 71
Germain, Greg, 169
Germinet, Gabriel, 237

Gérome, Raymond, 157
Gerout, Nicolas, 72
Gerrold, David, 56
Gessler, Rudolph, 102
Ghelderode, Michel de, 142, 167
Giafferi, Anne, 156
Gianotti, Anna, 123
Gignoux, Hubert, 50
Gilbert, Ariette, 129
Gilbert, Aurélie, 168
Gilbert, Charles, 225
Gilberti, Lilas-Rose, 30
Gillet, Jérémy, 82
Gilley, Jeremy, 137
Gillioz, Roger, 118
Gillot, Pascal, 146
Gilot, Yolande, 176
Gingembre, Jean-Guy, 65
Giordano, Arnaud, 60
Girard, Danièle, 83
Girard, Marcel, 122
Girard, Marianne, 112
Girardot, Ana, 110
Giraud, Claude, 78, 97
Giraud, Guy, 120
Giraud, Pierre, 142
Giraudeau, Bernard, 21, 83
Giret, Françoise, 32
Girouard, Anne, 84
Giroux, André, 17
Gisquière, Serge, 109
Giudicelli, Jean-Claude, 163
Gnilka, Walter, 42
Goasguen, Jacques, 50

Gobbi, Sergio, 54
Gobert, Fabrice, 110
Gobin, Gabriel, 42, 109
Godebert, Georges, 225, 237, 238, 239
Godet, Danielle, 57, 63
Godin, Jacques, 122
Gogol, Nikolai, 74, 194, 201, 219
Goimard, Jacques, 145
Goldenberg, Daniel, 24, 229, 231, 240
Gomes Devauchelle, Mickaël, 134
Gonsalez, Jean-Luc, 123
Gordeaux, Paul, 211
Goscinny, René, 193
Gossart, Jean-René, 82, 136
Gotlib, Marcel, 182
Gouix, Guillaume, 110
Goulard, Didier, 179
Goupil, Charles, 228
Goupil, Frédéric, 110
Goupil, Jeanne, 23, 59
Gourdon, Stéphane, 72
Gourmet, Olivier, 100
Goutas, Pierre, 16
Gouy, Antoine, 73
Gouzenne, René, 124
Govy, Georges, 215, 218
Graczyk, Bernard, 127
Grad, Geneviève, 115
Gradziel, Adrianna, 55, 99
Grammont, Georges, 20
Grandclaude, Claude, 125
Grandidier, Marcel, 171
Grandjouan, Jacques, 166
Grandsart, Delphine, 54
Grangier, Gilles, 59
Granier, Olivier, 151
Granotier, Sylvie, 137, 167
Gras, Jean, 17
Graveleau, Gilles, 85
Gravier, Georges, 212, 213, 222, 240
Gréco, Juliette, 36
Green, Julien, 182
Green, Marika, 22, 113, 116, 131, 158
Greggory, Pascal, 114
Grégorio, Annie, 109
Grello, Jacques, 80, 155, 178
Grenier, Roger, 76, 77, 83
Grenon, Macha, 123
Grigorieff, Nathan, 20, 21
Grimaldi, Eva, 27
Grimaldi, Sophie, 184
Grinberg, Barbara, 98
Grinberg, Claude, 168
Grinberg, Jean-Claude, 34, 50, 146
Gripari, Pierre, 7, 237
Gripel, Jacques, 172
Grisales, Amparo, 136
Grosso, Guy, 142, 148
Groulx, Richard, 123
Groyne, Pili, 121
Gruault, Jean, 113, 179
Grube, Hellmut, 43
Gruel, Armand, 154
Gruel, Brigitte, 154

Gruel, Emilie, 154
Gualdi, Pierre, 44, 52, 136
Gueble, Danièle, 144
Guedj, Vanessa, 84
Guei, Cyril, 72
Guélis, Jean, 120
Guemy, Jean-François, 122
Guérin, Gilles, 59
Guérin-Tillié, Stéphan, 69
Guerra, Ruy, 76
Guerrab, Soufiane, 29, 100, 135
Guerre, Claude, 200
Guers, Paul, 38, 68, 146, 187
Guertchikof, Louba, 186
Guesmi, Samir, 110
Guèvremont, Paul, 33
Guèvremont, Richard, 124
Guignard, Olivier, 121
Guillain, Bruno, 29
Guillaume, Gérard, 161
Guillaume, Laurent, 114
Guillaumin, Patrick, 132
Guillemot, Claude, 12, 44
Guillet, Michel, 171
Guillet, Raoul, 104, 131, 170
Guillo, Roger, 130
Guillot, Gilles, 70
Guinard, Philippe, 212, 214, 215, 216, 218, 219, 223
Guiomar, Julien, 112, 113, 161, 170
Guiot, Fernand, 166, 173

Guiraud, Stéphane, 185
Guisol, Henri, 84, 161
Guybet, Christophe, 66
Guybet, Henri, 154
Hacquard, Daphné, 58
Hadmar, Hervé, 30
Hagen, Mar celle, 221
Hagen, Marcelle, 222
Hahn, Hugo de, 234
Hahn, Jess, 32, 81
Haïm, Victor, 173
Hamel, Pascal, 230
Hamidi, Youcef, 58, 134
Hamilton, Charles, 224
Hammenecker, Jan, 100
Harari, Clément, 41, 78, 161, 173
Harden, Jacques, 32
Hardy, Linda, 155
Harrington, Prudence, 21
Harrouch, Victor, 28
Hart, Michel, 124
Hary, Elisabeth, 132
Hassoun, Deborah, 114
Hatet, Pierre, 129
Haudepin, Didier, 137
Haudepin, Sabine, 137, 174
Hauduroy, Jean-François, 222
Hauer, Rutger, 98
Haurey, Guy, 230
Hazanavicius, Raïka, 114
Hébert, Solène, 62
Heikin-Pepin, Nancy, 54
Heinlein, Robert A., 207
Heinzl, Anastasia, 108

Held, Raoul, 123, 124
Heliman, Thomas, 123
Hellens, Franz, 223
Heller, Dagmar, 22
Hembert, Jean-Christophe, 84
Henneberg, Nathalie, 213, 214
Hénon, Alexis, 84
Hentz, Pierre, 50
Heran, Daniel, 133
Herbert, Jean, 48, 50
Herbert, Sylvie, 168
Herce, Jean-Pierre, 130, 131
Herlin, Jacques, 119
Hernandez Boudet, Broselandia, 27
Hérold, Gérard, 184
Herpoux, Marc, 30
Herviale, Jeanne, 112
Hesme, Clotilde, 29, 110
Hettmann, Annabelle, 176
Hey, Yuming, 107
Heymann, Bernard, 118
Heynau, Jean, 112
Heynemann, Laurent, 57
Hiegel, Catherine, 161
Hiet, Sophie, 58, 128
Hill, Dedan, 122
Hilling, Jacques, 225
Hirsch, Jean-Claude, 134
Hirt, Eléonor, 137
Hiss, Nicole, 133
Hitchcock, George, 77
Hochet, Timothée, 46
Hoffmann, Catherine, 110

Hoffmann, E.T.A., 74, 181, 198
Hoffmann, Susanna, 24
Hogg, James, 201
Holdener, Pierre, 118
Holgado, Ticky, 119
Hollenbeck, Pierre-Alexis, 146
Holt, Hans, 20
Holterbach, Jean-Marie, 150
Homewood, Ben, 99
Hondo, Med, 32, 39
Honoré, Julien, 176
Hooymaayer, Sjoukje, 19
Horowicz, Bronislav, 201, 202
Horowicz, Bronislaw, 194, 201, 215, 219, 221, 223, 225, 235
Horrer, Olivier d', 215, 216, 220, 222, 225, 235
Hossein, Robert, 185
Houbé, Jean, 43, 172
Houlet, Gérard, 229
Houplain, Jules, 108
Houssin, Jacques, 79
Houssin, Joël, 54, 62, 159
Howard, Ronald, 181
Hoyle, Fred, 196
Hoyle, Geoffrey, 196
Hua, Khan, 123
Hubeau, Catherine, 142, 150, 202
Hubert, Jeannette, 181
Hubert, Jean-Pierre, 158, 159

Hubert, Lucien, 42
Hubert, Yves-André, 129, 132
Hubrenne, Beernard, 16
Hue, Huguette, 142
Hugo, Victor, 123, 199, 200
Hunebelle, André, 84
Hunnicut, Gayle, 63, 78
Hussenot, Olivier, 116, 155
Husson, Albert, 52, 131, 155, 161, 182
Hutin, Patrick, 67
Iacobesco, Loumi, 159
Idier, Jacques, 228
Iglésis, Roger, 17, 116, 147
Imbert, Laurence, 23, 153, 179
Imhof, Marcel, 83
Inkijinoff, Valery, 119
Interlenghi, Franco, 57
Inutine, Natacha, 148
Ionescu, Carmen, 185
Isker, Akim, 135
Isker, Myriam, 105
Issolah, Malik, 71
Ivoi, Paul d', 197
Izard, Christophe, 135
Jabbour, Gabriel, 57, 60, 74, 171
Jablonka, Simon, 107
Jackson, Shirley, 76, 77
Jacob, Jacques, 122
Jacobs, Delinda, 51
Jacobsen, Catherine, 45

Jade, Claude, 49, 81
Jakubisko, Jurad, 119
Jamain, Olivier, 59
Jamain, Patrick, 56
James, Henry, 179, 185
Jamet, Frédérique, 124
Jamiaque, Yves, 150, 200
Jampanoï, Mylène, 176
Janerand, Philippe du, 120, 152, 163
Janney, Georges, 181
Jansen, Maike, 131, 171
Jaquemont, Maurice, 106
Jaquet, Roger, 70
Jaquin, Abel, 147
Jarry, Annick, 151
Jatet, Pierre, 48
Jaubert, François, 31
Jawad, Saïda, 142
Jeanneret, Anaïs, 153
Jeanneret, Valérie, 154
Jean-Philippe, Claude, 44
Jeanson, Laure, 185
Jefford, Jacqueline, 129
Jendly, Roger, 175
Jentet, René, 216, 224, 238
Jeury, Michel, 163, 165
Jezequel, Julie, 118
Jiroyan, Arsène, 64
Joano, Clotilde, 150
Joffroy, Pierre, 220
Joirkin, Charlie, 51
Jolibois, Christian, 37
Jolly, Hervé, 138, 159
Jorré, Guy, 113

Jorris, Jean-Pierre, 116, 150
Josselin, Julien, 73
Jouannet, Thomas, 51
Joubert, Sylvain, 130
Jouf, Henri, 48
Jourdan, Catherine, 83
Jourdan, Eric, 35
Jourdan, Raymond, 70, 175
Jourde, Cédric, 122
Jousset, Bernard, 70
Joyet, Arnaud, 70, 71, 136
Joyeux, Odette, 146, 161
Jugnot, Arthur, 62
Jugnot, Gérard, 118, 142, 170
Juin, Hubert, 216, 220
Julien, André, 173
Julien, Pierre, 53
Jullian, Marcel, 111
Juvet, Nathalie, 49
Jyl, Laurence, 150
Kaack, Sabine, 25
Kady, Charlotte, 28
Kafka, Franz, 170
Kahane, Roger, 129
Kalfon, Jean-Pierre, 54, 79, 163
Kali, Salem, 109
Kamilindi, Gaël, 107
Kammenos, David, 58
Kammerscheit, Renée, 149
Kane, Carol, 137
Kané, Pascal, 150
Kantof, Albert, 24, 26, 27, 28
Kappes, Stéphane, 98, 169
Karyo, Tchéky, 114
Kassak, Fred, 230
Kassovitz, Mathieu, 46
Kassovitz, Peter, 53, 69, 74, 138
Kast, Pierre, 159, 206
Katajisto, Martti, 32
Kaufmann, Christine, 77
Kay, George, 29
Kaza, Elizabeth, 152
Kearns, Billy, 38, 102
Keigel, Léonard, 29
Keim, Claire, 62
Keita, Daouda, 101
Keller, Marthe, 17, 109, 137
Kellerson, Philippe, 133
Kempf, Tobias, 151
Kenny, Paul, 52, 53, 54
Ker, Evelyne, 115
Kerani, Abbie, 119
Kerbrat, Patrice, 27
Kerchbron, Jean, 12, 113, 143, 158, 177, 180, 185
Kergall, Dominique, 238
Kerne, Erwan, 131
Kerr, Charlotte, 22
Kéruzoré, Valérie, 84
Kervin, Maureen, 144
Keyes, Daniel, 156
Khan, Anton, 58
Kieffer, Roland, 147
Kier, Udo, 84
Kikoïne, Elsa, 54

Kindfors, Viveca, 119
Kindt, Fernand, 166
Klein, Gérard, 212, 213, 216
Klein, Nita, 132
Knippenberg, Herbert, 39
Kobrynski, Lazare, 231, 238
Kohler, Gilles, 102
Kohout, Pavel, 120
Kolldehoff, Reinhard, 39, 41
Koltaï, Robert, 138
Komi, Soila, 32
Korber, Maria, 22
Korian, Hervé, 51
Kosteikko, Eero, 32
Koundé, Hubert, 68
Kovacs, Mijou, 159
Kovacs, Muranyi, 72
Kownacka, Gabriela, 25, 26
Kozak, Katarzyna, 25
Kramer, Barbara, 136
Kravina, Herta, 32
Krawczyk, Gérard, 182
Kremer, Marie, 82
Krief, Bérangère, 72
Krier, Jacques, 160
Krol, Pierre André, 50
Kruck, Helga, 39
Kruger, Christiane, 23
Kubler, Ursula, 164
Kuhn, Sylvie, 17
Kunstmann, Doris, 84
Kupissonoff, 125
Kurys, Diane, 133

Kuttner, Henry, 185
L'Italien, Serge, 107
La Boulaye, Agathe de, 59
La Rochefoucauld, Sophie de, 68
Labbé, Guillaume, 108
Labelle, Marie-Chantal, 124
Labelle, Michel, 123
Labonté, François, 121, 123
Laborde, Catherine, 202
Laborit, Maria, 173
Labourdette, Elina, 117, 177
Lacamp, Isabelle, 57
Lacassin, Francis, 24, 49, 129, 132, 142
Lachance, Laurent, 107
Lachaud, Dorothée, 114
Lachhab, Samira, 59
Lacombe, André, 134
Lacombe, Georges, 169, 179
Lacombe, Julien, 99
Lacoste, Roland, 172
Lacroix, Evelyne, 172
Lacy, Bertrand, 64
Lafitte, Xavier, 102, 121
Lafond, Catherine, 117, 130, 180
Laforêt, Marie, 179
Lagarde, Jean-Jacques, 50
Lagay, Gil, 127
Lagneau, Jean-Charles, 113, 141

Lagrange, Jean-Jacques, 151, 183
Laisne, Martine, 134
Lajarrige, Bernard, 147
Lalande, Jacques, 129
Lalanne, Sébastien, 70, 71, 110
Laloux, Daniel, 57, 142
Lambert, Claude-Henri, 158
Lambert, Georges, 128
Lambert, Henri, 35, 97
Lambert, Jonathan, 71
Lambre, Frédéric, 103
Lambrichs. Gilberte, 199
Lamny, Maurice, 71
Lamole, Marc, 44
Lamorlette, Christine, 157
Lamour, Marianne, 124
Lamoureux, Sophie, 154
Lan, Truong, 85
Lancelot, Patrick, 50
Landais, André, 74
Landler, Karl E., 98
Landowski, Marcel, 154
Landry, Simone, 132
Lang, David-André, 134, 160
Lange, Bernadette, 129, 130
Langeais, Jacques, 195
Langelaan, George, 49, 151, 183, 212, 214, 216, 218, 219
Langlet, Daniel, 124, 163
Laniel, Gaétane, 107
Lanier, Jean, 70
Lannoo, Vincent, 128
Lanoux, Armand, 143, 148, 175
Lapparent, Hubert de, 44
Laprès, Lena, 107
Laquière, Toinette, 102, 121
Larcebeau, Gérard, 50
Larec, Yves, 126
Larivière, Michel, 123
Laroque, Michèle, 27
Larré, Vanessa, 62
Larry, Pierre, 124
Lartigau, Gérard, 45
Lary, Pierre, 15
Lasalle, Martin, 75
Lass, Barbara, 184
Lassalle, Thierry, 141
Latin, Frédéric, 126
Latour, Bernard, 213, 214, 215, 216, 217, 218, 219, 220, 221, 224
Latour, Pierre, 169
Lauby, Chantal, 105
Laudenbach, Philippe, 63, 79, 164
Laudenbach, Roland, 23
Laudière, Hervé, 69
Laurent, Christiane, 161
Laurent, Gilles, 231
Laurent, Jacqueline, 61
Lavalette, Bernard, 18, 193
Lax, Francis, 142, 157, 174
Lazure, Gabrielle, 164
Le Bail, Françoise, 179

Le Beal, Robert, 116
Le Bon, Charlotte, 46
Le Bris, Michel, 166
Le Couey, Catherine, 130
Le Délézir, Sébastien, 62
Le Fanu, Sheridan, 116, 147, 151
Le Gal, Yann, 101
Le Gall, André, 234
Le Gardeur, Pierre, 122
Le Goff, Jean-Louis, 182
Le Guillou, Jeanne, 135, 141
Le Hung, Eric, 181
Le Luhen, Claire, 55
Le Mouel, Jean, 82
le Paillot, Jean, 127
Le Person, Paul, 23, 26, 74, 157
Le Pottier, Justine, 72
Le Poulain, Corinne, 22, 78
Le Poulain, Jean, 120, 167
Le Quellec, Pierre, 237
Le Rouge, Gustave, 12, 103, 202, 205
Le Roy, Irving, 218
Le Royer, Michel, 138, 173
Le Rumeur, Pierre, 75, 83, 132
Le Sec, Alexis, 58
Le Tellier, Sophie, 98
Le Youdec, Annie, 34
Léandri, Bruno, 119
Léane, Fernand, 126
Lear, Amanda, 143
Léaud, Jean-Pierre, 159
Lebeaut, Olivier, 45
Leblanc, Éric, 65, 66, 67
Leblanc, Maurice, 12, 17, 20, 23, 26, 29, 60, 81, 82
Lebrun, Danièle, 48, 97, 161
Lecaplain, Baptiste, 72
Lecène, Marianne, 183
Lechien, Arnaud, 98
Leclerc, Ginette, 13, 75
Leclerc, Guy, 125
Leclère, Coline, 167
Lecompte, Daniel, 185
Leconte, Patrice, 118
Lecoq, Bernard, 77, 176
Lecourtois, Daniel, 83
Lecuyer, Guy, 33
Ledoux, Fernand, 174, 220
Ledoux, Mathias, 105
Ledoux, Patrick, 125, 126
Ledoyen, Germaine, 36
Ledoyen, Virginie, 82
Lee, Thean-Jeen, 58
Lefèbvre, Jean, 48
Lefebvre, Monique, 44
Lefèvre, Margot, 162
Lefèvre, René, 50, 113, 146
Lefèvre, Yves, 83
Legal, Patrick, 83
Legault, Vincent, 122
Léger, Sophie, 121
Légitimus, Pascal, 72
Legras, Jacques, 148

Legris, Pierre, 124
Lehérissey, Christiane, 65, 66
Leibovici, Roch, 124
Lemaire, Philippe, 57, 79
Lemaître, Anne, 197, 198, 199, 200, 201, 225, 238, 239
Lemaître, Jean, 31
Lemarchand, Lucienne, 117
Lemelin, Roger, 17
Lemler, Christine, 28
Lemmel, Dieter, 19, 20
Lemoine, Jean-Luc, 72
Lencquesaing, Louis-Do de, 145
Lenoir, Alban, 70, 71, 85
Lenôtre, G., 122
Léonard, Antoine, 164
Leone, Marcello, 149
Lepage, Jean, 157, 161
Leprince, Catherine, 56, 104
Leprince, Isabelle, 145
Leproux, Pierre, 78, 181, 186
Lergenmuller, Claude, 171
Leroux, Gaston, 12, 48, 60, 78, 113, 116, 149, 155, 195, 198, 206
Leroux, Jean-Pierre, 70
Leroux, Maxime, 68, 145
Leroy, Darlan, 17
Leroy, Serge, 165
Lesaffre, Roland, 24, 27
Lescot, Jean, 73, 133, 160

Lesieur, Patrick, 78
Lessertisseur, Guy, 129
Leterrier, Louis, 29
Letexier, Eddy, 85
Leuthreau, Nathalie, 80
Leuvrais, Jean, 97, 130
Levantal, François, 85
Leverd, Dominique, 103, 109, 131
Léviant, Léa, 101
Levie, Françoise, 128
Levie, Pierre, 125
Levignac, Sylvain, 36
Levin, Côme, 99
Levine, Michel, 29
Lewartowski, Joseph, 151
Lewin, Jeremy, 107
Lewis, Martin, 229
Lhermitte, Thierry, 187
Lhorca, Serge, 49
Libert, Jean, 52
Libolt, Alain, 117
Liegebel, Patrick, 229
Ligure, Claude, 165
Limonchik, Macha, 28
Lind, Jakov, 215
Lindinger, Natacha, 96, 161
Liotard, Thérèse, 21, 50, 74, 106, 177
Lippe, Jacques, 126
Lisowski, Georges, 221
Loiret-Caille, Florence, 136
Loisy, Jean, 235
Lombard, Jean-Robert, 84
Lombard, Robert, 31, 36

Londez, Vincent, 99
Londiche, Pierre, 29, 79, 164
London, Jack, 232
Lonsdale, Michael, 156, 179
Lopert, Tania, 113
Lopoukhine, Maricha, 145
Loran, M., 197
Lorenzi, Stellio, 183
Loret, Alexis, 51
Loria, Edith, 197, 198, 202
Lorin, Gérard, 164
Lorit, Jean-Pierre, 97
Lorrain, Jean, 205
Lorrain, Jean-Pierre, 31
Lot, Alfred, 62
Louane, 135
Louka, Paul, 126
Louki, Pierre, 142
Louret, Guy, 121
Lourson, Laurent, 204
Lovecraft, H. P., 150, 212
Loyer, Raymond, 113
Lubrano, Guillaume, 98
Lubtchansky, Jean-Claude, 57
Luc, Jean-Bernard, 141
Lucas, Gérard, 17
Lucas, Laurent, 110
Lucot, René, 70, 142
Lude, Christian, 36
Ludig, Grégoire, 72
Lugagne, Françoise, 157, 172
Lunati, Audrey, 68

Lutz, Marianne, 40
Lycan, Georges, 109
Maas, Sybille, 45
Macario, Ermanno, 217
Macnish, Robert, 223
Madeleine-Perdrillat, Clémence, 108
Madigan, Sylvain, 182
Madinier, Bruno, 109
Madral, Philippe, 53
Mage, Jean-Luc, 160
Magnan, Pierre, 227
Magnin, Claire, 123
Magre, Judith, 34, 114, 153
Mai, Fabienne, 141
Maigrot, Bernard, 173
Mailfort, Maxence, 63
Mailhot, Michel, 122
Maillard, Vincent, 161
Maistre, Armand, 52
Maistre, François, 22, 23, 61, 113, 116, 130, 147, 169, 172, 224
Maïwenn, 104
Malapa, Carl, 101
Malard, Stella, 218
Malet, Laurent, 114
Malet, Pierre, 63, 187
Malfille, Pierre, 40, 41, 42, 43
Malherbe, Arnaud, 100
Malignon, Jean-Pierre, 54
Mallat, Roger, 211
Mallet, Laurent, 177
Mallet, Odile, 145
Malleval, Denis, 168

Malliarakis, Matila, 110
Malo, Jean-Pierre, 79
Maltravers, Michael, 214
Mancuso, Alessandro, 108
Mandel, Georges, 77
Manez, Raoul de, 20
Manlay, Jacques, 165
Mann, Claude, 161
Manson, Héléna, 78
Manuel, Denis, 143, 202
Manuel, Robert, 171
Manzambi, Jonathan, 80
Manzor, René, 118
Marais, Jean, 84
Maratrat, Alain, 57
Marbot, Nicky, 82
Marc, Henri, 210
Marc, Myrielle, 237
Marcel, Odile, 226
Marchal, Catherine, 69, 114
Marchal, Georges, 16, 81, 134, 149, 170
Marchal, Olivier, 114
Marchand, Guy, 106, 118, 172
Marchand, Mélanie, 124
Marchesson, Patrick, 122
Marcillac, Jean, 19
Marcotte, André, 58
Marek, Félix, 66
Mareuil, Philippe, 23, 31
Margollé, Sylviane, 166
Margot, Stéphane, 84
Mari, Philippe, 98
Marielle, Jean-Pierre, 195
Marillier, Garance, 15

Marin, Antoine, 43, 48
Mariotto, Eric, 120
Marivin, Anne, 135
Marleau, Louise, 68, 84, 124
Marpeau, Elsa, 82
Marquand, Christian, 158
Marquand, Serge, 61, 159
Marquez, Luis, 69
Marsais, David, 72
Marsan, Jean, 120
Marsters, James, 98
Martel, Serge, 187, 193, 195, 203, 239
Martelet, Stéphanette, 70
Marthouret, François, 57, 74, 186
Martin, Alexis, 122
Martin, Dave, 137
Martin, Frances, 43
Martin, François, 146
Martin, Jean, 50, 61, 74, 77, 130, 142, 148, 149, 157, 164
Martines, Alessandra, 175
Martinetti, Thomas, 58
Martinez, David, 114
Martini, Renzo, 136
Martinolli, Christophe, 58
Martins, Jean-Pierre, 168
Marville, Sylvie, 194
Mary, Renaud, 155
Maslidor, Lisette, 149
Massicotte, Yves, 47
Massimi, Pierre, 18, 172
Masson, Loys, 159, 215, 218, 224

Mathieu, Bénédicte, 66
Mathieu, Claude, 180
Mathieu, Ginette, 176
Mathieu, Yves, 52
Mathot, Olivier, 32, 44
Mathy, Mimie, 176
Matta, Paloma, 113, 163
Matthieu, Xavier, 71
Mauclair, Dominique, 212
Mauclair, Jacques, 177, 225
Maugendre, Anthony, 96
Maul, Garrick, 150
Maunier, Jean-Baptiste, 98, 170
Maupassant, Guy de, 161
Maurel, Jean, 200
Maurette, Marcelle, 131
Maurey, Nicole, 113
Maurice, Robert, 144
Maurier, Claire, 39, 162
Maurier, Daphne du, 180
Maurin, Dominique, 182
Maurin, Marie-Véronique, 142
Maurin, Yves-Marie, 117
Maurois, André, 184
Maury, Jean-Louis, 77
Mauvais, Jean, 36, 48
Mavor, Freya, 80
Max, Harry, 35
Max, Jane, 128
Max, Zappy, 191, 234
Maxence, Pierre, 49
May, Claude, 163
Mayan, Kerian, 145
Mayne, Ferdy, 119

Mazani, Nacer, 123
Mazauric, Éva, 111
Mazeas, Bernard, 230, 241
Mazéas, Bernard, 174
Mazeau, Jacques, 59
Mazoyer, Robert, 113
Mazzotti, Pascal, 36
McCall, Catriona, 104, 175
Meaux, Joséphine de, 170
Mebrouk, Omar, 108
Meerson, Myron, 204
Meffre, Armand, 80
Mehadji, Dominique, 198
Meirieu, Emmmanuel, 85
Meisner, Gunter, 41
Melasniemi, Pertti, 32
Mélinand, Monique, 181
Ménard, Arlette, 179
Menard, Jean-François, 226
Mendel, Deryeth, 156
Menez, Bernard, 154
Mercier, Annie, 200
Mercier, Charlotte, 148
Mercure, Isa, 131
Mercy, Louis, 128
Meriko, Maria, 113, 129, 148
Méril, Macha, 60
Mérimée, Prosper, 186
Merle, Robert, 168
Merlin, Serge, 132
Mermet, Jedan, 155
Mermoud, Frédéric, 82, 110
Mesguich, Bernard, 157

Mesguich, Daniel, 16
Mesnil, Christian, 125
Mesplé, Mady, 148
Messe, Patrick, 169
Messer, Charlotte, 198
Messner, Claudia, 64
Mestral, Armand, 150, 157
Meunier, Denise, 199
Meunier, Raymond, 116, 148, 179
Meyer, Florent, 82
Meyrinck, Gustav, 12, 158, 199
Meyssignac, Emmanuelle, 147
Mezger, Theo, 25
Michaël, Jean-Pierre, 54
Michael, Pierre, 74
Michaud, Jean, 36, 41
Michel, Aimé, 103
Michel, André, 119
Michel, Marc, 29, 150
Michelangeli, Jean-Marc, 51
Miege Simansky, Denise, 219
Miège Simansky, Denise, 218
Mienniel, Xavier, 122
Miesch, Jean-Luc, 56
Migueault, Charles, 122
Miguras, Agnès, 108
Millardet, Patricia, 53
Miller, Monique, 33
Miller, Walter M., 213
Millot, Charles, 18

Mills, Juliette, 19, 130
Mills, Julikette, 164
Milo, Quentin, 125
Minazzoli, Christiane, 146
Minier, Alain, 185
Miranda, Isa, 156
Mirat, Pierre, 173
Misserly, Hélène, 131, 132
Missiaen, Jean-Claude, 79
Mitsouko, 42
Mittendorf, Hubert, 20
Mitterand, Frédéric, 118
Mitton, Henri, 227
Mlekuz, Mathias, 99, 161
Mnich, Geneviève, 74
Moatti, Yveline, 52
Modo, Michel, 49, 142
Modot, Gaston, 184
Moine, Patrick, 155
Molenes, Thalie de, 222
Molina, Vidal, 81
Molinaro, Édouard, 77
Molinier, Arthur, 170
Moller, Gunnar, 19
Mollien, Elsa, 62
Moncorbier, Pierre, 16
Mondolfi, Eva, 53
Monestier, Marianne, 223
Monge, Marie, 133
Monjanel, Pierre, 58
Monnier, Philippe, 56
Monod, Jacques, 35, 50, 131, 184
Monod, Roland, 49, 131, 170
Monot, Louise, 109

Mons, Maurice, 124
Monsaingeon, Grégoire, 128
Montalembert, Thibault de, 61
Monti, Nino, 37
Montier, Yvette, 30
Montillier, Georges, 48
Montoute, Édouard, 54
Montuel, Gonzague, 109
Mony, Georges, 126
Moore, Catherine L., 185
Moosmann, Daniel, 104, 180
Moran, Kate, 133
Morel, Geneviève, 16
Morel, Jacques, 61, 193, 195
Moreux, Jean-Pierre, 132
Morgensztern, Noam, 82
Morissette, André, 123
Morley, David, 51
Moro, Alicia, 26
Morrissette, Julie, 124
Mortensen, Sara, 51
Moscardo, Jean-Pierre, 105
Moszko, Myriam, 65
Mottet, Alain, 36, 49, 163
Moulin, Charles, 130
Moulin, Jean-Paul, 182
Moulin, Jean-Pierre, 141, 163
Moulinot, Jean-Paul, 16, 35, 112
Moulinot, Jean-Pierre, 158
Mounier, Sébastien, 15, 128
Mourat, Jean, 166
Mourier, Davy, 73, 110
Mourthé, Anny, 178
Mourthé, Claude, 178, 212, 215, 216, 217, 220, 221
Moussy, Marcel, 83, 163
Moutier, Gilberte, 146
Moutoussamy, Laure, 102
Muel, Jean-Paul, 57
Mugnerot, Robert, 169
Muharay, Piroska, 125
Muliar, Fritz, 22
Muller, Germain, 150
Muller, Henri, 160
Muller, Michel, 34, 142
Munch, Richard, 68
Muni, Marguerite, 36
Münster, Helga, 41
Munz, Michel, 65, 67, 68
Murat, Napoléon, 75
Murgier, Philippe, 149
Murzeau, Robert, 130
Murzeau, Thierry, 49
Musset, Régis, 54
Mussier, Jacques, 145
Nadal, Michèle, 186
Nadeau, Claire, 37, 50
Nahmias, Robert, 236
Nahum, Alain, 26, 27, 28
Nahum, Jacques, 18, 23, 24, 25, 26, 27, 28
Nambotin, Swann, 110
Napoli, Marc di, 59

Nat, Lucien, 113, 129, 130, 155
Nauer, Bernard, 119
Navarre, Louis, 79
Nebout, Claire, 53
Neel, Pierre, 103
Negroni, Jean, 112
Nehr, Jean, 179
Nell, Nathalie, 74
Nelson, Charlie, 185
Nerval, Gérard de, 49, 223
Nerval, Nathalie, 36
Nervbazl, Edouard, 118
Nesle, Jean de, 145
Neuvic, Thierry, 97
Neuwirth, Chantal, 124
Niang, Philippe, 155
Nicati, Adrien, 118
Nicaud, Philippe, 81
Nicloux, Guillaume, 80
Nicoloff, Serge, 151, 170
Nicot, Claude, 155, 161
Niculescu, Miron, 196
Nisic, Hervé, 152
Nivollet, Pierre, 84, 103, 120
Njo Lobé, Daniel, 51
Nkake, Sandra, 98
Nobis, Alain, 29, 40
Noblecourt, Noële, 40, 75
Noblet, Émilie, 114
Nocher, Jean, 204
Noël, Emile, 196, 199, 213, 218
Noel, Huberet, 36
Noël, Magali, 117
Noël, Philippe, 70
Noël, Serge, 141
Noël-Noël, 12, 138
Noguéro, José, 41
Nolin, Olivier, 133
Norden, Nicole, 49, 148
Norin, Olivier, 150
Norman, Jean-Daniel, 115
Normand, Philippe, 174
Novak, Veronica, 69
Novovitch, Nena, 127
O., Marie, 226
O'Brien, Fitz James, 222
Obé, Jean, 34, 130
Ogier, Bulle, 78, 131
Ogouz, Philippe, 35, 113, 114
Olaf, Pierre, 149
Olbrychski, Daniel, 53
Oldelaf, 71
Ollier, Claude, 235
Ollier, Daniel, 76
Ollivier, Franck, 102
Ommaggio, Maria Rosaria, 57
Orcier, Sylvie, 54
Oriane, Françoise, 128
Osterrath, Jacqueline H., 214
Otero, Isabel, 58
Othernin-Girard, Dominique, 137
Ottum, Bob, 37
Oudart, Gysèle, 126
Oumansky, André, 31, 69, 136, 177, 186
Oury, Gérard, 161
Outalbali, Sami, 101

Outin, Régis, 132
Ovion, Jacques, 199
Owen, Thomas, 125, 126, 127, 128
Ozenne, Jean, 183
Ozeray, Madeleine, 76, 185
Pacôme, Maria, 115, 155
Page, Alain, 13, 50, 102, 236
Pagett, Nicola, 137
Pagliai, Ugo, 27
Pailhas, Géraldine, 108
Paillette, Laure, 176
Paillot, David, 58
Palau, Pierre, 36
Palec, Yvon, 124
Paliotti, Anthony, 80
Pallascio, Aubert, 33
Palmade, Pierre, 72
Palmer, Renzo, 103
Palud, Xavier, 82
Paoletti, Claire, 58
Papagalli, Serge, 85
Paqui, Jean, 181
Parasites, Les, 61
Parent, Gilles, 122, 123, 124
Paret, Roland, 121
Paris, Jacques, 122
Paris, Laurent, 173
Parisot, Henri, 142
Parsons, Jacques, 200
Party, Robert, 131
Pascal, Caroline, 84
Pascal, Philippine, 76
Pascal, Valérie, 23

Pascaud, Sylvie, 122
Paster, Joseph, 147
Pastor, Lucas, 46
Pastor, Marina, 37
Patachou, 53
Patakia, Daphné, 108
Pataut, Claire, 177
Patrick, Janine, 20
Patrick, Jean, 212
Patron, Emmanuel, 54
Paturel, Dominique, 74
Paulhac, Jean, 217
Pauly, Marco, 64, 66, 67
Pauly, Rebecca, 150, 156
Pauthe, Serge, 134
Pauwels, Louis, 116, 149, 158, 177, 180
Pavaux, Marc, 153
Pavic, Milorad, 214
Payet, Manu, 72
Payton, Barbara, 58
Peake, Mervyn, 199
Péché, Jean-Jacques, 127
Pedersen, Vytte, 116
Pedri, Jade, 108
Pelegri, Pierre, 76
Pélissier, Raymond, 131
Pellegeay, Frédéric, 54, 168
Pelletier, Gilles, 33
Pelletier, Raymond, 146
Pelletier, Roger, 142, 184
Pellotier, Jean, 121
Pelot, Pierre, 169, 171
Peltier, Philippe, 145
Perdrière, Hélène, 83
Peretti, Thierry de, 186

Pernel, Florence, 141, 154
Pernet, Pierre, 155
Péron, Denise, 183
Perrault, Charles, 144, 147
Perret, Edith, 81, 173
Perrier, Pierre, 110
Perrin, Francis, 98
Perrin, Jacques, 96, 159
Perrin, Marco, 23, 34
Perron, Claude, 175
Perrot, François, 23, 76, 104, 109, 116, 153, 181
Personne, Fred, 105
Peschar, Hannah, 174
Peskine, Brigitte, 145
Pesnot, Patrick, 117, 138
Petersen, Karin, 157
Petit, Françoise, 141
Petit, Roland, 154
Petrof, Serge, 220
Petrolacci, Jean Pierre, 103
Petterson, Allan Rune, 119
Peufaillit, Nicolas, 110
Peycharand, Hélène, 57, 63, 75
Peyrelon. Michel, 79, 186
Peyrou, Georges, 198, 199, 200, 202, 222, 232
Philippe, Julie, 81, 152
Philippon, Franck, 114
Philipponnat, Florence, 154
Philippot, Marcel, 37
Phoenix, Philypa, 107
Piat, Colette, 226

Pibouleau, Robert, 203
Picard, Michel, 56, 117
Picard, René-Maurice, 232, 233
Piccolo, Ottavia, 56
Piégay, Henri, 112, 114
Piéral, Pierre, 61, 111, 136
Pierauld, Guy, 130
Pierre, Hervé, 29, 159
Pierre, Jacques, 150, 156, 171
Pierre, Roger, 120, 207
Pierrot, Frédéric, 104, 110
Pigault, Roger, 150, 176
Pignol, Jean, 48, 153, 161
Pignon, Nicolas, 102
Pilar, Mario, 112
Pilartz, Yara, 110
Pillaudin, Roger, 201
Pillet, Marie, 168
Pilorge, Michel, 186
Pinon, Dominique, 82, 98, 111
Piquet, Odette, 182
Pirol, Pierre, 135
Pisani-Ferry, Isaure, 133
Pistorio, Pierre-François, 83
Pitiot, Frank, 84
Pitoëff, Sacha, 21, 109, 116, 148, 155
Pittard, Constance, 71
Pitti, Stéphane, 107
Pivin, José, 219, 222
Planchon, Paul, 111, 134, 144, 147, 150, 160, 162
Planchot, Dominique, 59

Plancon, Chantal, 199
Plante, Raymond, 121, 123
Plas, Olivier de, 104
Plumecocq-Mech, Juliette, 72, 121
Plunian, Philippe, 177
Pluot, Fernand, 15
Pocchard, Werner, 59
Podalydès, Denis, 175
Podetti, François, 70
Poe, Edgar Allan, 75, 159, 178, 215
Poiret, Jean, 207
Poirier, Aurélia, 110
Poirier, Henri, 117
Poisson, Alix, 110
Poivre, Annette, 142, 148, 153
Polet, Philippe, 69
Politoff, Haydée, 102
Pollet, Jean-Daniel, 161
Polly, Nina-Paloma, 134
Polvey, Patrick, 111
Pomarat, André, 134, 147, 151, 162, 171
Pons, Maurice, 166
Ponson du Terrail, Pierre-Alexis, 112, 134, 195, 206
Ponsot, Clara, 175
Pontremoli, David, 57
Popesco, Valérie, 117
Porges, Arthur, 212
Porte, Robert, 169
Portehaut, Aurélien, 71, 84

Porterat, Maurice, 183
Portiche, Roland, 29
Possot, François, 164
Potocki, Jan, 61, 202, 239
Potok, Rebecca, 138
Pottier, Alexandre, 105
Poujoly, Georges, 163
Poulain de Saint Père, Thibault, 120
Poupaud, Melvil, 108
Pourteyron, Aurore, 70
Pozzuoli, Alain, 151, 199, 200, 205
Pradeau, Jean, 184
Pradier, Perrette, 115
Prat, Jean, 144, 152, 153
Préfontaine, Claude, 28
Preissac, Émilie de, 168
Préjean, Patrick, 78, 119, 129
Prévert, Jacques, 176
Prévert, Pierre, 12, 50, 176
Prévost, Daniel, 34
Prévost, Sören, 55
Price, Vincent, 161
Princi, Mark, 68
Proslier, Jean-Marie, 138
Prost, René, 134
Proulx, Marc, 124
Proust, Olivier, 123
Provence, Denise, 16
Prudon, Hervé, 197
Prune, Véronique, 29, 69
Prunier, Yves, 134
Puech, Jean-Baptiste, 175
Puget, Claude-André, 158
Puterflam, Michel, 112

Putzulu, Bruno, 143
Puydebat, Patrick, 72
Puydorat, Richard, 215
Quéderosse, André, 240
Quéneau, Raymond, 187
Quester, Hugues, 103
Questi, Giulio, 69
Queysanne, Bernard, 166
Rabourdin, Olivier, 128
Radcliffe, Ann, 83, 224
Rademakers, Fons, 19
Raës, Gaël, 58
Raffaelli, Bruno, 28, 64, 65, 67, 68
Ragon, Laurence, 177
Rahouadj, Farida, 68
Raimbourg, Lucien, 113, 138
Raiola, Guido, 223
Rais, Asil, 62
Rajot, Pierre-Louis, 168
Rake, Joachim, 32
Rambach, Anne, 107
Rambach, Marine, 107
Rambal, Jean-Pierre, 23, 67
Ramberg, Catherine, 143
Ramonet, Yves, 59
Randax, Georges, 125
Ranson, Marcelle, 36
Rapace, Ola, 114
Rault, Fabien, 86, 87, 88
Ravalec, Blanche, 169
Ray, Jean, 125, 126, 127, 196, 219
Ray, Nicolas, 115
Rayer, Maud, 132, 187

Raynal, Patrick, 121, 153
Ré, Michel de, 61, 144
Réa, Robert, 186
Read, Douglas, 39
Rebbot, Philippe, 61
Rebbot, Sady, 169
Rebot, Sady, 188
Recoing, Aurélien, 128
Redon, Martine, 50
Reen, Katharina, 116
Reggiani, Serge, 162
Remacle, Amélie, 51
Remberg, Erika, 39
Rémi, Jean-François, 30
Rémy, Albert, 183
Rémy, Chantal, 73
Renard, Maurice, 11, 49, 138, 154, 167
Renard, Max, 125
Renaud, Francis, 114
Renaudet, Vincent, 107
Renauld, Isabelle, 53
Renault, Brune, 121
Rénier, Yves, 36
Renoir, Jean, 183
Renoir, Magali, 165
Renty, Paul, 182
Respati, Harline, 41
Reumaux. Patrick, 199
Revel, Valentine, 72
Reverend, Frédéric, 67
Reverho, Christine, 65, 66
Revillon, Mariannik, 165
Revon, Bernard, 63, 64
Rey, Fernando, 68
Reybaz, André, 49

Rey-Magnan, Emmanuelle, 109
Riaboukine, Serge, 62, 67
Riberolles, Jacques, 131, 183
Ribowska, Malka, 48, 185
Ribowski, Nicolas, 27
Ricard, Olivier, 143
Rich, Catherine, 130
Rich, Claude, 68, 155
Rich, Pierre, 131
Richard, Claude, 129, 164
Richard, Firmine, 101
Richard, Jacques, 170
Richard, Jean, 115
Richard, Jean-Pierre, 105, 177
Richard, Roger, 215, 217
Riche, Daniel, 79, 159
Richemont, Chantal, 196
Richert, Carole, 154
Richet, Raphaëlle, 108
Ridremont, Patrick, 62
Rieffel, Jean, 120
Rieger, Paul, 165
Riera, Albert, 160, 212, 213
Riesner, Laurence, 207
Riffard, Roger, 45, 104, 117
Rigault, Timoté, 108
Rignault, Alexandre, 16, 40, 48, 52, 156, 175
Rimbaud, Robert, 103, 106, 185
Ripert, Colette, 117
Riquier, Georges, 129

Risch, Pierre, 40
Rispal, Jacques, 174
Rist, Christian, 181
Riva, Antoinette, 217, 223
Rivault, Pascale, 142
Rivemale, Alexandre, 144, 153, 172
Rivers, Dick, 143
Rivet, Gilberte, 173
Rivière, Jean-Marie, 45
Rivière, Marie, 166
Robak, Alain, 120
Roberge, Hélène, 115
Robert, Antonin, 147
Robert, Benoît, 146
Robert, Yves, 159
Roberts, Pascale, 23, 106, 141
Robichez, Cyril, 145, 153
Robillard, Serge, 221
Robin, Anastasia, 82
Robin, Michel, 57, 142
Robineau, Katherine, 226, 231
Robinson, Edward G., 217
Robinson, Madeleine, 170
Robiolles, Jacques, 114
Robles, Emmanuel, 241
Roblin, Louise, 146
Robutti, Enzo, 103
Rochefort, Jean, 195, 212
Rocher, Benjamin, 108
Rodriguez, Ruddy, 53
Roger, Noelle, 233
Rognoni, Louis, 103, 195, 217, 220, 227, 230, 231
Rohmer, Sax, 207

Roland, Denise, 180
Roland-Manuel, Claude, 195, 197, 198, 201, 205, 213, 216, 218, 219, 220, 222, 225, 236
Rollin Weisz, Jeanne, 212, 213, 214, 215, 217, 218, 219, 221, 223, 224, 225, 236, 239
Rollin, Dominique, 153
Rollin, François, 85
Rollis, Robert, 34
Roman, Malya, 104
Rome, Claude-Michel, 142
Roncoroni, Jean-Louis, 127, 151, 183
Ronet, Maurice, 75, 178
Roos, Eddy, 134
Roqueplo, Lola, 101
Roquevert, Noël, 155
Rosier, Cathy, 109
Rosny, Jacques, 97
Rosset, Camille, 114
Rosset, Frédéric, 114
Rossi, Jacques, 123
Roth, Julie-Anne, 100
Rouaud, Jean, 168
Roudaut, Raphaëlle, 58
Roudy, Pierre, 220
Rougé, Florence, 66
Rougerie, Jean, 35, 119
Rouillard, Jacqueline, 109
Rouleau, Philippe, 29
Rouleau, Raymond, 185
Roure, Francis, 227
Rousseau, Pierre, 151, 166

Roussel, Anne, 138
Roussel, Nathalie, 71, 173
Roussel, Thérèse, 69
Rousselet, André, 50
Rousselet, Bernard, 183
Rousselet, Monique, 221
Roussillon, Baptiste, 173
Roussillon, Jacques, 168
Roussillon, Jean-Paul, 34, 154, 168
Rouvel, Catherine, 21
Roux, Thibault, 84
Rouyère, Bruno, 122
Rouzière, Michel, 176
Rozes, Gilbert, 176
Ruchaud, Frédérique, 130
Rudaz, Alain, 58
Rudel, Roger, 30
Rudychenko, Diana, 145
Ruegg, Pierre, 170
Ruhl, Michel, 112
Ruini, Marine, 51
Ruire, Max, 134
Rumilly, France, 146
Rupert, Jean, 43, 109, 180
Russo, Daniel, 74
Ruyssen, Monique, 225
Ryan, Michelle, 98
Saad, Margit, 42
Saadoun, Alexandra, 85
Saadoun, Magali, 85
Saba, Tony, 84
Sabatier, William, 18, 185
Sacha, Jean, 31, 32
Sachot, Jean-Claude, 123
Sadjo, Babetida, 100
Saedeleer, Olivier de, 128

Safi, Alaa, 80
Saglio, Patrick, 117
Sagnier, Ludivine, 29
Sagols, Jean, 156
Said, Marcela, 29
Saint-Jean, Robert de, 182
Saint-Julien, 234
Saint-Macary, Hubert, 70, 98
Saint-Mor, Anne, 165
Saintons, Pierre, 172
Saint-Ourens, Roman, 185
Saint-Paul, Eva, 32
Saint-Pierre, Renaud, 166
Salata, Rosetta, 27
Salerne, Anne-Marie, 112
Salier, Edouard, 101
Salkin, Lucien, 125, 126
Salles, David, 55
Sallette, Céline, 110
Salomone, Bruno, 85
Saltel, Roger, 16
Salviat, Catherine, 69
Samie, Catherine, 119
Sammel, Richard, 167
Sammut, Richard, 185
Sanche, Guy, 17, 47
Sanchez, Thomas, 59
Sand, Hervé, 48
Sanders, Dirk, 154, 172
Sanders, Sarah, 40
Sandrelli, Sandro, 217
Sanson, Charlotte, 114, 133
Santelli, Claude, 12, 80, 81, 165, 174, 181
Santini, Pierre, 160

Santon, Marie-France, 120
Sapritch, Alice, 142, 179
Sarcey, Martine, 68
Sardou, Emmanuelle, 175
Sarfati, Julien, 97
Sarfati, Maurice, 148, 150, 151, 162, 171, 173, 181, 201
Sarray, Yvon, 129, 131
Sarrazin, Dominique, 64, 153
Sarry, Daniel, 21
Sartchadjiev, Joseph, 28
Sassi, Roland, 203, 204
Sassy, Jean-Paul, 184
Sattmann, Peter, 68
Saudray, Jean, 42, 48
Saurel, Jean-Baptiste, 108
Saury, Alain, 164, 169
Sautrec, Philippe, 179
Sauvegrain, Didier, 156
Sauvion, Serge, 33
Savarin, Annie, 114
Savignac, Ida, 230
Saxel, Bernard, 212, 214, 217, 220, 222, 225, 237
Scalese, Laurent, 54
Scalondro, Paolo Maria, 28
Scantanburlo, J.-P., 123
Scasso, Claude, 121
Schaake, Katrin, 38
Schäfer, Bernd, 19
Schapira, Manuel, 15
Scheigam, Boris, 135
Schiffman, Némo, 101

Schiltz, Maryvonne, 97, 104, 175
Schitzer, Arthur, 228
Schlegel, Paulette, 147
Schmidt, Julien, 73
Schneider, Aliocha, 133
Schneider, Charles, 120
Schneider, Jean-Paul, 164
Schneider, Marcel, 185
Schneider, Niels, 15
Schwarzmaier, Michael, 25
Schwilden, Maurice, 126
Sciamma, Céline, 110
Scipion, Robert, 22, 25, 81, 109
Scob, Edith, 109, 117, 178
Scotlande, Fred, 72
Scott, Alan, 31
Scott, Walter, 201
Seban, Paul, 83
Sébastian, Micky, 167
Séchan, Edmond, 176
Seck, Ibrahim, 80
Segal, Gilles, 143, 157
Seidenschwan, Franz, 59
Seignolle, Claude, 168, 170, 179, 216, 220, 224, 225, 236, 237, 238
Seiler, Jacques, 112, 174
Sélignac, Arnaud, 143
Sellers, Catherine, 50, 224
Sellier, Georges, 142
Sellier, Pascal, 146
Semenoff, Ariel, 151
Semler, Peter, 81
Semonin, Jérémie, 146
Semprun, Carlos, 152
Senarica, Pier, 27
Sénéchal, Arthur, 82
Senges, Pierre, 204
Sentier, Jean-Pierre, 168
Séraphine, Thomas, 177
Serbedzija, Rade, 26
Sergue, Gérard, 79
Sermonne, Claire, 80
Serrault, Michel, 34, 35, 158
Serre, Henri, 138, 151
Serreau, Jean-Marie, 166
Serres, Jacques, 45, 121, 163
Servais, Sonia, 128
Setbon, Philippe, 56, 68, 69, 167
Setti, Clémence, 46
Séty, Gérard, 46, 105
Seuzaret, Hélène, 51, 96
Séverin, Gaston, 161
Sevilla, Joëlle, 84, 88, 90
Seyrig, Delphine, 153
Seyvecou, Sabrina, 62
Sharif, Omar, 81
Shelley, Guy, 149
Shelley, Mary, 157, 199, 207
Shelley, Percy Bysshe, 202
Shepherd, Jack, 137
Sherif, Kamel, 66
Sicard, Marcel, 220
Sichov, Dounia, 145
Siclier, Jacques, 70
Sicotte, Madeleine, 47

Sidoroff, Michel, 197, 203
Siegrist, Paul, 17
Siegrist, Vincent, 29
Sihol, Caroline, 103
Silberg, Nicolas, 60, 157
Silva, Luna, 107
Silverberg, Robert, 180
Simaga, Léonie, 128
Simak, Clifford D., 223
Simenon, Marc, 186, 211
Simmonet, Eva, 131
Simon, François, 19, 177
Simon, Jean-Daniel, 103, 163
Simon, Maïa, 70
Simon, Naïa, 202
Simonet, Julien, 177
Simonin, Albert, 19, 21, 23
Simono, Albert, 45, 145
Simourre, Gilbert, 228
Sinicorni, Giorgia, 99
Siniglia, Annie, 70
Sinoué, Gilbert, 97
Sire, Gérard, 234
Sisser, Pierre, 29
Sisti, Vittorio de, 28
Sivadier, Jean-François, 110
Slotine, Henri, 37
Smith, Cotter, 180
Sola, Catherine, 54
Soler, Anne-Valérie, 85
Solignac, Vincent, 175
Sommers, Barbara, 102, 183

Sonnendrucker, Paul, 144, 162
Sonnier, Georges, 181
Sorel, Jean, 159
Soskin, Henry, 78
Soubeyran, Henri, 206, 215, 218, 225, 238
Souchon, Janine, 132, 145
Soulet, Bernard, 215
Soulez Larivière, Hadrien, 58
Sourzac, Katia, 64
Sousa, Alexandre, 25
Souvestre, Pierre, 12, 63, 64
Souza, Roger, 124
Sow, Slony, 168
Specht, Marcel, 134
Spegt, Marcel, 150, 162
Speiser, Kitty, 20
Spiegelman, Léon, 216
Spiero, Christiane, 64, 65, 67, 68
Spilmont, Jean-Pierre, 199
Spiraux, Alain, 222, 231
Sporrle, Gunther, 23
Spriel, Stephen, 232
Stahl, Yvette, 144, 147, 160
Stameschkine, Michel, 125
Steen, Jean, 200
Steen, Jean-Jacques, 176, 227
Steger, Babsie, 102
Stephane, Idwig, 102
Sterling, Alexandre, 117

Stern, Sarah, 69, 128
Sternberg, Jacques, 7, 223, 240
Stévenin, Jean-François, 82, 137, 145, 150
Stévenin, Robinson, 135
Stévenin, Sagamore, 145
Stevenson, Robert-Louis, 148, 183, 184
Stewart, Alexandra, 78, 159
Still, Aline, 135
St-Jacques, Diane, 122
Stoica, Luana, 185
Stoker, Bram, 198, 200, 212
Stora, Bernard, 26
Storoge, Dimitri, 108
Strauss, Nicole, 195
Stroh, Valérie, 69
Sturgeon, Theodore, 56, 57, 77, 206
Subiela, Michel, 13, 24, 48, 49, 128, 129, 130, 131, 132, 133, 149, 162, 172
Subor, Michel, 174
Sue, Eugène, 201
Suffran, Michel, 161, 216
Sundberg, Yann, 102
Surgère, Hélène, 124
Sutto, Janine, 123
Sy, Omar, 29
Sydney, Olivier, 149
Sylla, Assa, 101
Sylvair, Luc, 231
Sylvia, Gaby, 144, 147

Sylvie, 36
Szabo, Laszlo, 138
Tabard, Pierre, 50, 158
Taffin, Tony, 165
Taglioni, Alice, 108
Taillandier, Françoise, 175
Tainsy, Andrée, 185
Talbot, Anne, 164
Talmone, Fanny, 101
Tanakil, Isabelle, 109
Taroni, Jacques, 198, 202, 225, 236
Tavernier, Nils, 79
Taylor, Arch, 131
Tchenko, Katia, 48
Tcherina, Ludmilla, 143
Tchernia, Pierre, 34, 35, 115, 158, 187
Temple, William, 57
Tennant, Victoria, 69
Tennberg, Jean-Marc, 35
Tephany, Arlette, 165
Tephany, Jacques, 156
Térac, Solange, 39, 40, 41, 42, 43
Terral, Boris, 62
Terrangle, Jean-Louis, 135
Terzieff, Laurent, 161
Tessari, Duccio, 19
Tessé, Jean-Philippe, 145
Testa, Karina, 120
Testud, Sylvie, 167
Tété, 73
Teynac, Maurice, 131
Teyssedre, Anne, 163
Thénault, Bob, 157
Thévenon, Pierrette, 81

Thiam, 27
Thiam, Jenna, 110
Thibault, Jean-Marc, 187, 207
Thiérée, Jean-Baptiste, 167
Thirion, Louis, 224, 225
Thiry, Marcel, 126
Thomas, Anaïs, 101
Thomas, Bernard, 29
Thomas, Louis C., 118
Thomas, Pascal, 154
Thomé, Martine, 204
Thor, James, 184
Thorson, Linda, 175
Tichy, Gérard, 81
Tielrooy, Élise, 109
Tientcheu, Steve, 121
Tilière, Christian de, 132
Tillieux, Maurice, 234
Tilly, François-Louis, 168
Timperley, Rosemary, 218
Tinti, Gabriele, 81
Tioulong, Boramy, 157
Tiphaine, Bernard, 148
Tirli, Bernard, 52
Tissot, Rodolphe, 58
Titre, Claude, 38, 131, 162, 179
Todeschini, Bruno, 161
Toeplitz, Krzysztof Teodor, 25
Toesca, Maurice, 184, 188, 240
Toledano, Philippe, 53
Tolstoï, Catherine, 227, 230

Tonecki, Michal, 221
Tonietti, Anne, 35
Tonnelier, Norman, 46
Topart, Jean, 101, 112, 130, 161, 184, 202
Topin, Tito, 53
Tornade, Pierre, 34, 113, 175, 182
Toublanc-Michel, Bernard, 102
Tougas, Sébastien, 122
Tourneur, Jacques, 233
Tourneur, Maurice, 233
Tourneur, Michèle, 227, 229, 238
Toussaint, Dominique, 159
Touzet, Corinne, 28, 79
Trabaud, Pierre, 120
Tragarz, Daniel, 176
Tran, Steve, 80
Tranquilli, Silvano, 27
Trapp, Nataël, 114
Travail, Maurice, 50
Traversi, Valentin, 37, 85
Trébouta, Jacques, 68, 159, 174
Tréjean, Guy, 84, 129, 130, 174, 202
Tremblay, Ghyslain, 47
Trondheim, Lewis, 110
Trotta, Margarethe, 77
Trujitto, Renato, 123
Tsamere, Arnaud, 70
Tubb, E. C., 172
Tugot, Michel, 34
Tulasne, Patricia, 122

Turenne, Henri de, 97
Turgenev, Ivan, 74
Turlier, Jean, 50
Turp, Gilbert, 123
Tybo, Edmond, 188
Tyborowsky, Edmond, 169
Tyczka, Igor, 184
Tzvetkova, Vania, 28
Uderzo, Albert, 193
Ughetto, Bastien, 61
Ulchan, Philippe, 182
Ulliel, Gaspard, 46, 80
Ulysse, Fred, 111
Umgelter, Fritz, 22, 23
Uritescu, Valentin, 185
Uytbrock, Eric, 125
Uzan, François, 29, 55
Vacth, Marine, 100
Vaillard, Pierre-Jean, 146
Val, Pierre, 168
Valdeneige, Bernard, 49, 142, 148
Valentini, Marian Georges, 239
Valera, Dominique, 79
Valéry, Paul, 171
Vallée, Didier, 144
Valles, Étienne, 196
Vallier, Hélène, 115, 162
Valmary, Capucine, 58, 108
Valmy, André, 129, 130, 131, 146, 156, 162, 163
Valois, Arnaud, 100
Valorbe, François, 174
Valota, Patrice, 136

Valtier, André, 133
Valton, Jean, 52
van den Driessche, Frédéric, 177
Van Doude, 132
Van Eyck, Kristina, 53, 63
Van Ghendt, Andy, 127
Van Parys, Agnès, 29
Vandenpanhuyse, Gaston, 52
Vandevelde, Christophe, 72, 99
Vaneck, Pierre, 30, 76, 151, 156, 165, 180, 202
Vaneck, Sylvie, 129, 179
Vardier, Josette, 35
Varoujean, Jean-Jacques, 227, 229
Varraut, Loïc, 85
Varte, Rosy, 34, 74, 130, 157, 158
Vassort, Cécile, 112
Vattier, Bérangère, 188
Vattier, Robert, 138, 181
Vattier, Roger, 48
Vaudaux, Maurice, 103, 164
Vaur, Georges, 124
Vavilova, Irina, 203
Vaylord, Vanessa, 117
VDB, Thomas, 55
Veillon, Astrid, 54
Veillot, Claude, 49, 54, 68
Veillot, Justine, 98
Velle, Louis, 78
Venantini, Venantino, 69
Venel, Jean-Paul, 176

Ventura, Claude, 174
Vérat, Eric, 55, 58
Verde, Patrick, 165
Verdier, Julien, 50, 109
Vergne, Marie-Blanche, 151
Verhaeghe, Jean-Daniel, 154, 170, 173
Verhoeren, Emile, 125
Verlant, Louis, 127
Verley, Bernard, 131, 133, 181
Verley, Monique, 127
Vermorel, Marie-Claude, 37, 38
Vernal, Irène, 126
Vernay, Robert, 38, 39, 40, 41, 42, 43, 44
Verne, Jules, 11, 12, 59, 80, 81, 120, 147, 148, 163, 164, 168, 172, 174, 181, 197
Verne, René, 17
Vernes, Henri, 38, 39, 40, 41, 42, 43, 44
Vernier, Claude, 131
Vernier, Jean-Frédéric, 199
Vernier, Pierre, 45, 112
Vernillat, Francette, 147
Vernon, Anne, 150
Verset, Alice, 100
Versini, Marie, 22
Versins, Pierre, 203
Versois, Odile, 83
Vervoort, Jean-Marc, 141
Véry, Pierre, 157

Vézina, Mathieu, 122
Vial, Alice, 114
Vial, Pierre, 168
Vialle, Max, 142, 150, 184
Vian, Boris, 159
Viard, Henri, 30, 32, 33, 169
Viard, Karin, 182
Vibert, François, 76, 158, 174, 179, 186
Vicas, Victor, 30, 31, 32, 33
Vierne, Jean-Jacques, 196, 198, 199, 206, 225, 239, 240, 241
Vigne, Daniel, 145
Vigneron, Eliane, 51
Vignon, Jean-Paul, 144
Vignon, Virginie, 45, 48
Vigny, Jean, 118
Vilers, Vania, 176
Villalonga, José-Luis de, 61
Villard, Juliette, 116
Ville, Jacques, 71
Villé, Paul, 46
Villers, Claude, 154, 203
Villiers de l'Isle Adam, Philippe-Auguste, 198
Villiers de l'Isle-Adam, Philippe-Auguste, 200
Viltange, Jean-Pierre, 135
Vincent, Dominique, 146, 164, 219
Vincent, Fernand, 153, 187
Vincent, Mirès, 131, 132

Vincent, Renaud, 154
Vinci, Jean, 130, 147
Violette, Jean, 129
Virlojeux, Henri, 17, 18, 20, 21, 114, 144, 182
Vitez, Baptiste, 146
Vitold, Michel, 78, 97, 124, 131, 181, 184, 224
Viviès, Hélène, 99
Vo, Patrick, 71
Vogel, Jacques, 124
Vogel, Nicolas, 36
Voizard, Marc F., 28
Volson, Patrick, 145
Von Thun, Max, 96
Vrigny, Robert, 170
Vuillemin, Odile, 58
Vuillermoz, Michel, 108, 170
Wagner, Agnieszka, 26
Wagner, Paul, 117
Wahiche, Dominique, 199
Walker, Jennie-Anne, 70
Walker, Pierre, 151
Walle, Aïna, 152, 163, 170, 184
Wallery, Géo, 113
Walpole, Horace, 202, 218
Walter, Kararzyna, 26
Warnecke, Gordon, 137
Watton, Christian, 28, 170
Weber, André, 17, 167
Weber, Jacques, 96, 159, 165
Weber, Stanley, 82
Weingarten, Isabelle, 144
Weingarten, Romain, 144
Weitzmann, Henri, 229, 231, 236
Wheeler, René, 18
White, Michael Jai, 98
Wickline, Dan, 98
Wiener, Elisabeth, 112, 176
Wiener, Jean, 202
Wiik, Aurélien, 28
Wilde, Oscar, 155
Wilkinson, Roderick, 178, 221
Willcocks, Nathan, 99
Wilson, Georges, 34, 78, 149
Winling, Jean-Marie, 109, 167
Winterhalter, Vincent, 145
Wod, Georges, 109
Wojtowicz, Stéphan, 72
Wolf, Valérie, 151
Wolfsberger, Peter, 64
Woodward, Shane, 99
Woolrich, Cornell, 217
Woringer, Bernard, 35, 102
Worthalter, Arieh, 121
Wronecki, Daniel, 168, 179
Wul, Stéfan, 103
Wyn, Michel, 24, 25, 78, 135
Yakovlev, Anton, 167
Yanne, Jean, 193
Yefsah, Slimane, 62
Yerlès, Bernard, 154, 155, 168

Youri, Isabelle, 101
Youri, Jean-Claude, 101, 147, 174, 186
Zaccaï, Jonathan, 82
Zamberlan, Anne, 118
Zamire, Anne, 178
Zamyatin, Yevgeny, 203
Zanini, Fannie, 170
Zaoui, Vanessa, 176
Zardi, Dominique, 75, 77
Zehnacker, Jean-Paul, 63, 81, 109, 157, 187
Zelde, Jacques, 79
Zenoni, Fabio, 54

Zentara, Edward, 26
Zerki, Daniel, 228
Zevaco, Michel, 203
Zidi, Malik, 104
Zimmer, Pierre, 17
Zinga, Marc, 100
Zobda, France, 53
Zola, Jean-Pierre, 36, 39
Zoller, Pierre-Henri, 178
Zubert, Karol, 163
Zucca, Jérôme, 106
Zucca, Pierre, 181
Zucchi, Augusto, 28

www.ingramcontent.com/pod-product-compliance
Lightning Source LLC
Chambersburg PA
CBHW030135170426
43199CB00008B/80